£ 1-50

Social Services Departments

13\8

Also published on behalf of
Brunel Institute of Organization and Social Studies $\boxed{\textbf{\textit{BIOSS}}}$

Hospital Organization
Ralph Rowbottom
with
Jeanne Balle, Stephen Cang,
Maureen Dixon, Elliott Jaques,
Tim Packwood, and Heather Tolliday

Social Services Departments

Developing Patterns of Work and Organization

Social Services Organization Research Unit,
Brunel Institute of Organization and Social Studies BIOSS

Principal Contributors
Ralph Rowbottom
Anthea Hey
David Billis

 Heinemann · London

Heinemann Educational Books Ltd
London   Edinburgh   Melbourne   Auckland   Toronto
Hong Kong   Singapore   Kuala Lumpur
Ibadan   Nairobi   Johannesburg
Lusaka   New Delhi   Kingston

ISBN o 435 82771 5
© Ralph Rowbottom, Anthea Hey, and David Billis 1974
First published 1974
Reprinted 1978

Published by Heinemann Educational Books Ltd
48 Charles Street, London W1X 8AH

Printed in Great Britain by
Richard Clay (The Chaucer Press) Ltd
Bungay, Suffolk

Foreword

One outstanding feature of contemporary industrial society is the formation of large-scale employment systems. Nowhere is this development more true than in the public and social services in Great Britain. The new organizational structure for the personal social services is a good example, covering as it does some two hundred thousand staff in nearly two hundred local authorities.

The sound organization and management of these vast institutions is a chronic problem. In the attempt to improve their effectiveness, changes in organization are continually being introduced. This process of change is particularly striking at the present time. Many Social Services Departments are about to undergo further radical change in the impending reorganization of local government which will affect about two million people in total. The reorganization of health services will affect three quarters of a million people, and the complete implementation of the Fulton Report for the Civil Service nearly half a million more.

All these people are more or less affected by the inevitable personal uncertainty which accompanies change in organization. The problem then is first how to ensure that the changes are worth the trouble they cause, and second how to reduce to a minimum the disturbance to individuals. To achieve these effects requires clarity of perception and of definition of the changes to be introduced.

Unfortunately, however, the mere decision to bring about large-scale organization changes with their far-reaching effects is no guarantee that the proposed changes will be formulated in a manner comprehensible either to those responsible for producing a change or to those affected by it. Changes are introduced without those responsible knowing what they are doing – not because of foolhardiness or irresponsibility – but because organization science is itself as yet so undeveloped that there are no well-established organization models or concepts to hand with which administrators can effectively describe either existing organization or the changes to be brought about in it. Lack of clarity causes much unnecessary uncertainty and confusion about what is to happen. Effects which are undesirable, or even the opposite of those intended, can be produced as readily as the effects sought after.

Examples of difficulties of this kind are much too easy to find – nearly any organizational change will serve. The Fulton Report on the Management of the Civil Service was concerned with increasing managerial accountability. However, because of lack of clarity about the distinction between management levels and grades, its implementation was concentrated upon grading and career structure with a consequent blurring rather than clarification of managerial organization and accountability.* The Bains Report on the Management and Structure of Local Authorities tackled the question of whether each local authority should or should not appoint a Chief Executive Officer – but in the absence of any established and commonly accepted and used definitions it is impossible to know from the report whether the recommendation is for a person who would be a manager accountable for the work of the professional department heads, or for a person who would be a professional co-ordinator of the work of the various departments but not the accountable manager (an issue commented on by the authors in Chapter 9).

One can go on with example after example, but this is not my object. The point is that in the absence of established meanings for such concepts as manager, management level, grade, rank, chief executive, responsibility, superior, administrator, staff specialist, matrix organization, monitor, co-ordinator, chairman, professional autonomy, delegation, reporting, appraisal, assessment, bureaucracy, authority, participation, policy and policy-making, decision, payment by results, and so on; it is literally impossible to couch reorganization plans in sufficiently comprehensible terms to get within shooting distance of an intended target.

So it is that the nation goes from one reorganization to the next, conceptually ill-equipped and I believe floundering. The chief quality of the present book is that it attempts to overcome some

* See Elliott Jaques 'Grading and Management Organization in the Civil Service': *O & M Bulletin*, Vol. 27, No. 3, August 1972.

of these difficulties. Its approach to organization is through the tasks to be achieved. The authors start by giving useful detailed attention to the social policies which are to be implemented – to the services which the new social services departments are to provide for the community. Social work with individuals and families, residential work, and day-care and domiciliary services are analysed in more fundamental terms of basic social work, basic services, and supplementary services.

Starting from consideration of the work to be done, and drawing on their own field work with various departments, the authors proceed to construct a series of models for deploying the human resources of the departments to serve community needs. These models are of two main kinds – their Model A in terms of type of function, and Model B in terms of geographical deployment. In both kinds the various supporting services – such as planning, administration, finance, logistics, and staffing – are dealt with separately.

One of the most fundamental issues discussed is the vexed question of the consequences of the professionalization of social work for organization. In particular, research work has rigorously explored the widely canvassed idea that professional freedom is inconsistent with hierarchical management organization. The Research Unit has found that no such inconsistency exists, at least in this particular context. The professional freedom of the social worker has been confused with the clinical autonomy which for example, is accorded to medical consultants and general medical practitioners. The authors explain why clinical autonomy is inconsistent with a managerial hierachy, and why professional freedom is not. Tentatively, they construct an additional organization model for a Social Services Department, given that social workers were to gain the additional professional recognition that would allow genuine professional autonomy.

These models of organization are described in terms of a systematically defined family of concepts, and a glossary of these concepts is provided at the end of the book. The variety and precision of concepts employed is such as to allow an appropriately complex analysis of the special organizational requirements of field social work, residential care and day care, and domiciliary services. The analysis is concerned not only with the main lines of departmental division and management but also with the means of effective lateral interaction between these services, and between the social services as a whole and the reorganized National Health Services.

The organizational patterns described should help to deploy the members of the service so that they can best use their talent in providing services. Moreover, they should help to provide descriptions of any reorganizations which may be planned in terms which once understood can be used unambiguously by all concerned. The effort of initial mastery of the terms and concepts presented will demand some work on the part of the reader – but the time is long past when organization and reorganization could be treated as matters of simple common sense accessible to everyone with a modicum of managerial experience.

The pilot studies described in the book give some indication of how a teased-out picture of organization can be of help to people involved. They also demonstrate how flexibility and adaptability are increased. Clearly formulated concepts can be tested in practice, and where found to be wanting they can be modified or rejected. By this process of testing through experience, the steady emergence of improving organization may be anticipated. It is a matter of more than passing importance to the people of any nation.

July 1973   *Elliott Jaques*
                                Director, Brunel Institute of
                           Organization and Social Studies

Preface

As will be apparent from the text, the findings upon which this book is based come from field work carried out by all members of the Social Services Organization Research Unit. Equally, the fashioning of concepts derives from that field work and from continual discussion within the research team. The three members of the Unit whose names appear upon the title page have, however, been responsible for the preparation of the book, and their particular roles have been as follows.

Ralph Rowbottom has been the team leader since the inception of the research, and its director since 1972. He was responsible for writing the manuscript. He is also a member of the Brunel Health Services Organization Research Unit.

Anthea Hey has been a member of the team from its inception, coming from the position of Senior Assistant Children's Officer in Cheshire. She has been project officer in charge of the East Sussex Project. She was made a Senior Research Fellow in 1972.

David Billis joined the team as Research Fellow one year after the research began. He is project officer in charge of the Brent Project.

In addition to the authors of this book, the following have been or are members of the Research Unit, and have contributed by their field work and participation in project discussions:

Dorothy Jerrome (Senior Research Assistant)	1969-70
Jacob Fachler (Senior Research Assistant)	1970-71
John Evans (Research Fellow)	1971-72
Geoffrey Bromley (Research Fellow)	1973-
Helen Fergus (Research Fellow)	1973-

It will be noticed in reading the book that references are made by name to the specific local authorities with whom we have worked (though not to any individuals by name with whom we have worked). The Department of Health and Social Security, our sponsors in this project, normally insist on anonymity of both persons and places in research reports. Given, however, the special method of work employed in this project (described in Chapter 1), with its focus on specific problems in specific departments, and its emphasis on maintenance of confidentiality for all material until clearance is obtained, they have agreed to relax their general rule. It has been accepted in this particular instance that the identification of real places is likely to enhance the value of the material presented, given that its publication has been agreed by all the people concerned.

In registering our debt to those who have helped this project, our prime acknowledgement must be to the many hundreds of people from Social Services Departments throughout the country who have joined with us both in specific field projects and in conferences at Brunel University in the attempt to reach better understanding and control of some of the organizational problems which now face the social services. Without their willing collaboration this work would simply not have existed. Thinking of the field projects specifically described in this book, we should not fail to give particular thanks to the Directors and staffs of the Social Services Departments in Brent, East Sussex, and Wandsworth, and to the Chief Officers and their staffs from the former Children's Departments in Essex and Wandsworth, and the former Mental Health and Welfare Departments also in Wandsworth.

Amongst conference members, too, have been many staff of the Social Work Service of the Department of Health and Social Security who, within these events (and often outside them as well), have considerably helped us to orientate to the social services field as a whole and its problems. We have a particular debt of gratitude to express to Gillian Browne-Wilkinson, Janet Cole, John Cornish, Lillien Davidson, Barbara Kahan, Robert King, John Locke, Frederick Taylor and their colleagues who have provided on behalf of our sponsors, the DHSS, a sympathetic and sensitive steering mechanism for the project as a whole over these first years.

Within the University we have been helped at innumerable points by the advice and ideas of Professor Elliott Jaques, as designated supervisor of the project and Director of the Institute, and also those of Professor Maurice Kogan, many of whose research interests abut on our own.

Finally we would like to record our profound thanks to Mollie Parish and her staff, not only for their help in the considerable mechanics of producing a book of this kind, but for their general administrative support to the project since its inception.

R.W.R

A.M.H

D.B

1973

Contents

xiii

1 Introduction

This is a book with an unfashionable approach. Its subject is the new unified Social Services Departments (SSDs) that came into being in local authorities (counties, county boroughs, and London boroughs) in early 1971. It is not concerned with the huge problem of discovering exactly what needs these departments have to meet in their various localities or with what resources are needed to meet them. It is not concerned with the urgent question of the supply of trained social workers and how this may be increased, or for that matter with whether trained workers are more effective than untrained, or whether elaborate techniques of intervention in social problems are better than simple ones. It is not concerned with the ideologies or attitudes of social workers and other associates, or with how social workers and others interrelate (or fail to interrelate) at a personal level in various group situations.

This book is concerned essentially with how workers at all levels in these departments see their own roles, the roles of their fellow workers, and the roles of their departments as a whole. It is concerned with a worker's view of the necessary work to be carried out, and the proper and most valid distribution of functions and authority to get it carried out effectively. In short, it is concerned with organizational structure and procedure from the viewpoint of those who constitute the organization.

There is little doubt that such a concern is unfashionable at present amongst the bulk of the commentators and onlookers – the social administrators, sociologists, psychologists, and management theorists. Their interests in social services are for the most part of the kind indicated above – in social need and the proper level of provision to meet it, or in social work technique, or in the study of the formation of professional attitudes, and their effects on work, or in the psychology of behaviour in organizations. The organization structure itself tends either to be discarded out of hand by theorists in terms such as 'merely the *formal* structure' or if given any serious consideration at all, dealt with in the grossly over-simple terms of 'classical' management theory of the 1930s and 1940s – 'span of control', 'unity of command', 'line-and-staff organization', and so on.[1]

On the other hand it is quite evident that practitioners – workers and managers in the field – do not find the consideration of organization structure unfashionable. They cannot ignore it: it conditions their every daily act and every working relation. Many of the problems of work which they spontaneously present are quite overtly in organizational terms, and many others can readily be demonstrated to have some immediate organizational cause. Nearly always problems which are overtly ones of clarifying needs, reallocating resources, developing training programmes, introducing new methods of work, dealing with 'personality' issues, and so on, turn out in the end to require some consideration of organizational machinery if they are to be adequately dealt with.

The Development of the Project

Significantly the origin of the project was a request in 1968 from the Home Office to Brunel University to undertake a programme of management training for officers from local authority Children's Departments, which at the time came under the wing of the Home Office. (Significantly, for 'management training' too is a subject in high esteem in the fashion of the day.) We readily agreed to collaborate provided that we could also be financed to carry out research work in Children's Departments. Such work would have two aims. First, it might enable us, and the department concerned, to get a clearer view of organizational and management problems, so that training programmes might be more realistic and useful. Second, it would allow us to see what change, if any, actually resulted from training, or more directly, from the preliminary research itself.

Instead, then, of some static or isolated kind of management

[1] The work of writers such as Urwick, Mooney and Reilly, Graicunas, or (at any earlier date) Fayol. See, for example, Gulick and Urwick (1937).

training based on the exposition of general management 'principles', we conceived an approach geared to specific needs and problems, and built of interlocking elements in a way that may be illustrated as follows:

With the sponsorship of the Home Office and the willing collaboration of the Children's Departments concerned, work was actually started in the autumn of 1969 in two local authorities, the London Borough of Wandsworth and the County of Essex, and a little later a first series of six two-week 'conferences' for senior staff from the then Children's Service was launched.

The word 'conference' rather than 'course' was a considered choice. Throughout the first series, and subsequent ones, we have regarded the events concerned quite as much as opportunities to test and generalize research findings from specific projects as occasions to train and inform participants through the straightforward exposition of established truths. In fact, the dual elements of research and training are surely inseparable in any adequate process of so-called 'action research' on the one hand or 'formal training' on the other. The difference is merely in the balance between the two, and in the situation of the group of people involved.

With the approaching amalgamation of separate Children's, Welfare, and Mental Health Departments into unified Social Services Departments, it became increasingly unrealistic to think only in terms of children's work. Our brief was appropriately extended with the agreement of the Department of Health and

Social Security (DHSS) who were to take responsibility at national level for all personal social services following reorganization. The DHSS took over sponsorship of the work. Conference membership was extended to staff from all branches of the social services. New financial arrangements allowed us to build up a larger project team.[2]

Our project work extended to the London Borough of Brent; to the County of East Sussex and thence to three County Boroughs in the East Sussex area to be amalgamated with the County Authority in 1974 – Brighton, Eastbourne, and Hastings; and also to Berkshire. Steering Committee arrangements were established within the DHSS to allow general guidance of all our work, as well as providing a definite place to which findings could be fed for assimilation at national level.

The Social-analytic Method

The method of work we have adopted is called 'social analysis'. It was pioneered by Elliott Jaques in the Glacier Project, and has been employed also in the Health Services Organization Project undertaken at Brunel University which runs in parallel to the project described in this book.[3] In each of these three projects,

[2] Initial financing in the Children's Department Project allowed for two researchers full-time or equivalent. Present financing (March 1973) allows for up to four, under a part-time director.

[3] For leading references to the Glacier Project see Brown (1960), Brown and Jaques (1965), Jaques (1967). The work in hospitals of the Health Services Organization Research Unit is described in Rowbottom et al. (1973). Social analysis as a method is considered in detail in an extended appendix in the latter work, and also in 'Social Analysis and the Glacier Project' – a paper by Jaques (Brown and Jaques, 1965).

Looking for parallels in social services, the method of social analysis is comparable in some respects with 'action research' as employed, for example, by Leissner et al. (1971) in their study of Family Advice Centres. The approach has much in common with the strategies of intervention in organizations increasingly referred to as 'organization development' (see for example Beckhard, 1969, and Bennis, 1969). However it is noteworthy that practitioners in the 'O.D.' field, having made due obeisance to the need to include consideration of 'formal' organizations in areas of possible development, usually concentrate on social psychological matters like developing personal and group attitudes and skills in dealing with communication, conflict, and the negotiation of change. More broadly, social analysis may be related to a whole array of methods of social intervention in a variety

there has been a heavy, though by no means exclusive, concern with the role-structure of organizations. (Although there is nothing in social analysis as a method which demands this particular emphasis. It seems that it might be employed in relation to any aspect of organizational life that could in principle be institutionalized – its functions, its role-structure, its procedures or its policies.)

As a method, it is first and foremost client-orientated – like social work or psychotherapy. It starts from the client's own statement of his problems and must therefore be distinguished from the systematic survey, or even the case-study, both of which are usually shaped and planned by the researcher. On the other hand, it must be distinguished from management consultancy, since explicit recommendation about what action to take in particular circumstances is never offered.

The approach is collaborative and rests therefore on the continuing confidence of all those with whom the researcher-analyst works. It follows that the latter must respect the confidentiality of work until such time as the client of the moment 'clears' material for more general release. In the collaboration, the analyst offers analysis and only analysis: responsibility for action remains at all times with the client, as does responsibility for collection of any necessary supplementary data, or responsibility for evaluation of the results of action. (The researcher cannot step out of his analytical role to act at the same time either as servant on one hand or monitor on the other.) What the analyst contributes is, first, his own analytic skills, second his experience of similar situations, and third his knowledge of social structure and processes in general.

In practice, having been accepted for work in a department – a process which will usually involve introductory discussions with various groups of staff from the department – the researchers then wait for members of the department to take the initiative in suggesting particular problems for investigation. In some departments in which we have worked, it has been considered desirable to establish a Project Steering Committee with wide representation

---

of fields which share in common the existence of a change agent, some kind of client or client system, and the attempt to apply scientific knowledge to the client's problems (Lippitt et al., 1958; Bennis et al., 1969; Hornstein et al., 1971).

from within the department to endorse any proposed projects and to keep an overview of subsequent progress. Naturally such a Committee includes the Director.[4] In other departments it has been considered sufficient for the Director and his immediate assistants to act as such a steering group.

Typically, the sanctioning of specific project work is carried out in three stages. First the steering group within the department endorse the proposed project and decide its urgency and priority. Then discussions are held with the group of staff most immediately concerned (for example, all the staff in an Area Office, or perhaps a mixed group of residential and field staff). Finally, a preliminary discussion is held with each individual participant, to see whether or not he personally wishes to become involved. In principle, he may decide not to, although it is only realistic to recognize at this stage the likely pressures on him to join, from either peers or superiors.

Having thoroughly tested in this way the strength and reality of the desire to collaborate in an attack on the proposed problem, the actual work of analysis starts in individual discussions. The emphasis on confidentiality allows a free airing of views, and ephemeral or personal issues can be filtered out to reveal the more basic or structural problems.

As the analysis proceeds deeper views of the problem are revealed, layer by layer. First, consideration is given to various starting assumptions about how the organization is supposed to deal with the problem on hand – the public facts as it were. Then the question is pursued with the client of how the organization tends to work in practice, which may well be different – the 'real' facts so to speak. From there, questions can be pursued about what organizational machinery is in fact desirable to help to deal with the problem on hand, given existing circumstances and constraints. Finally, questions can be pursued, as far as is realistic, of how these arrangements might be further improved given relaxations in certain constraints or changes in circumstances.[5] If all goes well,

[4] For example, a Steering Committee exists in Wandsworth consisting of the Director, three Assistant Directors and elected representatives from the Area Officers (one), the senior social workers (one), the social workers (three), and the administrative staff (two).

[5] In the language of the Glacier Project (Brown, 1960) discussion can proceed from the *manifest* situation, i.e. as formally described and displayed; to the situation *assumed* by the participant; to the *extant* situation, i.e. the

both parties – the analyst and the client – extend their insight and at some stage (perhaps after several discussions) the analyst can commit to paper a joint analysis of the situation, based on the particular perceptions of the person with whom he has been working, and clear it for release. After individual discussions, the analyst produces a general report for the whole group, and this itself will then be discussed and revised in one or more group sessions. Often such sessions reveal still better the true nature of the problem, and in doing so clear the way for the formulation of new possibilities for remedial action (samples of typical individual and group reports are given in Appendix C).

Sometimes the group itself has authority to act; or sometimes, with the agreement of the group concerned, the various reports can be released to higher levels of the department where authority rests to decide appropriate action. What now exists is an analysis of the problem, together with possible lines of attack drawn from the direct experience of those who live with the problem. It has very different weight from any 'recommendations' from some external expert (although it is true that the analyst has necessarily influenced what has been produced). Nevertheless, any action which results is inevitably experimental in nature, and after some agreed period of time, perhaps three or six months, the effects of the action concerned can be assessed and the benefits evaluated.[6]

---

situation 'revealed by systematic exploration and analysis'; and hence to the *requisite* – the 'situation as it would have to be to accord with the real properties of the field in which it exists'. The general drift of this description is highly valuable to the social analyst, though certain practical and philosophical problems arise from these precise definitions as they stand. However, the analysis is certainly many steps forward from the crude dichotomy of 'formal' and 'informal' organization embraced by many writers from the Hawthorn Project onwards (see for example, Blau and Scott, 1963).

[6] It has been argued against social analysis as a method that it ignores objective evaluation of changes. In fact, the method does not at all preclude the gathering (by the client department) of objective data to assist evaluation, where such is realistic. But it must be recognized that whatever supporting data is available evaluation, by its very name, is ultimately a subjective process. In the end, we have to choose between various subjectivities – the researcher's values, the values of the workers in the client department, the values of elected members of local authorities who employ the workers, or the values of the clients whom the departments serve, assuming that these latter can be articulated other than through elected representatives.

Again, the researcher-analyst joins in, and again his role is to help analyse any residual problems which still remain, or any new problems that have arisen.

It is thus very important that the researcher should maintain long-continuing contact with client departments. For this reason, our research strategy has been to work intensively and for long periods with a few authorities, rather than in a broader and more ephemeral way with many. It was judged that the conference programme would give us the necessary opportunities both to extend our knowledge of a wider range of departments, and to test the wider generality of our findings.

Sorts of Problems Considered

In principle, it seems that social analysis might be applied to a very wide range of problems which affect a group of people in their common work. As stated, in this project, so far at any rate, the process has been applied mainly to problems of role-structure (i.e. the roles which people are to play, and their interrelationships) though to some extent as well, to problems of organization procedure.[7] However, it can hardly be stressed too strongly that questions of organization role and interrelationships cannot be divorced from consideration of the nature of the work to be done by the department as a whole; and the interplay of these two factors will be seen in what follows to be a constant theme of this research.

Here are examples of some of the main problems we have encountered. Each has arisen in one or other of our main field projects, but discussion in conferences has shown that nearly all are widespread causes of anxiety and uncertainty.

Role of the 'Senior'
What, basically is the job of the senior social worker? Is it in some sense managerial, is it more properly that of guide and mentor, or is it both? Does the senior have the right to interfere with the social

[7] In principle, for example, there is no reason why we could not, if asked, examine problems of pay or grading (as was done quite explicitly in the Glacier Project) or even problems of detailed working methods (as was done, for example, in the analysis of pricing procedures in the Glacier Project). Whether the emphasis so far on role-structure has resulted from our own conscious or unconscious biases in interest, or from our client's urgent need to sort out basic organizational problems before tackling others, is difficult for us to judge.

workers 'own' cases? Should seniors be forced to carry supervisory or administrative responsibilities in order to progress in terms of status and pay?

Intake and Transfer
How can departments control their workload, given the (no doubt) perennial situation of a demand greatly outstripping the resources available to meet it? Is there a case for specialist intake workers? If so how can referral of cases be smoothly effected, where long-term case work is needed? What is the essential distinction between intake and duty work, if any?

Clerical Staff in Area Teams
Who controls clerical staff in area teams? Are they a genuine part of the area team, or are they merely outbranchings of central administration?

The Area Team as a Whole
What is the role of the Area Team as a whole? Is it merely that of an outposted case work unit, or ought it to aspire to a more complete role in relation to its local 'community'? Ought it to be concerned with evaluation, planning, and development of local services and with community work (so called)? Ought it to encompass domiciliary and day care staff, or even residential establishments; and, if so, what might 'encompassing' mean in hard organizational terms?

Residential and Day Care Establishments
Where do residential and day care establishments fit in the total organizational structure? Who is the immediate manager of each head of establishment, i.e. who at the next level carries full and continuous accountability for how that establishment as a whole flourishes? Are residential workers appropriately the 'equal' of field workers or, alternatively, are there any good reasons for recognizing the latter as carrying special authority and status?

Residential Placements
What is the most efficient system for finding residential and day care placements, given the particular needs of clients on the one hand, and the particular characteristics of various establishments on the other? How far should field social workers be involved with the client in residential care? Who should co-ordinate continuing activity?

Role of Administration
What is the role of central administration departments? Should they

carry or share in a real managerial role; or should they be recognized as simply secondary or service-giving, with no executive authority whatsoever?

Role of Central Advisers and Specialists
What is the proper role of the various central advisers and specialists to be found in many departments – residential advisers, mental health specialists, adoption specialists, and so on? Do they have a purely consultative role; or should they too be given executive authority, and if so, of what kind?

Role of Assistant Directors
What does the title 'assistant director' imply over and above a certain grade or status? Does it necessarily imply a full managerial relationship to other more junior staff? Must directors act only through their assistants, or may they properly establish direct working relationships, for example, with divisional or area officers?

Development of New Services, Policies, Procedures
How is the department as a whole to develop and introduce new services in a systematic way? How can it develop systematic policies and procedures to govern everyday activities, so as to rescue senior staff from a daily and untamed flood of minor emergencies and contingencies?

Representation
Given the size of the new departments (typically now running into thousands of staff) how can those at the top keep adequate contact with the views and feelings of all those at the bottom? What place is there for a system of elected representatives of various kinds and groups of departmental staff?

Conceptual Clarification

Let us consider exactly what we, the research team, hope to contribute to the solution of these problems. As has been stated, we certainly do not pose as experts in the sense of offering specific solutions in specific situations. For in any case the most appropriate immediate response to any of these problems in various specific authorities may be quite different, depending on a host of local and temporary factors – personnel, financial, geographical, and so on – which only those who live in the situation and who carry continuing responsibility can judge. On the other hand, we aspire to more than being merely the means of bringing groups of staff together to solve their own problems in their own way, or (at a lower level still) merely to helping them indulge in some form of mutual emotional catharsis. What we try to do in fact is to help the people concerned to a better mastery of their problems through the recognition, definition, and establishment of the necessary conceptual tools with which to grasp their problem-situations.

Now this may sound very abstract – a mere exercise in semantics – but in fact it is a very down-to-earth activity. The value of conceptual analysis can be illustrated in an introductory way by two examples drawn from the problems listed above. One relates to organization structure, and the other to procedures.

In several places above, the terms 'management' and 'managerial' are used in stating problems – as they are commonly in everyday organizational life. Now it is obvious that none of the questions posed in these terms can be adequately dealt with until the terms are clarified; not just until some arbitrary definition is laid down, but until some explicit understanding and agreement is reached of a *concept* of manager or management which takes account of real features of the social situation, and of the kinds of behaviour or action necessarily required of actors in this situation.

Here we draw on a particular conception of the managerial role which was developed in previous projects,[8] though in fact the definition shown below has evolved somewhat as a result of more recent work in this project itself.

Managerial Role
A managerial role arises where A is accountable for certain work and is assigned a subordinate B to assist him in this work. A is accountable for the work which B does for him.

A is accountable:
  – for helping to select B
  – for inducting him into his role
  – for assigning work to him and allocating resources
  – for keeping himself informed about B's work, and helping him to deal with work problems
  – for appraising B's general performance and ability and in con-

[8] See reference above to the Glacier Project and to the project work of the Health Services Organization Research Unit of Brunel University.

sequence keeping B informed of his assessments, arranging or providing training, or modifying role.

A has authority:
- to veto the selection of B for the role
- to make an official appraisal of B's performance and ability
- to decide if B is unsuitable for performing any of the work for which A is accountable.

With this definition established, certain questions raised above – for example, whether central administrative staff should play a managerial role in relation to either field or residential staff – appear in quite a new light. Clearer choices emerge (does one *really* want central administration to be accountable for the kind and quality of work carried out in residential establishments?) and possible action becomes more apparent (who then *should* be required to carry out a managerial function in respect of heads of establishments?).

This particular clarification is only one of many similar ones relating to organizational structures. Building on the work of previous projects we have now established a list of some dozen or so different executive role-types over and above managerial roles, whose existence can be demonstrated with more or less precision in social service and other organizations. Thus to say that an administrator or specialist does not carry a managerial role is by no means the same as saying that he carries no authority; many other choices exist as later discussion will reveal. We have already established the existence in social services departments in addition to managerial roles, of *supervisory roles, staff officer roles, co-ordinating roles, monitoring roles, service-giving roles,* and a further range of roles in what we describe as *dual-influence* situations. Using these organizational elements or 'modules' in various combinations gives rise to the possibility of a rich variety of more or less complex organizational forms and thus a whole range of practical alternatives for organizational definition.[9] A list of the complete

[9] This is a far step from the simplified 'line-and-staff' or 'functional' models of the classical management theorists and, we suggest, is more specific and practical than the broader classifications used by the latter-day writers: 'organic' and 'mechanistic' organization (Burns and Stalker, 1961) 'professional', 'semi-professional' or 'non-professional' organization (Etzioni, 1964), 'hierarchy' and 'arena' (Hunter, 1967) 'hierarchy' and 'polyarchy' (Algie, 1970) and so on.

range of organizational modules at present established, with precise definition, and illustrations, is shown in Appendix A, and referred to for frequent use throughout the remainder of the book.

It may be noted that all these definitions of role-types employ the same kinds of terms: 'duties' or 'functions', 'authority', and 'accountability'. It is at this point that many conference members from social services have cavilled. What has happened to the full person, they ask? Where is the place in this analysis for inter-communication, for the subtle play of personality on personality, for the recognition of the voice of experience or expertise?

The answer is, naturally, that all these things do exist and do matter: indeed that they constitute the very flesh and blood of organizational life – as they do of all social life. But to see organiza-tional life only in these terms is exactly to miss the bone structure underneath the flesh and blood. Organizational roles can be con-ceived and described in the absence of individuals to fill them, and they can only be described in such terms as above. More or less well conceived and understood they *do* greatly condition the inter-action of people within the organization. To be concerned with designing them well is not to ignore the spontaneous flow of human intercourse but to attempt to provide the sort of channels which best facilitate it. (It is perhaps the case that the professional social workers by their very training are apt to analyse organiza-tional problems only in personal and psychological terms, and not also in terms of social structure.)

So much then for the managerial role and its counterparts. A second example of conceptual clarification in the field of organiza-tional procedures rather than role-structure arose in project work concerned with referral processes. At a certain point in one field project we discovered that problems were arising in the referral of cases from a specialist 'intake' group to a 'long-term' case work group (the project is described in Chapter 8). The exact mechan-ism of referral was far from clear. There were times when appa-rently nobody was responsible for the case, and the upshot was that intake workers became inhibited about action on cases which really should have been referred to the long-term group.

A necessary insight was the distinction of the *referral* process from the *transfer* process and their separate and precise definitions. Social workers may often refer cases for advice, services, collabora-tion, or even (as in this case) for possible transfer. But until such time as accountability has been accepted by the new party, transfer is not complete, and accountability therefore remains with the original party. (Other conceptual clarifications were needed too in this situation, for example a clarification of exactly what was meant by 'short-term' case work and 'long-term' case work.)

The Present Position

In a very real sense the following pages constitute a progress report on a continuing project. What is described are the findings that have crystallized in the first three and a half years of project work, i.e. up to the spring of 1973.

At the time of writing work continues in Wandsworth, Brent, Berkshire, and the complex of authorities in the geographical area of East Sussex. (Work in Essex ceased with the coming to an end of the Children's Department in 1971.) Although the various projects concerned started at different times and vary in character and intensity, in general it has been possible to establish deep and continuing relationships with the departments concerned. The point has now been reached where action and change intimately linked to project work is beginning to occur in all of them.

The first four years of conference events (mostly one to two weeks each in length) will have brought us into contact with nearly five hundred senior staff from social services throughout the country.[10] As a result of this conference work, we have begun to establish more tenuous links with a number of other departments where we are carrying out what might be described as intermittent consultancy. Furthermore, through conferences and publications, and through our continuing contact with our steering groups within DHSS, we have begun to work with various central

[10] Conferences have drawn staff from 97 Children's Departments, 12 Welfare Departments and 13 Mental Health Departments (as they were), and from 75 Social Services Departments. In all, staff from some 120 of the 174 authorities in England and Wales have attended. In addition 59 staff from the Social Work Service group of DHSS (and its predecessors) and a number of senior research and teaching staff from the field have attended. Staff from SSDs have been drawn mainly from the range from Area Officers (or its residential or day care equivalent) up to and including Director-level.

agencies in the social work field such as the Central Council for Education and Training in Social Work.

Altogether then, we envisage the possibility of continuing work at three successive levels:

(1) continuing intensive social-analytic project work in a small number of departments, which it is hoped will extend in the course of time to all parts and all levels in each, in order to generate and test new fundamental understanding of how departments as a whole can best function;

(2) intermittent contact in a consultancy-type relationship with a number of other departments, to spread ideas and test them further in particular sites;

(3) the more general dissemination and testing of ideas through conference activity, publications, contact with professional and other staff in central government, and the like.

Outline of the Book

The subject matter in the coming pages is broken into a number of main headings – the work of SSDs, organization of field work, organization of residential care, and so forth. Under each heading we offer a general analysis of problems in the area concerned, and in each case we draw heavily on various examples from field project work. Sometimes the project work has done little more than indicate the true nature of the problem. Sometimes it has moved to the point of identifying remedial action or alternatives for remedial action. Sometimes we are reporting from fields of work in a state of change as a direct result of the analysis that has been undertaken. In addition, in each chapter we draw freely on general views that have been expressed within our conferences on the nature of the problems concerned or the adequacy of various possible solutions.

Thus each chapter is firmly rooted both in direct project work in the field and in conference discussion. Together they span many aspects of the work of present social services departments, but where we have no direct project experience (as in for example the field of community work, or of home-help organization) then we have kept our comment or speculation to a minimum.

The following chapters fall into several broad groups. The next three chapters consider the department as a whole, its social environment, its general range of work, and the various possibilities for its general structure. The following four chapters examine various parts and processes in more detail – field work, residential care, domiciliary and day care, and procedures for co-ordinating work with particular cases that may involve several or all branches of the department. The penultimate chapter describes expanding project work in broader fields such as the relationship of the department to the local authority as a whole, to health services, and to its employees seen as a number of separate occupational groups in their own right. Finally, in the last chapter we summarize the main conclusions from our work so far.

To keep a clear narrative flow, the main text is reserved as far as possible for actual project descriptions and immediate commentary on them. Academic discursions and references to other literature are relegated to footnotes.

2 The Social and Organizational Setting

The New Social Services Departments

The Social Services Departments of local authorities in England and Wales came gradually into existence in 1970 and 1971 following the recommendations of the Seebohm Report.[1] Although that major report projected a full and glowing vision of what a comprehensive social services agency might be, the legislation that followed it[2] was somewhat bare, consisting of little more than a detailed specification of all the particular pieces of existing welfare legislation for which a new department would be responsible. However, several new points of substance were established. First, each local authority – county, county borough, or London borough – was to appoint a special committee concerned wholly and solely with social services matters (this in spite of a plea by the earlier Maud Report[3] for a reduction in the proliferation of committees that already existed in local authorities). Second, each authority was to appoint a Director of Social Services who again would be wholly and solely concerned with social services. No joint appointments of Medical Officer of Health and Director of Social Services would be tolerated, for example – the implication was that Directors would be immediately accountable to social services committees. Third, the appointment of individual Directors was to

[1] Home Office *et al.* (1968) *Report of the Committee on Local Authority and Allied Social Services.*
[2] Local Authority Social Services Act (1970).
[3] Ministry of Housing and Local Government (1967).

be subject to the scrutiny of the appropriate Secretary of State, and if necessary to his veto.

In essence the new legislation gathered under one roof most of the personal social services previously carried out in children's departments, health departments, and (where separate) in welfare departments. It did not adjudicate, however, on whether or not personal social services carried out by welfare workers in education or housing departments should also be incorporated, although scope for doing so was not specifically excluded. It did not suggest what should happen to social workers in hospitals (although it has since been stated that these workers are to be transferred to the employment of local authorities). It did not include the probation service.[4]

When appointed, Directors found themselves at the head of departments employing many hundreds, or in the case of the largest departments, some thousands of staff. These included former child care officers, welfare workers, and mental health workers; the staff of various homes and hostels for children, the old, the mentally disturbed, and the handicapped; the staff of various day centres and nurseries; large numbers of home-helps (mostly working part-time); and large numbers of supporting administrative and clerical staff. To help co-ordinate and manage this diverse empire a new range of assistant directors and advisers were created. Of all the staff, however, only a small proportion had any formal qualifications in social work, though they brought collectively a considerable wealth of practical knowledge and experience.[5]

In the following chapters the work and the internal structure of these new departments will be studied in detail. In this chapter we shall start by establishing a broad picture of the kind of organization under consideration and how it stands in relationship to its social and political environment.

By way of introduction it might be stressed that SSDs do not carry out their work in social isolation. Their clients go into hospital, attend or fail to attend schools, are subject to legal pro-

[4] Appendix F of the Seebohm Report gives a detailed account of the nature, distribution, and organization, of personal social services in statutory authorities at the time of the Report (1968).

[5] It was estimated that only about 40% of main grade field workers had a professional qualification, ignoring trainees and assistants (Department of Employment, 1972), and less than 4% of residential staff (Central Council for Education and Training in Social Work, 1973).

ceedings, suffer from evictions, run into difficulties with social security benefits, and so on. Any long-term view which does not take into account links with other local authority departments and with various other statutory and voluntary agencies is unlikely to be either comprehensive or useful.

Nor can departments be viewed realistically without taking account of the true nature of their relationship to the bodies which support and govern them. For whilst departments are not simply outcrops of some universal self-generating bureaucracy neither are they associations of uncontrolled self-supporting 'professionals'. Whilst they are not simple obedient agents of social control, neither are they unrestrained instigators of social change.

The Conventional Sociological View

Before expanding these points it is perhaps as well to lay to rest one particular ghost. This might be called the *conventional sociological view* of social services organizations. The essential image that remains after reading much of the sociological literature is as shown in Figure 2.1.[6] It may be interpreted as follows.

The entity under discussion is something called an 'agency' whose output is simply something called 'social work'. Essentially it contains two groups: the professional social workers and the administrators. By and large the former identify with clients and are primarily concerned with their needs. They bring into the situation 'professional values' which they have imbibed in training and in association with their fellow professionals. Their professional background gives them something called 'professional authority'. On the other hand, the administration tend to identify with 'bureaucratic values'. They see rules and regulations as most important. Their desire is to contain costs and their instinct is to repel what they see as extravagant demands for service. They fill the higher levels of the agency, and so by definition carry 'bureaucratic authority'. Many administrators are admittedly ex-profes-

[6] See for example leading works by Blau and Scott (1963) and Etzioni (1964). Reading such present day sociological textbooks for social work students, as those of Leonard (1966), Smith (1970) or Heraud (1970), the framework or paradigm depicted below is so taken for granted that one might not only describe it as the conventional sociological view but indeed, in Galbraith's famous phrase, as *the conventional wisdom* of the day.

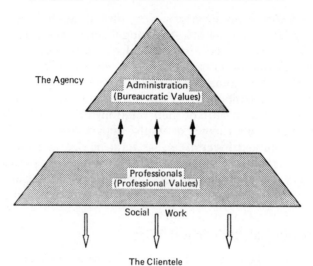

Figure 2.1   Overview of Social Services Departments
– A Simple Stereotype

sionals but their *professional* competence is assumed to be less than that possessed by those who remain in practice. (Of the two groups there is little doubt as to who is on the side of the angels!)

Now this is no doubt an oversimplification and perhaps even a distortion of the conventional sociological view. The main thing to emphasize is that although some such general overview or orientating framework is necessary, such a one as this leaves many serious gaps.

First, although the word 'agency' is used, there is little or no pursuit of what might seem the obvious questions – on whose behalf the agency operates, and on what, as it were, is the nature of the social linkage upwards and outwards.[7] Again, there is an

---

[7] As Kogan and Terry (1971) have observed, local authority social service agencies do not appear from nowhere. They are intended as the executive arms of democratic government. If indeed there were substantial conflict between the values that motivate professionals in their work, and those inherent in the bureaucratic process, there might well be good grounds for giving preference to the latter, deriving as they do (or ought to do) from the goals and policies sanctioned by democratically-elected representatives of the communities to be served. However, as they go on to observe, if the agency did not want and intend professionals to work professionally and according to their professional norms it would scarcely go to the trouble of employing them.

assumption that 'social work' is a self-explanatory term. Social work is taken to be what all professional employees are trained to carry out, and the question whether this is what and only what the agency wishes to undertake is left unexamined. Further again, there is little thought as to exactly who constitute the 'clientele'. The word is taken again as self-explanatory, and whether the agency has an obligation to undertake work with or on behalf of those who are not immediate and obvious clientele is left unexamined.

Overall, there is the assumption that departmental employees can usefully be divided into 'professionals' and 'administrators'. However valid this organization apartheid may have been in earlier days, in Britain at least the bulk of 'administrative', i.e. managerial, positions are now filled from professional ranks and it is highly questionable to conceive people in such positions as either no longer professional or as in some way failed professionals. Nor does it help to be forced to draw sharp lines where 'professionals' end and 'administrators' begin. Is the senior social worker who 'leads' a team but carries his or her own caseload, an administrator or a professional?

A Pluralistic Alternative

Surely the overview shown in Figure 2.2 provides a more realistic base for detailed organizational exploration.

Instead of the monolithic 'agency' a whole complex of separate but interacting social structures must be recognized. At the centre is the main structure of the department, a system of work-doing roles headed by the Director. Associated with this at successive stages of remove are the Social Services Committee, the Local Authority as a whole, and Central Government. Together the last three can be thought of as constituting a complex governing institution which establishes in the main departmental structure an executive system to forward its aims. The governing institution finances the department and authorizes its monitors and work.[8]

[8] As Donnison and Chapman (1965) observe in their series of case studies of social services agencies ' "*the* bureaucracy" breaks up on serious inspection into a variety of separate, competing and bargaining organizations; and these organizations do not present a monolithic face to "the public" but are interpreted and allied with a variety of "publics" which exercise considerable influence on their operations' (p. 254). They too note the distinc-

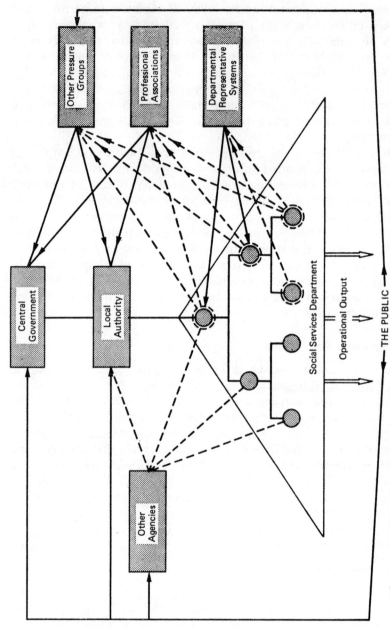

Figure 2.2 Overview of Social Services Departments – A Complex of Interacting Social Systems

Ultimately, this complex governing institution is linked to the general public who elect its members at local and national level. Also, the department must work and interact with many agencies, some subject to the same governing institutions and some independent.[9]

Other social structures arise by virtue of the linkage of members of departments at many levels – not only the lowest – with various professional associations or trade unions.[10] Professional associations give quite concrete and explicit expression to the otherwise rather abstract idea of a profession as a shared system of ideals, methods, and knowledge. These professional associations and unions have a clear interaction with, and influence on, both central and local government. Over and above this, individual departmental members will often choose to join special pressure groups of more or less militant outlook.[11] Finally, yet a further piece of social structure may exist in the form of a staff representative system particular to each department, as discussed in more detail in Chapter 9.

Rather than the simple dichotomies of 'administrators' and 'professionals', of 'establishment' and 'others', this is a 'pluralist' view of the social environment. Moreover, it embraces both conflict and consensus within its scope. Any one institution (for example a local authority committee) will often find itself facing conflict in the form of pressure or opposition from many others (for example, central government, a professional association, or even the members of its own department). In meeting this pressure

tion between the role of the 'governing body' and the 'executive system'. The latter is not just the passive instrument of the governing body but itself creates and continually modifies the service (p. 234) – but it must get the support of the 'resource providers'. The job of the governing body is to approve, modify, or reject, proposals for significant change in objectives or re-allocation of resources (p. 250). Elsewhere, Parsons (1960) makes much the same point in a more general context when he emphasizes the need to distinguish the 'community' or 'institutional' system of any organization from its 'technical' and 'managerial' system.

[9] See Evan's (1966) concept of the 'organizational set'.

[10] For example, the British Association of Social Workers, the Association of Directors of Social Services, or the National Association of Local Government Officers.

[11] Such organizations on behalf of children, the mentally disordered, the homeless, as (respectively) the Child Poverty Action Group, the National Association of Mental Health, 'Shelter', or, of course, straightforward political parties.

it will tend to move towards a consensus. Any individual member of the department may feel the influence of several conflicting roles – for example, executive role, or role as member of professional association – and he will, in his own life, seek some equilibrium in the pulls which these various roles generate.

In general terms, the function of the department will be to provide to the public and for the public such 'social services' as its governing institution determines following the various interactions described above. Whether or not the resulting definition coincides completely with 'social work' as advocated by a particular professional association, or with the sort of activity advocated by a particular pressure group will be another matter, depending on the power of the group concerned to impress its view. In general all groups might be expected to hold somewhat different views of the proper functions and priorities of departments – this is the implication of a pluralist society.

In other words, in the language of systems theory, no department is a closed system in its own right. Various loops are built into the social structure which as it were allow direct or indirect pressure from the service receivers to be fed back through more or less powerful linkages to the main body of the department. And this is over and above such 'feedback loops' of systematic evaluation as the department may itself see fit to establish.[12]

[12] It may be tempting at this point to try to fit this approach into one or other of the main established sociological frames of reference for organizational studies – 'systems', 'structural-functional', 'psychological', 'action', 'inter-actionist', etc. (Silverman, 1970; Cohen, 1968). It is our belief in fact that the approach draws something from all these schools, but subscribes wholly to none. A systems-view of organization is offered at this point, but we would agree with Silverman that 'organizations' do not react to their environment: it is their members who do. Chapter 3 explicitly employs a functional analysis, but again it is understood that it is the various participants who must in the end define and legitimate the functions required and not we, the independent observers. The psychology of supervision is studied in Chapter 5, but it is not assumed that organizations are shaped simply to satisfy the personal or social needs of their employees. The detailed accounts of participants' various expectations of their colleagues in various working situations given in Chapters 5–8 capture something of the flavour of an 'interactionist' approach. Overall the general strategy of social analysis as a method of research and intervention in its own right, with its built-in expectation of existing conflicts in view, interpretation, and ideology, amongst various organizational members, can be recognized as cognate with an 'action' frame of reference.

Of course in practice any particular part of this system may fail to work well or as it should. To say that in general it is the function of a governing institution in the welfare field to mediate between the public which is served and the 'agency' which serves them is not to suggest that the existing democratic machinery in Britain has reached its final perfected form – or indeed to be dogmatic on whether or not other supplementary machinery such as an 'ombudsman' or a system of consumer councils may not be needed as well. What we have here is not so much a blueprint for the future as a broad description of the kind of social geography that already exists.

The Quality of Departmental Structure

The next major question is that of the general nature or quality of the departmental structure itself. It is noticeable that workers employed in departments regularly talk of 'the hierachy' as an existent fact, though not always, be it said, in terms of total affection. It is evident too that departmental organization charts are regularly drawn in a familiar hierarchical form. But should one take the assumption of hierarchical structure so easily for granted? And even if taken for granted as a matter of fact for the present, may one not question its desirability as a permanent feature?

Before answers to these questions can be attempted it is necessary to step back a little to consider more carefully the whole question of hierarchical organizations and what it means.

Towards a Rigorous Definition of 'Hierarchy'

Again, it is interesting to start by taking account of the conventional wisdom amongst writers and theorists on this subject. Broadly it may be said that hierarchical organization is seen not just as a neutral description, but as a conception tinged with dubious, if not positively undesirable, characteristics. Psychologists have emphasized the dehumanizing effects on those who serve within it, and offered other (apparent) possibilities which give greater scope for individual creativity and growth.[13] The sociologists have claimed that the proper form of organization must depend upon a variety of factors such as kind of technology, rate of

[13] See for example McGregor (1960). Likert (1961), Argyris (1964).

environmental change, and degree of professionalization.[14] Directly, or by implication, they too have offered apparent alternatives to hierarchy. On the whole, in their writings hierarchy emerges as a rather humdrum option, associated with static environment and simple technology. In the British social services scene, two recent writers have scorned the hierarchy altogether as an outdated conception, and offered in its place their own restyled models, the 'polyarchy' and the 'arena' respectively.[15] In a world-wide movement the new radicals[16] have unhesitatingly lumped hierarchy with bureaucracy, authority, the establishment, manipulative-technology and the many other bad things that are to be abolished in the sweeter, greener, time to come. Even technologists and business men are reported as beginning to see dynamism (and profit) in moving from the static 'pyramid' to the 'constellation' of semi-autonomous divisions.[17]

'Hierarchy' is often used interchangeably with 'bureaucracy'. The latter is generally taken to imply such characteristics as a high degree of regulation, impersonality taken to the point of lack of concern for those at the bottom of the organization (let alone the clientele), an overwhelming preoccupation with the production of written records, and so on. There is an implicit assumption that hierarchy (or bureaucracy) if pursued to the limit, completely curtails the freedom of the individual employee, professional or other.

Surely, however, any view of hierarchical organization which purports to show the complete centralization of decisions, the complete determination of actions, the complete specification of objectives and values, is so far from any existing or possible truth as to be paranoid phantasy. In reality all workers at whatever level are continuously having to make personal judgements on actions to be taken or priorities to be observed, accepting that in doing so they have indeed to stay within certain boundaries or constraints which are set from above more or less broadly and more or less explicitly. The appropriate image, surely, is not that of a cast-iron frame which locks each worker in a fixed relation to his fellow and predetermines his every action. It is rather that of

[14] See for example Burns and Stalker (1961), Lawrence and Lorsch (1967), Hage and Aiken (1970).
[15] See Algie's (1970) 'polyarchy' and Hunter's (1967) 'arena' organizations
[16] See for example Marcuse (1964): Reich (1972).
[17] Schon (1971).

a membrane-like structure which allows each worker some particular cell or space in which he may freely operate (Figure 2.3)
Sometimes those above allow the membrane to expand at a particular point, and sometimes.they pull it in. This leaves quite aside
any value judgement as to how well any particular structure is
designed to meet the needs and abilities of its workers on the one
hand, or of the work to be carried out on the other.

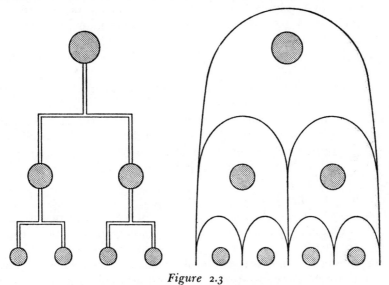

Figure 2.3

Such a picture allows for a degree of difference in the goals and
priorities held by different people and groups employed within
the organization, and moreover for a degree of real-life overlap
or duplication of work. At the same time, unless there can be
some consensus, however broad, on common aims, and some consensus on the main divisions of work, then the word 'organization'
can hardly be employed to describe the situation.[18]

[18] This leaves open the question of how far the consensus extends, or
whether published versions of organizational aims accurately reflect the
existing consensus at any time – the distinction between 'real' and 'stated'
goals made by Etzioni (1964); or between 'official' and 'operative' goals
made by Perrow (1961). At the same time a clear distinction must be made
between the *motivations* of employees and the *aims* and *objects* implicit in
their organizational roles as things of quite different nature and status.
(Simon, 1964).

The main point to be grasped at this stage, however, is that neither the concept of hierarchy nor the concept of bureaucracy can be put to any effective use in precise analysis until the meaning to be assigned to each of them is very considerably refined. Since the concept of bureaucracy is open to so many interpretations [19] we shall not attempt to use it further here as a possible tool of fine analysis.

As far as hierarchy is concerned, at least one specific and useful interpretation can be made. This is the notion of hierarchy as meaning nothing more or less than a structure of successive *managerial* roles. Here managerial role is taken in the particular sense already defined in the previous chapter (see also Appendix A). Using such a clearly bounded definition enables one to say exactly what does or does not qualify as hierarchical organization. As defined here, it does not for example relate to the relative pay or status of various posts – nor to the relative qualifications or degree of professional orientation of the people in them. In particular – and most importantly – it is neutral as far as *managerial style* is concerned.

For it is in this latter area, one suspects, that most of the so-called alternatives to hierarchy really apply. So much of the talk about 'organic' organization, 'group' management, and 'teamwork', is really about participative and democratic styles of management as opposed to more obviously directive ones. At any rate, hierarchical organizations as defined above would encompass the range from most autocratic, narrow, status-ridden, and unimaginative, management style at one extreme, to the most permissive, status-free style at the other – provided that the basic conditions remained of one manager at each level, with ultimate rights to approve or sanction the work being carried out by those of his colleagues for whose work he was accountable.

Hierarchy in Social Services

With the precise conception of hierarchical structure in mind one can now report a striking observation from our own project work – that nearly without exception the members of the staffs of SSDs

[19] As Mouzelis (1967) and Albrow (1970) have separately shown.

with whom we have explored this question over the past years [20] have firmly accepted the present structure of SSDs as fundamentally hierarchical in the sense defined above. They recognize, for example in the role of Director, full accountability for all that takes place within the department, and full accompanying rights to determine the selection of staff, appraise their performance and react accordingly. They also recognize his right to prescribe their work as needs be within the bounds of given statute, regulation, and policy. It may be observed in passing however, that what has not always been so easy for staff to identify, is exactly how the managerial structure expresses itself at levels below the Director – an issue we shall return to later.

In fact, a further finding of significance can also be reported. Drawing on work in other fields being undertaken at Brunel University we have been able to formulate two fundamentally distinct alternatives to hierarchical organization – organization based solely on the *co-ordinated group* (as found frequently in the health care field), and a possible further conception, the true *co-operative*. In exploring these alternatives with departmental staff in conferences at Brunel, we have discovered no firm view at all that either might suitably form the basic texture of SSD organization, given its particular social characteristics, either now or at any foreseeable time in the future. (This whole issue is explored and elaborated in more detail in Appendix B.) Indeed, more positively, the strong consensus has been to support the hierarchical form (as here defined) as the most appropriate one for this particular social situation.

Given certain obvious characteristics of the social work ethos – an emphasis on the value of personal autonomy, and a tendency to play down reliance on the exercise of authority – these findings may seem surprising. Certainly our own instincts were to test the applicability of the hierarchical model with caution in the first instance, until faced with the strong and repeated reaction described above. In view of the strength of the response, however, the assumption of the basic hierarchical structure of SSDs is taken

[20] We have raised this question in conferences and field projects with something of the order of seven hundred staff from some 120 of the 174 authorities in England and Wales. Although the majority of these staff held positions equivalent to senior social worker status or above, those of lower status formed a significant group in themselves, and also concurred with the view quoted when this issue was raised with them:

for granted in various detailed discussions of organization in the chapters that follow.

Matrix Organization

One important proviso must be added. As reported, our work has led to the strong conclusion that the *basic* texture of departmental structure is hierarchical in the sense defined. However, our work has also increasingly brought to light the existence, or desirability in some cases, of a further network of organizational relationships in addition to the basic hierarchical structure, in which the leading roles are *co-ordinative* rather than *managerial*. As later chapters describe, the need to co-ordinate the work of many different groups of clients (e.g. the mentally handicapped, the elderly) or particular fields of work (e.g. group work, community work, adoption and fostering work) creates a need for people with the specific role of pulling all the threads together in each case. Or to take another example, given the extended team of people who may be working with a particular client, embracing staff from a number of disciplines and perhaps from a number of agencies, there is an obvious need for one to act as the chief co-ordinator at any time. In neither case can the role readily be filled by a person who is in a managerial relation to all other actors.

The particular definition of co-ordinative role around which turns this conception of the co-ordinated group reads as follows at its present stage of evolution:

Co-ordinating Role

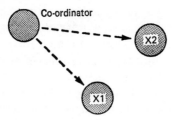

A *co-ordinating role* arises where it is felt necessary to establish one person with the function of co-ordinating the work of a number of others *in some particular field* and where a managerial, supervisory, or staff, relationship is inappropriate. The activity to be co-ordinated might, for example, be:

- the production of a report, estimate, plan, or proposal;
- the implementation of an approved scheme or project;
- the overcoming of some unforeseen problem affecting normal work.

The co-ordinator can only carry out his role to the full within the framework of some generally agreed task, although he amongst others may propose such a task for the group where a need is discerned.

The co-ordinator is accountable:
- for proposing appropriate tasks where a need is discerned;

and following general acceptance of this or any task-proposal:
- for negotiating the general form and content of co-ordinated work programmes;
- for arranging the allocation of existing resources where necessary;
- for keeping himself informed of actual progress;
- for helping to overcome problems encountered by X_1, X_2, etc.;
- for providing relevant information to X_1, X_2, etc., including information of progress;
- for reporting on progress to his superior (if such exists) or to those who established the co-ordinating role.

In carrying out these activities the co-ordinator has authority to make firm proposals for action, to arrange meetings, to obtain first-hand knowledge of progress, etc., and to decide what shall be done in situations of uncertainty, but he has no authority in case of sustained disagreements to issue overriding instructions. X_1, X_2, etc., have always the right of direct access to the higher authorities who are setting or sanctioning the tasks to be co-ordinated.

In comparing this with the definition of the *managerial* role (Appendix A) it is important to emphasize that the co-ordinator has no right to make appraisals of personal performance, no right to override sustained disagreements, and no duty to forward general career development.

What results in the department then, is a basic hierarchical structure which is overlain or accompanied by many other co-ordinated groups established for various specific purposes – see Figure 2.4. In keeping with this, any member of the department can be a member of many different working groups established for different purposes at different times. This is an organizational form increasingly described in the literature as *matrix* organiza-

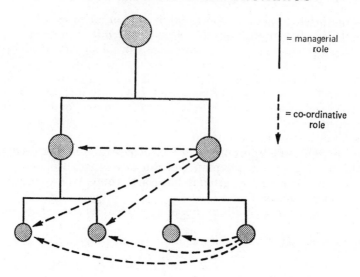

Figure 2.4   Multi-Dimensional or Matrix Organization

tion,[21] although the point is not always grasped that it does not necessarily replace, but usually complements, hierarchical structure.

Conclusion

In essence we have suggested that to talk of social services departments simply as 'bureaucracies' is to miss the enormous complexity of the many distinguishable social structures involved. It is true that the basic textures of this central departmental structure appear to be hierarchical, in a defined sense, and likely to remain so. But 'hierarchy' here must certainly not be taken as synonymous with 'bureaucracy'. The degree of formalization, centralization, impersonality etc., is a matter of separate determination. Moreover, the basic hierarchical structure is not the only one of account in SSDs. Increasingly, recognition must be given to further group structures which cut freely across main hierarchical lines. In these groups the leading roles are *co-ordinative* rather than *managerial* in nature.

[21] See, for example Kingdon (1973). Algie's (1970) 'polyarchy' for social services too, is essentially a matrix structure.

Beyond this central structure other systems arise which are certainly not hierarchical in the sense that has been defined. *Representative systems*, where they arise, have their own distinctive forms, and do not involve *managerial* roles. Local authorities themselves are based on a genuine *committee* structure (see Appendix A), as indeed is usual in governing institutions. Other sorts of structure which one might provisionally call *coalitions* occur where joint bodies of two or more authorities arise.[22] Just as it is dangerous to conceive SSDs simply as bureaucracies, so it is dangerous to conceive their members simply as 'bureaucrats'. True, that as members of departments they carry particular executive roles. But in other simultaneous phases of their social life, they are members of professional associations, voluntary agencies, pressure groups, and political parties. What they bring to the performance of their executive role will be much affected by the experiences and expectations of these other roles. If each is a 'bureaucrat' then he is (or is potentially) a 'professional' too, a political citizen, an individual.

Our overview, then, is a picture of many different social systems, some hierarchical in form and some not, all in interplay and interaction. Rather than the attractive simplification of bureaucrat versus professional, establishment versus underdog, and the rest, this more complex model forces us to the real question of organization and social structure. How *large* a hierarchy? What *form* of public control? What *links* with other agencies? What *relation* to professional associations? And so forth.

[22] As for example, in existing Regional Planning Committees for provision of residential accommodation for children; or, for another example, as in the Joint Consultative Committees to be established in 1974 between Local Authorities and Area Health Authorities.

3 The Work of the Department

It is intriguing to discover in casual conversation with interested acquaintances just how little general knowledge there appears to be about the nature and scope of social work. The informed layman knows well enough, in general terms, what goes on in a school, a hospital, a prison, or an employment exchange, but he is often somewhat at a loss to know exactly what might go on in a present-day social services department.

Possible reasons for this are not difficult to suggest; for a start there is doubt even as to the proper phrase to describe the field concerned – should it be called social services, social work, social welfare, or just welfare? What does it contain that is not already some part of education, health, penology, housing, or employment services? Is it to do with helping people materially; that is, by supplementing their income or providing goods or services? Is it to do with changing people's attitudes and behaviour? Or is it to do with improving the general environment in which they grow up and live?

It need hardly be added that such questions often perplex those working in the field no less than the casual observer. The constant stream of publications on the 'true' nature of social work, social case work, community work, residential work, or whatever it may be, is a significant indication in its own right; and a phenomenon not quite paralleled by discussion of the 'true' nature of other better-established areas of social provision, for instance, health care, or education?[1]

---

[1] The underlying uncertainty is also indicated by the continuing debate as to how far social work is truly a 'profession' – see Wootton *et al.*, (1959), Toren (1969). Presumably a true profession is at least clear what its basic work is!

Fortunately we are not obliged here to attempt a direct answer to such general questions. The more limited question we shall broach in this chapter is that of the proper range of functions of a very particular agency, the present-day Social Services Department in England and Wales.[2]

As it happens, this task has never been posed for us in precisely these terms in any one field-project. However, in practically every project which we have undertaken in a specific area – intake work, residential care, administrative work, and so on – it has sooner or later become necessary to get to grips with the precise nature of the work involved in order to understand the procedural or organizational question at issue. As time has gone on and as various pieces of analysis have been converged, we have come to see that there can be no completely satisfactory answer to any specific questions of organization or procedure without preliminary understanding of what the department as a whole is trying to do – *what it is in business for.*

For example, such an understanding is needed when studying general departmental structure. (What sorts of activities are implied when terms like 'field work', 'residential work' and 'domiciliary and day care' are used to identify various main divisions; and what activities, if any, are in danger of being overlooked when employing such terms?) It is needed when considering the role of the trained social worker and how this is differentiated from the role of the social work assistant or the occupational therapist or home help. (Does the term 'social work' encompass all that SSDs have to do; and if so what activities are carried out by these other kinds of staff?)

Functions and Purposes

Before attempting to define the business of SSDs, it is necessary to clarify one general point about the nature of the terms used. We shall be listing what we shall call the 'functions' of SSDs. How, it may be asked, do such things differ in their nature from 'purposes', 'aims', 'goals', 'objects', 'objectives', 'duties', or 'tasks'?

[2] Social Work Departments in Scotland have a slightly different constitution under law. In any case, though much of the analysis in this study may be applicable to them, they have not been included within the formal terms of reference for our particular research.

All these words are purposive in tone, and in many contexts they are interchangeable. As will be discussed in a later chapter we have found it necessary to assign a special meaning at any rate to one of them – task – as a specific piece of work to be completed in a specific period of time. The meaning to be assigned to 'function' is as follows. In establishing any organizational structure some basic assumptions have to be made about the general and continuing aims, goals, or objects, which are to be served. It is these basic and continuing goals underlying organizational structure which we shall refer to as 'functions'.

Having said this, however, it must be stressed immediately that decisions about these basic goals by no means exhaust all the decisions which have to be made about ends and values. Statements of functions merely settle decisions of goal or value which are inescapable if organizational structure is to be devised in a rational way. Thereafter, the various individuals who man the structure so devised will necessarily spend much of their time in further discussion and arguments about ends and values, indeed, making value judgements which often imply a radical reallocation of resources and reorientation of direction. On occasion, of course, they will wish to reassess the very functions which are to be performed, and then over and above reallocating resources and priorities, new or modified organization must be brought into being.[3]

In essence we are drawing attention to three quite separate stages in establishing the total framework within which work is carried out in organizations in general, or SSDs in particular:

(1) decisions about *organizational functions* (i.e. fundamental and continuing goals);
(2) decisions about the *organizational structure* necessary to carry out these functions;

[3] Again we might warn against a too-hasty jump from the word 'function' to the assumption that in sociological terms, a 'structural-functional' approach is being adopted. Again we must stress that the attempt in this project is to help various *participants* – local authorities, legislators, members of SSDs – to reach consensus on the kind of work to be carried out; not to deduce the necessary functions of SSDs from some abstract consideration of the role required of them in contributing to the maintenance and so on of society as a whole (Parsons, 1960), or in order for their continuing survival in an environment of change (Miller and Rice, 1967).

(3) decisions within given organizational structure about general working objectives, standards, and priorities, in given circumstances at given periods of time – what might be called *operating policies*[4].

Harking back to the previous chapter, it is evident that social analysis as a method of work is likely to have a maximum contribution in clarifying decisions in the first and second areas listed above. Decisions in the third area are often quite heavily 'political' in character. They depend on knowledge and understanding of specific circumstances and specific needs, and are necessarily shot-through with intuitive feelings about what is valid and desirable for particular localities at particular times.

The Functions of Social Services Departments and Their Relationship to Legislation

Our analysis of the functions of present-day SSDs is shown in Table 3.1. As has been said, it has not arisen directly out of any one field-project, but has been created in response to a growing need to have some general framework against which to set more specific problems and discussion.[5] Before examining it in detail several preliminary points must be made.

First, such a list should not be taken as in any way an attempt to prescribe for all places and for all time what are the proper functions of social services agencies. It is intended as a list of the typical activities of one particular kind of social service agencies – local authority SSDs in England and Wales – under the given conditions of legislation and social setting in which they find themselves for the present. Such a list might easily be modified for the particular circumstances of any given authority, and it

---

[4] The distinction here between *organizational functions* and *operating policies* has some resemblances to the distinction between 'official goals' and 'operating goals' made by Perrow (1961). However, we believe that an extended statement of basic functions such as that suggested below, can be put to specific practical purposes, in contrast to his image of official goals as essentially vague and abstract, and without significant practical consequences.

[5] Its main testing has been in conference discussions with senior officers from social services over several years, during the course of which it has gone through considerable evolution from earlier versions.

TABLE 3.1

ANALYSIS OF THE PRESENT FUNCTIONS OF SOCIAL SERVICES DEPARTMENTS

General Function – the prevention or relief of social distress in individuals, families, and communities, in liaison with other statutory and voluntary agencies.

This general function is split into a number of more specific functions:

Research and Evaluation
(Ascertainment of the extent and nature of social distress and evaluation of the adequacy of existing operational activities to meet this distress.)

Strategic Planning
(Planning, in conjunction with other statutory, private, or voluntary, agencies in the field, new or improved operational activities to meet needs.)

Operational Work at the Community Level
(Work at the community level directly aimed at the prevention or relief of social distress.)
    assisting voluntary welfare activity
    stimulating self-help groups amongst those in need
    registration and inspection of the activities of individuals or agencies engaged in private or voluntary welfare work
    mass screening for individual social distress
    creating public knowledge of services and rights.

Operational Work with Individuals and Families
(Work with individuals, singly or in groups, aimed directly at prevention or relief of social distress.)

    basic social work
    (the basic or central core of social work with individuals)
    – making assessments of need and of appropriate response
    – providing information and advice
    – monitoring and supervision
    – helping to maintain and develop personal capacity for adequate social functioning
    – arranging provision of other appropriate services

basic services
- providing money and goods
- providing meals
- providing accommodation
- providing transport
- providing help in daily living
- providing recreation, social, and cultural life

supplementary services
- providing aids and adaptations
- providing communication and mobility training
- providing occupational training and sheltered employment
- providing management of clients' property
- providing an adoption agency service
- providing medical and paramedical treatment*
- providing formal education*
(*in some degree).

Public Relations
(Maintenance of a good general social environment through press contact, lectures, etc.)

Staffing and Training
(Recruitment, general training, and welfare of staff.)

Managerial and Co-ordinative Work
(Selection and induction of staff, prescription of work, co-ordination of work, monitoring of work, personal appraisal, staff development, etc.)

Logistics
(Provision of premises and equipment, materials, and other supporting services to enable operational and other work to be performed.)

Finance
(Collection and disbursement of cash, accounting, budgeting, and budgetary control.)

Secretarial
(Recording and communication of decisions, actions, and events.)

---

would obviously require extension were substantial new legislation to appear. The list has not been produced, then, by some process of grand deduction from the general aim reproduced at its head. On the contrary, it has come from consideration of all the activities that already appear to be being undertaken (more or less adequately) in SSDs, and the statement of general aim has arisen from an attempt to generalize them.

Second, its relation to legislation must be noted. Properly, according to the *ultra vires* principle, no local authority can undertake any (substantial) activities which it is not obliged or allowed to do in legislation, although some deviations from this weighty ruling probably occur in practice in a minor way from time to time.[6] There is no question, then, of the work of any local authority department being split into two parts, the statutory and the other. All the detailed functions listed in Table 3.1 are, in fact, reflected more or less closely in legislation. There is, however, some divergence in two respects. It is an interesting fact that the legislation that brought the new SSDs into being contained no statement of overall purpose or aim.[7] Instead a heterogeneous collection of duties was gathered together from existing legislation, ranging from those as broad as promoting welfare of the physically handicapped[8] and welfare of the mentally disordered[9] to those as specific as providing supervision of wards of court,[10] providing burial or cremation for vagrants or others found dead, providing temporary protection of property belonging to people in hospital, and recovering from putative fathers costs of providing assistance for illegitimate children.[11]

In offering a statement of general aim or function, the list in Table 3.1 therefore stimulates consideration of the *development* of further specific legislation, as further specific needs are identified

Where there is also some question of divergence between the

---

[6] Some social workers from former children's departments suggest that advisory and preventive work with families often went beyond existing legislation prior to the 1963 Children's Act. Presumably local authorities of the time were somehow able to satisfy their District Auditors as to the propriety of the expenditure involved!

[7] See the Local Authority Social Services Act 1970. This may be contrasted with other social legislation, for example, the National Health Service Act 1946 or the Social Work (Scotland) Act 1968 which do contain such general statements. The latter speaks of the duty of every local authority 'to promote social welfare by making available advice, guidance and assistance on such a scale as may be appropriate for their area ...' (Section 12).

[8] National Assistance Act 1948, Sections 29 and 30.

[9] Mental Health Act 1959, Section 8.

[10] Family Law Reform Act 1969, Section 7.

[11] National Assistance Act 1948. Sections 50. 48. and 43.

bounds of present legislation and the suggested statement, is in the definition of the kinds of persons for whom these functions may be invoked. All existing legislation is in terms of closely-defined clientele, be they children, the elderly, the chronically sick and disabled, or the mentally ill; and not just in terms of the 'needy'. Certain classes of needy persons such as the single homeless vagrant or the childless couple with marital problems are not specifically covered by legislation, though it may very well be argued that these people, too, give rise to, or suffer from, 'social distress'. The problem is, of course, well known, and each department in practice already has to make up its mind on who does and who does not count as eligible for its help or intervention, and under which of the broader items of legislation it is going to justify any expenditure if questioned.

The third general point that must be made is that in producing a formulation we have attempted to avoid the trap of confusing *functions* with *occupations*. Thus to suggest, for instance, that SSDs must carry out 'residential work' or provide 'occupational therapy' is to do little more than say that they must (or do) employ residential workers and occupational therapists. For the most part it is true that specifying a profession or occupation amounts to the same thing as specifying the functions to be carried out. However, it is just in cases where occupational groups – like residential workers or occupational therapists in fact – are most unclear about their own identity and role that there is most need for a clear specification of the functions to be carried out in various employing agencies, so that the occupational groups concerned may judge what recruitment and training should be staged accordingly. In fact, as we shall see, some of the functions which are identified cut right across established groups such as 'field' social workers and 'residential' social workers.

Generally, too, we have avoided the use of all common terms like 'case work', 'social work', and 'community work' precisely because there are so many extant interpretations of these terms. (Some possible equivalence between the terms shown in Table 3.1 and those more commonplace terms are discussed later in this chapter.) These and other general points made so far in this chapter may be summarized as shown in Figure 3.1.

What is being said in essence, is that the analysis of the required functions of SSDs is not only a necessary preliminary to the

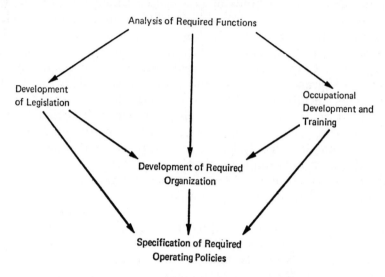

Figure 3.1

development of required organization, but it is also a stimulus to considering necessary developments in legislation, and a point of reference from which to chart developments in occupational structure and training.

The General Function of Social Services Departments

Proceeding to the actual content of Table 3.1 it may be seen that the proposed statement of the general or overall function of SSDs is:

> the prevention or relief of social distress in individuals, families, and communities, in liaision with other statutory and voluntary agencies.

Naturally such a broad statement raises many questions. What, for a start, is 'social distress' and how does it differ simply from 'distress'?

Whilst it is difficult to answer this directly, it certainly appears necessary to register the fundamental distinction between the sort of needs expected to be met by, for example, a social services

agency and those expected to be met by a health service, an
employment service, an industrial conciliation service, or a church;
all of which are also in some degree in the business of offering
to relieve distress of one kind or another.

'Social distress' is the best phrase we have to distinguish a certain sort of need from what is customarily classified as physical
or mental ill health on the one hand, or on the other from those
personal problems which have not yet reached the point where
the social functioning of the person concerned has fallen below
what at any time is regarded as a generally acceptable level.[12] (To
distinguish these is not to deny that such needs frequently arise
in combination. Ill-health for example, is often accompanied by
social distress.)

A criticism sometimes raised is that such an aim is too narrow,
and that some positive phrase such as the 'enhancement of the
quality of life' is more appropriate than the seemingly dismal concern with 'social distress'. The broader aim is tempting, but once
again the real need is to distinguish the function of SSDs from
that of many other agencies also concerned with the quality of life.[13]
Education departments, housing departments, planning departments, are also concerned with the quality of life – in fact, this is
the concern of all branches of the local authority. One could perhaps say that SSDs by their inclusion in (general purpose) local
authorities are in that way associated with a general quest for the
enhancement of the quality of the social life of their locality. One
could also add more specifically, that to the extent that Directors
and other officers of SSDs are involved in strategic planning for

[12] There is no formal statement of the proper aims of SSDs in the
Seebohm Report, but para. 139 refers to the responsibility for 'the prevention,
treatment, and relief of social problems' and para. 140 refers to a comprehensive approach to 'the problem of individuals and families and the
community in which they live'. Elsewhere, frequent use is made of the
phrase 'social distress' (e.g. para. 142, para. 427).

[13] Wootton's (1959) classic attack on the social caseworkers' pretensions
to 'omniscience and omnipotence' in seeking to define the scope of their
role (as opposed to the reality of what they do in practice) is an obvious
reference here. The natural desire of social services to deal with the whole
man, the whole family, the whole neigbourhood, the whole community,
leads logically to a takeover bid for all other agencies in the public sector.
The desire may be natural enough, but the end result of amalgamating
all interacting social agencies, as Kogan (1969) points out, is the absurdity
of a 'Ministry of the People'.

the authority as a whole their function transcends a mere concern with actual or potential social distress or malfunction (see further discussion in Chapter 9). These provisos apart, we come back to the point that all activities for which the SSD has specific account-ability do seem to be concerned with actual social distress or with the prevention of incipient social distress.[14] SSDs are obliged to be selective where and with whom they work. In this respect, they are different from education, library, parks, or planning, depart-ments, for example, whose concerns are universal in the sense that they are obliged to be thinking continually of how they may enhance the quality of life of all who live in their locality.

Responsibility for the provision of play groups and day nurseries provides an interesting test case. To the extent that play groups and day nurseries provide pre-school education, they meet a uni-versal need. From this viewpoint they – in common with nursery schools – should be a responsibility of the education department. But they have another function, which is to meet 'social need' by taking care, for certain periods during the day, of young children whose families for one reason or another are not otherwise able to look after them properly. This obviously links with the work of SSDs, and here the need to be met is not a universal one.[15]

Again, on the subject of provision of temporary accommodation for the homeless[16] it can be and has been argued that it is the job of housing authorities to make universal provision for what is clearly a universal need – the provision of houses. The job of social services might better be defined as providing comprehensive support for those families which, quite apart from being simply without a roof over their heads, were for some reason or other

[14] The Seebohm Report (Chapter XIV) distinguishes what it calls *specific* prevention (which is the job of SSDs) from *general* prevention – 'com-munity-wide policies aimed at creating environments conducive to social well-being by improving work opportunities and conditions by assuring reasonable standards of living or educational attainments'. Such broad matters clearly involve many agencies other than SSDs.

[15] See the discussion of this issue in the Seebohm Report, paras. 200–205. The Committee argued on a majority view that since the main needs which were met by play groups and day nurseries were 'social' SSDs should assume responsibilty for them (as in fact they have).

[16] Under the National Assistance Act 1948, Section 21.

constitutionally incapable of making or keeping a proper home.[17]

Having said all this one notes the ultimate difficulty of capturing in precise definition the overall aim of any fundamental social agency. Indeed the constant interpretation and reinterpretation of basic aims is part and parcel of the process of evolution.

The Specific Functions of Social Services Departments

Proceeding to the specific functions of SSDs listed in Table 3.1 it will be seen that the phrase *operational work* is used at certain points. By this is meant the work which directly promotes the department's aims – in this case the prevention or relief of social distress. In other words, operational work is the 'output'.

The concept is important, for example, in defining what is meant by *research and evaluation*, the first item on the list. Here the phrase is taken to mean research applied to the field in which operational work is to be carried out, and subsequent evaluation of the success and adequacy of this operational work. Research – systematic research that is – can, of course, be in relation to any object of the department's work. It can be applied to management processes, to recruitment problems, to staff attitudes, and so on. Some restriction of definition is necessary if the term is to be meaningful in the organizational context. (Many actual 'research' sections probably lack just this clear focus. To establish 'research' sections without any closer definition of the field of work is surely as unrealistic as establishing, say, a special section concerned with 'communication' or with 'efficiency'.)

Strategic planning is seen as springing naturally from such specific research and evaluation.[18] It, too, is seen as having an operational focus. The use of the word 'strategic' implies planning that is long-term and comprehensive, and, if it is to be at all adequate, planning which takes due account of the physical facilities and resources of manpower required. By implication such planning is directed

[17] See Seebohm, paras. 401–405. The report even went as far as suggesting that social services might provide special 'recuperative units' for such problem families (para. 405).

[18] The picture of a continuous cycle of research, planning, delivery, and evaluation evoked here is similar in essence to that used by Foren and Brown (1971) as a starting point for their analysis of SSDs.

'upwards', that is, it is the sort of planning that requires political and financial ratification by higher organizational levels before it can begin to have effect. (Later, a different and more short-term species of planning will be distinguished, inherent in what will be called 'operational co-ordination', which is 'downwards' in the sense of being capable of implementation without further ado within agreed and established policy.) The phrase 'strategic planning' as used here is equivalent to what in the industrial context is more usually called corporate or long-range planning.[19] Since the work of SSDs interlinks so closely with that of other local authority departments (for example, housing and education), with existing voluntary agencies in the welfare field, and with many other statutory authorities (health, social security, police, prisons, courts, and so on), it is obvious that there can be no systematic and effective large-scale planning that is not undertaken in liaison with other such agencies.

The next main heading in Table 3.1 is *operational work at the community level*. This does not rest on any particular definition of 'community' (a slippery word) but is merely a convenient phrase to gather together all operational work that is not focused on any one individual, but rather on greater or smaller sections of local society as a whole or on the agencies who serve it. Within this main heading, the activity of *assisting voluntary welfare* includes the giving of financial aid to existing voluntary organizations (societies for the deaf, blind, or disabled, for example) or the stimulation of new voluntary organizations or groups. By and large, it refers to work with bodies of people who are not themselves in need, but who are proposing to work on behalf of others. By contrast, the subheading *stimulating self-help groups amongst those in need* refers to such things as helping those in deprived neighbourhoods to form housing associations, tenants' associations, or play groups, for example, in order to overcome some of their own problems. *Registration and inspection of the activities of individuals or agencies engaged in private or voluntary welfare work* includes both work with private agencies or establishments

[19] Although the phrase 'corporate planning', as used within local authorities, usually implies strategic planning which concerns the local authority as a whole, across all its departments (Stewart, 1971). Nevertheless, the process, and the orientation to needs and outputs rather than to internal problems, is the same at both departmental and local authority level.

(for example private homes for the elderly) and work with child minders. Though these two types of work are frequently carried out by different staff, we suggest that they are essentially similar in nature.

The subheading *mass screening for individual social distress* is intended to convey something distinctively different from *research.* The obvious analogies here are with such public health activities as mass radiography or mass cytology. It is certainly true that mass screening produces invaluable research data, but the purpose obviously goes well beyond mere research. The clear implication of any mass screening activity is that appropriate treatment or remedial action is to follow in *all* cases where deficiency or danger has been revealed. Research does not carry this specific implication; and indeed by various sampling techniques is often able to avoid the laborious chore of establishing and identifying each individual case of need. The best existing example of mass screening in SSDs is that which departments have undertaken in response to their statutory obligation to ascertain the number of all chronically sick and disabled people living within their locality.[20]

The final item under the heading of operational work at the community level, namely *creating public knowledge of services or rights,* may not be one that receives much attention in departments under present conditions, but there is little hesitation amongst those in the service with whom we have discussed the matter that such an item should be included in any such list. Again, the obvious example is the statutory obligation to disseminate to the chronically sick and disabled information of services available and their rights to them. Of course the inclusion of such an item as one of the proper and inescapable functions of SSDs says nothing about the desirable level or range of activity. The over-enthusiastic pursuit of such activities could obviously lead to circumstances in which the department was embarrassed with a surge of demand which it was then unable to meet.

Operational Work with Individuals and Families

The next main heading, *operational work with individuals and families,* describes what is perhaps the most publically evident of

[20] Chronically Sick and Disabled Persons Act 1970, Section 1.

all the department's work. However, the proper formulation of the specific activities it encompasses has proved to be extremely difficult.

Conventional analysis of the department's work at this point would, no doubt, employ terms like 'field work', 'residential work', 'day care', 'domiciliary care'. But these do not stand up in any hard analysis as distinct and independent entities. Residential work, for example, involves the provision of meals. So may domiciliary care. Day care may involve the provision of occupational training. So may residential care. Some clients may be provided with accommodation 'in the community' in the form of foster homes or in temporary housing; others receive accommodation as one part of 'residential care'. It is universally agreed that clients in any setting – in their own home, in foster homes or lodgings, in local authority homes, in hospitals or special schools – are likely to need some common thread of service at a higher or more intangible level, be it called 'case work', 'social work', or simply 'support'.

As will be seen from Table 3.1, an analysis is offered which cuts across these conventional distinctions. An attempt has been made to identify the various elements which are to be provided in various settings and in various mixes according to the particular need of the client concerned. They have been divided into three main groups: *basic services, supplementary services,* and what (for want of a better phrase) may be called *basic social work.*

Basic services is perhaps an obvious category. It includes all the more straightforward things which the department may provide in various settings – food, a roof, goods, help in dressing, washing, cleaning, and so on. Often these services are provided by ancillary, 'non-professional' staff. (Though one must resist the temptation to analyse by occupational groups rather than by the nature of the work itself.)

Supplementary services is used to describe a number of further specific services which may be provided in various settings over and above the basic services just discussed. Usually they involve staff with specialized skill or knowledge. As with basic services, they can be provided in separate elements as required. In looking in detail at what they comprise, it is interesting to note that to some extent present SSDs are not only in the welfare business as it might be narrowly interpreted, but are also in the education, health, and employment business. SSDs sometimes employ their own medical officers, chiropodists, physiotherapists. They employ teachers in some community homes (formerly approved schools). They themselves provide work for the disabled both at home and in day centres.[21]

Before passing on from these two areas of work it must be added that the distinction between basic services and supplementary services cannot be pressed too hard. By and large, as has just been observed, the activities described here as *supplementary services* are provided by staff with special qualifications or experience – though this would not be true of the management of property for those in residential care, or for the provision of certain simple aids. By and large *basic services* are provided by ancillary staff. But these distinctions are not definitive, nor can other definitive distinctions be offered. The important thing is the specific list of items prepared under these two main headings. However, it is convenient, as we shall see, to have some term – in this case 'basic services' – to describe a range of fundamental provisions which appear to be required (amongst others) in all residential establishments, of whatever kind.

Perhaps the most difficult work to come to terms with is that listed under the third subheading here, *basic social work*. Field social workers carry it out but so do some residential workers, and others, too. It will certainly include what is commonly known in the social work profession as 'case work', but as it is defined, will also include what is commonly known as 'group work'. Some of the more exacting or specialized parts will only be able to be performed by well-qualified and well-experienced workers, and in this sense, the adjective 'basic' is perhaps misleading. Other parts, like providing certain kinds of information or carrying out certain routine monitoring of the well-being of clients, will be capable of delegation to relatively inexperienced or less intensively-trained staff.

[21] Whether the employment of such staff might better rest with other agencies is an open question. At the time of writing it is assumed that the employment of all medical, paramedical, and nursing, staff will pass to Health Authorities, mirroring the move for SSDs to employ all social workers who carry out their work in health care settings.

It is perhaps surprising to see words like 'monitoring' and 'supervision' appearing as part of the description of what otherwise would appear to be a wholly permissive client-initiated activity. However, it is abundantly clear that there are many situations where departments must and do intervene whether the 'client' likes it or not. Such intervention is legislatively prescribed where children are being maltreated, where those with acute mental disturbance are in need of compulsory removal to hospital, and where the senile old, whether they know it or not, can no longer look after themselves.

We come then to the centre of the difficulty, the activity called here *helping to maintain and develop personal capacity for adequate social functioning.* Here we have in mind an activity designed to help better social functioning which may be distinguished from provision of material aid or even from the provision of simple information or specific advice. The word 'capacity' is crucial. The activity considered is addressed generally to the way the individual acts and responds; to his ability to use material aid or information adequately in various life situations; to his ability to establish healthy relationships with others with whom he comes into contact at various times; that is, to his own in-built constitution.

Now it is not part of our concern to enter the various controversies about how such 'people-changing' activities are best carried out; whether they ever rest on a truly scientific basis; whether they ought to yield first place to 'environment-changing' activities. It is not part of our concern to advocate a non-directive as opposed to an interventionist approach; a 'functional' as opposed to a 'diagnostic' approach; to advocate 'crisis-intervention' as opposed to long-term case work; to weigh the merits of 'interpretive' as opposed to 'ego-supportive' work; and so on.[22]

It is merely our concern here to note that such activities *are* carried out in SSDs, and to attempt to describe them in terms which are broad enough to be comprehensive of many schools of thought without being so broad as to be meaningless. In this way it may be possible to understand better how such work should be organized and ordered, and to decide what categories of staff are going to have to undertake it.

[22] For further references to these and other approaches in social case work see Roberts and Nee (1970)

Other Functions Carried Out Within Social Services Departments

The remaining functions listed in Table 3.1 are not themselves operational but either support or control operational work in some way. Each is evident not only in SSDs but in many other large-scale organizations in various fields of business, and all must presumably exist, in embryo at least, in all undertakings, however small. All organizations must in some degree attend to their general public image (*public relations*). All must recruit and train staff (*staffing* and *training*). All greater than one person in size find themselves involved in the activities of control and co-ordination *per se* which arise where two or more people work together in some complex role-structure (*managerial and co-ordinative work*). All must assemble various physical resources to promote their work (*logistics*), must maintain accounts of their expenses (*finance*), and maintain and transmit records and reports of their activities and achievements (*secretarial work*).[23] The detailed nature of these activities and the organizational arrangements necessary to undertake them are explored in depth in the next chapter.

Standards of Service and the 'Caring' Attitude

Considering the list in Table 3.1 as a whole, one can perhaps at this point anticipate a likely reaction. 'What' (many readers may ask) 'has happened to the *essence* of good social work? Where has the tender care gone, the loving nurture, the sympathetic support

[23] It way well be that the main headings on this list: research into needs and evaluation of services; strategic planning; public relations; staffing; managerial and co-ordinative work; logistics; finance and secretarial work; together with the operations themselves, form a useful analytical framework for any organization. At another level we have also found the list useful in this project when carrying out systematic analysis of the functions in any role – as in the production of job descriptions for example. Generally, the analysis at this point is in keeping with an 'open-system' view, seeing organizations as continuously in interaction with their environments in procuring and processing various inputs of money, materials, information, and human resources. More specifically, links will be obvious with Miller and Rice's (1967) identification of *operations, maintenance,* and *regulatory* activities; and with Katz and Kahn's (1966) identification of *production, supportive, maintenance, adaptive,* and *managerial* subsystems, a development of an earlier formulation proposed by Parsons (1960).

to those in distress, that a good department provides quite over and above all those concrete functions. What, in other words, has happened to the quality of the work?'

The main answer is that the analysis above is simply not about the particular *standards* of work which are adopted in any case, about the *way* in which activities are carried out, or about the *attitudes* and *outlook* of those who perform them.[24] Of course all these things are of vital importance, but such discussion simply goes beyond the basic analysis of function which is of concern here. An analysis of functions, at appropriate depth, will indicate what sort of department to create and what sorts of workers will be required to man it. It will not indicate what operating policies to adopt, what procedures to use, what standards to set and inculcate, or what sort of 'atmosphere' to create – though these are important things which must sooner or later be tackled by any department. But conversely – and this is the point – discussion of attitudes and outlook, and standards and 'atmosphere', are not in themselves sufficient to allow decisions on the structure of departments and the proper work of various occupational groups within them. As long as it is clear what is hoped to be done with an analysis of functions, and the limits of this, one need not be abashed that the discussion makes so little use of all the 'good' words, all the vivid, emotionally-positive, adjectives.

On a slightly different issue, it has been and continues to be a moot point whether or not some such function as 'nurture' or 'general care' should appear in this list. By and large we are persuaded – the value-charged descriptions apart – that, say, the activity of nurturing children in care is no more in functional terms than appropriate combinations of the various activities listed above. There are, however, those that argue that the function of 'nurture' or 'general care' does include elements which, though they may be difficult to define, nevertheless make it greater than the sum of any of these particular constituents.

[24] Thus, when Smith and Harris (1972) talk of *relief* functions, *treatment* functions, and *social control* and *moral reform* functions of social services departments, they are really addressing themselves to the ideologies of different individual social workers. Similarly Blau and Scott's (1963, p. 66) famous study of 'County Agency' is concerned with the *attitudes* of workers of different backgrounds to such things as career and agency policy and about their *orientations*. It is not about organization itself as defined here.

Field Work, Residential Work, Etc.

It remains to try and relate this analysis of the functions of SSDs to the more commonplace administrative or professional descriptions of social work. Let us consider for a start some of the conventional administrative classifications such as 'field work', 'residential work', 'domiciliary services', and 'day care'. The first point to make is that these terms do not (in our experience) refer to exactly the same activities in every department where they are employed. Furthermore, it has seemed impossible to produce any definitions of them which would be both precise and significant enough to deepen understanding of the essential nature of the work to be carried out. Nevertheless, if only because of their regular use it is necessary to come to terms with them as far as possible.

Some help in clarification is provided if a related area is considered in which clear distinctions are readily available (an area already mentioned earlier in the chapter), namely the *setting* in which the client resides at any time and around which his life is centred. The client might, for example, reside:

- in his own home
- in lodgings, or a foster home, or private home
- in residential care (in a local authority or voluntary home)
- in hospital
- in a boarding school.

In any of these situations, various packages of care or service of the kind described in the list above may be delivered to him, ranging from minimal intervention to what in effect is complete and comprehensive care. Not all elements in certain settings described above will be provided by the same agency, of course. For example, food, accommodation, and help in daily living are provided by health authorities for those in hospital.

From this viewpoint, the following equivalences can be established, bearing in mind that they are very broad indeed:

Field Work
　Basic social work with individuals living at home, in lodgings, in foster homes, hospitals, boarding schools, and (in some respects) *basic social work* also with those in residential care, *plus* various

elements of *operational work at the community level* as defined
above, i.e. stimulating self-help groups, assisting voluntary welfare
activity, etc.

Domiciliary and Day Care
Provision of various *basic services* and *supplementary services* for
those living at home, in lodgings, in foster homes, and occasionally
also for those in residential care (as in the provision of day centres
for the mentally handicapped who reside in local authority homes);
occasionally also the provision of *basic social work* for those who
attend day centres.

Residential Care
Provision of *basic services* and (in some respects) *basic social work*
for those who are in residential care.

The hazy nature of the boundaries between these categories becomes evident. Is the provision of *basic social work* for those in
residential care part of field work or part of residential work, or
(even in some cases) part of day care? In many ways the use of
these three terms obscures more problems than it clarifies. Since
they are in common usage, however, they will be employed in
the subsequent discussion where broad and general descriptions
are all that the argument requires.

Case Work, Group Work, and Community Work

The difficulties of precise definitions that arise with other commonplace terms used in professional discussions – terms like 'case
work', 'group work', and 'community work' – are, of course,
notorious. Far from making a direct assault on this Everest of a
problem, strewn with the litter and casualties of earlier pioneers,
one is diffident even to offer broad descriptions in the way just
attempted for 'field work', etc. Nor need we here be too concerned
with such a task. The important thing perhaps is to ensure that
any analysis of function like that offered above is comprehensive
enough to let each would-be explorer (to maintain the analogy)
define what line of attack he likes, in keeping with the particular
conception of case work, community work, etc., that he wishes
to promote.

Thus there is no need here to worry whether 'social case work',
in addition to what has been called *basic social work* in Table 3.1,

includes also the actual provision of some more material things described there as *basic services*.[25] There is no need to worry whether 'social work' is synonymous with 'case work', or whether it is equivalent to all the activities carried out by an SSD. There is no need to worry whether 'community work' means merely stimulating self-help groups amongst those in distress, and assisting voluntary welfare activity (in the language of Figure 3.1); or whether its essence is in planning to avoid future social distress by large-scale preventive actions by many different social agencies what has been called above 'strategic planning'.[26] The important thing is to make sure that any comprehensive list of departmental work makes provisions somewhere for *all* these activities to be carried out in whatever manner and proportions are judged best.

The same point can be made with regard to three other kinds of activity which are currently the subject of some special interest in professional discussion – 'social action', 'intermediate treatment'. and 'group work'.

A 'provisional definition' of social action offered by a Special Working Party set up by the British Association of Social Workers reads as follows: 'Social action means tactics and strategies used to achieve changes in the *social situation* of individuals, groups, and communities' (our italics).[27] Many of the particular activities which are then discussed by the Working Party readily fit into the framework established here, e.g. carrying out surveys of need,

---

[25] The literature on social case work is vast. A useful overview is provided by Hartman (1971). See also Roberts and Nee (1970).

[26] Again, the literature on community work is too great to be systematically quoted here. The Gulbenkian Report (Calouste Gulbenkian Foundation, 1968) on the training of community workers in Great Britain is a useful starting point. It suggests three main levels of activity:

(1) face-to-face work with local or neighbourhood groups (p. 35, p. 69);
(2) facilitating agency and inter-agency co-ordination and sustaining and promoting social groups (p. 35, p. 72);
(3) community planning and policy formation, based on research (p. 35, p. 74).

The first activity is referred to, in this country at any rate, as *community development* (Seebohm Report, para. 480). All these activities are, of course, covered at some point or other in the list developed above. The Gulbenkian Report (p. 34) emphasizes that not only professional community workers are concerned with community work thus defined, but also many other people concerned with social provision (p. 34).

[27] British Association of Social Workers (1971).

stimulating other agencies to action, public education, establishing
self-reliant and vocal groups in run-down communities. Most of
these are what we have categorized above as *operational work at
the community level*. But others, such as organizing political action
and demonstrations, making direct approaches to legislators and
the press, are more difficult to place. Of course, certain of these
'pressurizing' activities form a natural part of any organizational
life. It is commonplace for employees in many organizations to
put direct pressure on their managers or their employers to adopt
new policies, to allocate more resources or (as the employees see
it) to adopt a more enlightened outlook. In large organizations
such attitudes may often be undertaken through employee 'representative systems' and where the work is national in scope, indeed,
through professional associations as well (see Chapter 2).

Having isolated such specific activities which are relatively free
from problems, one is admittedly then left with a recalcitrant
remainder. How far can the employed social worker properly
step out of his organizational role to criticize or even to act against
the agency which employs him? Is he ultimately responsible to
his clients (however he defines them) or to his employers? The
broader ethical and social issues here are considerable.

As far as 'intermediate treatment' is concerned, as a particular
strategy for dealing with certain sorts of young people in need
of care, protection, or control,[28] we have had little or no chance so
far to explore its meaning in project work. We assume that this
activity too is capable of expression in some combinations of the
terms described above – helping to develop personal capacity for
adequate social functioning, monitoring, and supervision, etc.

The term 'group work' raises a slightly difficult question. First,
it must be assumed that work with clients in face-to-face groups
is always concerned with some specific end. The process may be
helping a group of mentally ill clients to achieve more normal
functioning, or helping members of a family to understand each
others' particular problems better, or helping groups of foster
parents to understand their particular roles better; but it is never
just 'working with a group'.

In reality group work consists of a whole bundle of techniques
which may be employed in a variety of situations to further cer-

[28] See the White Paper – *Children in Trouble* (Home Office, 1968) the
Children's Act 1969, and *Intermediate Treatment* (DHSS, 1972).

tain ends which are to be independently defined. The ends may be helping to improve capacity for social functioning, giving information, providing recreation, providing employment, or indeed, some combination. Sometimes these ends can best be served by working in one-to-one relationships, sometimes by working in groups, and sometimes by both together. On these arguments, group work is not a specific function in its own right, or any combination of the specific functions listed above.

Conclusion

Here, then, is a general statement of all the functions to be carried out in SSDs. It is a statement which eschews commonplace descriptions of activity, either in administrative terms (field work, residential care, day care, domiciliary services, and the like) or in broader professional terms (case work, group work, community work, and so on). It attempts to describe in sharp and realistic terms the various combinations of services and interventions that can be offered in many different settings; the home, the hospital, the residential establishment, and so on. It does not try to describe the standards, attitudes, or values, which should colour such work, but above all attempts to offer what is rarely offered in such discussions – a *comprehensive* statement of the work to be carried out; and not only immediate work with clients, but the broader work of planning, co-ordinating, and servicing the main operational work as well.

Such a statement, even though it may require modification in the light of further work, provides a proper and necessary basis for a number of more specific fields of exploration which are pursued in the chapters which follow – the kinds of organization and procedures needed in SSDs, the various kinds of occupational groups which are called for, and the orientation of training within such groups in order that they can play the part required of them, individually and in combination.

4 Alternative Departmental Structures

The unfortunate thing about designing organizational structures is that one inevitably tears apart in practice activities that can only too easily be shown to be inseparable in principle. No sooner had Seebohm's cause of integrated social services triumphed than committees and directors were faced with the job of how to divide them all up again, in allocating them to various divisions and branches of the new so-called integrated departments.

By emphasis on the overall requirements of the individual or family rather than on particular kinds of problems, Seebohm in effect said – however you organize, do not organize as you have in the past on the basis of separate work with children, the handicapped, the homeless, the mentally ill, and so on. Instead, prime emphasis was laid on the provision of comprehensive social work from Area Offices situated where they were most accessible, the 'one door' for the individual or family in distress. But social work in the community, so called 'field work', is not the only work that the department has to carry out. Residential care and various forms of day care and domiciliary support are needed, as well. Given the emphasis on such 'Area Offices', it was perhaps natural for those who had to organize the new departments to think first of organizing them all in one 'field work' division, and thereafter to assign the other work – residential care, day care, and domiciliary care – to complementary divisions. And in any case, the former departments, within their particular specialisms, had mostly been organized on this basis.

In fact, what was happening over and beyond putting personal social services under the co-ordinating control of one departmental director rather than many, can be conceptualized as a shift from organization primarily according to *kind of client* (more strictly, *client need*), to organization primarily according to kind of work, or more precisely, *function*. Though indeed the division of work *below* departmental level in children's welfare, and mental health, departments had already been functional.

However, these are not the only possible bases of organizational division. Stepping back to survey the subject broadly, it seems that at least five separate possibilities exist, at any rate in principle. Departments might be primarily organized according to:

- *function (purpose, kind of work)* (in whatever terms it might appropriately be described) e.g. field work, residential care, day care; or (in the terms used in the previous chapter) e.g. provision of accommodation, help to achieve personal capacity for adequate social functioning, provision of help in daily living;
- *place*, e.g. geographical division. area, 'patch';
- *kind of client*, e.g. children, the elderly, vagrants;
- *kind of worker*, e.g. social worker, occupational therapist, home help;
- *method of work*, e.g. work in groups, work with individuals, work with communities, etc.[1]

[1] The classic analysis of this was provided by Gulick (1937) whose framework was *purpose, process, clientele,* and *place*. Wilensky and Lebeaux (1965) extend a similar analysis specifically to the social welfare field where they suggest that the service provided under any particular *auspices* (or *sponsorship*) can be divided according to *purpose* (or *programme*), e.g. case work, group work, community organization; *clientele*; and *geography* (or *location*); and they discuss the pros and cons of each division (p. 248–259). In effect it is suggested above that *kind of worker (skill)*, and *method of work (process)*, ought to be considered as separate categories.

Note the distinction between *functions*, which refer to ends or purposes, even if they seem to be expressed in 'activity' words and *methods* which are references to how activities are carried out, or what kind of activities are carried out in pursuit of ends which remain to be specified.

Note also that *kind of client* is not quite the same as the client himself – the crucial Seebohm argument. Thus the same client, or client-family, may exhibit youthfulness, homelessness, mental handicap, or any number of states or conditions. Organization strictly according to the client with all needs considered would arguably constitute a sixth category, though one perhaps lacking credibility as a prime basis for organization in SSDs – one division for all clients A–F, one for all clients G–N, and so on!

Manifest Structures of the New Departments

The hundred and seventy new departments that came into existence were not all organized in the same way. Three examples of different departmental structure – at least as structure was officially described on paper – from authorities with whom we have worked are shown in Figures 4.1, 4.2, and 4.3.

The Brent organization (Figure 4.1) or something like it was a commonly adopted pattern.[2] One operational division was to deal with field work, through Seebohm-type Area Offices, whilst the other operational activities, residential work, day and domiciliary services were combined into a second division. A third division was to provide administrative support, namely secretarial and financial work. A fourth was to carry out the remainder of the 'non-operational' activities described in the previous chapter – research,

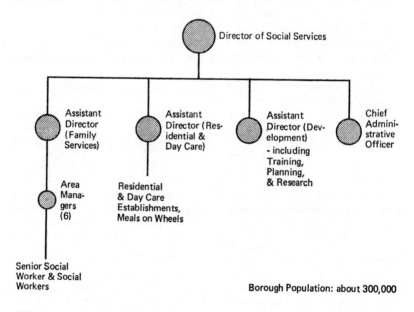

Figure 4.1 Social Services Department, London Borough of Brent – Main Outlines of Organization as Officially Described at Time of Formation (1971)

[2] To judge from various conference discussions on departmental structure with the staff from seventy-five of the new authorities concerned.

planning, and staff training. The Brent nomenclature was not typical in one respect, however. In most departments what in Brent were referred to as 'Area Managers' were referred to as 'Area Officers', 'Area Chief Social Workers' or sometimes (particularly in larger county authorities) 'Area Directors.'

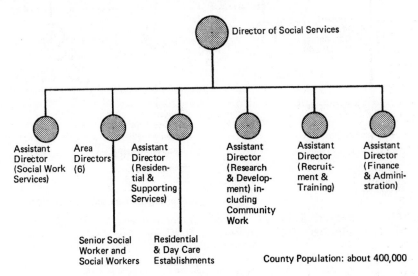

Director of Social Services

Assistant Director (Social Work Services)

Area Directors (6)

Assistant Director (Residential & Supporting Services)

Assistant Director (Research & Development) including Community Work

Assistant Director (Recruitment & Training)

Assistant Director (Finance & Administration)

Senior Social Worker and Social Workers

Residential & Day Care Establishments

County Population: about 400,000

Figure 4.2   Social Services Department, County of East Sussex – Main Outlines of Organization as Officially Described at Time of Formation (1971)

In East Sussex, a pattern was adopted that, on the face of things at least, was much less common. Here the Area Officers – called 'Area Directors' were explicitly declared to be directly accountable to the Director of Social Services, not to the Assistant Director (Social Work Services) and as such were regarded as members of the Director's immediate 'management group.' The Assistant Director (Social Work Services) was accountable for much general planning and co-ordination of departmental activity, but with some insignificant exceptions did not carry direct managerial accountability for any operational work.

In East Sussex, community work was associated with research and development, partly because of the background and experience of the particular officer who held the research post. In Wandsworth (Figure 4.3), on the other hand, adoption of the title Assistant

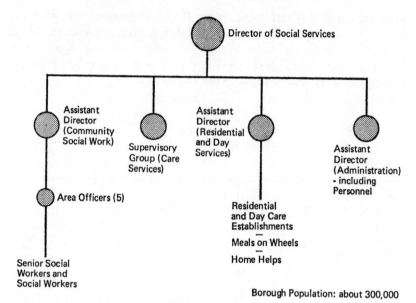

Figure 4.3   Social Services Department, London Borough of Wandsworth – Main Outlines of Organization as Officially Described at Time of Formation (1971)

Director (Community Social Work) was used to convey the fact that the post carried accountability not only for the case work carried out in Area Offices, but also for many of the broader classes of work at community level described in the previous chapter. One unusual feature of the organization in Wandsworth was the establishment of a small group of professionally-qualified staff know as the Supervisory Group whose role was described as 'the maintenance, improvement, and development of caring services, including staff selection and training'.

These brief descriptions may suffice to indicate something of the variety – and similarity – of patterns and titles adopted. Elsewhere operational activities were sometimes divided into three parts. Besides a field work division and a residential care division, a third division to encompass the provision of day centres of various kinds, meals on wheels, home helps, arrangement of transport, holidays, etc., would sometimes be formed. Sometimes separate 'research' posts would be established. Usually, however, particularly in smaller authorities, they would be combined with staff training as in the case of Brent. Sometimes a specific Deputy Director post would be established. Occasionally it would be shown as having certain designated sections within its aegis. Sometimes it would be shown in the main hierarchical line immediately under the Director. Often it would be displayed on charts in the classic manner: high but somewhat to the side of the main hierarchical line, and without indication of direct control of any specific sections.

These then are the sorts of structures that published charts and circulars indicated, but (and this will hardly be any surprise to those who have worked in such settings) what they *meant* in practice was often quite another matter.[3] First, it seems that many posts were established primarily to harness the particular availability of skills and knowledge amongst the group of staff inherited by the new departments at the moment of establishment. As further staff were recruited, or as existing staff acquired new skills, the demands on some of these posts shifted and diminished. Second, it turned out that not all the organizational 'lines' drawn on charts, although pictorially the same, represented the same relationship in reality. Sometimes, for example, the post of head of the field work division (by whatever title) shown clearly between the Director and Area Officers turned out to be one which was more or less frequently bypassed when the Director needed to do business directly with Area Officers, or vice versa. Sometimes it turned out that so-called heads of residential divisions, particularly where they were not professionally qualified, were heads for certain more 'administrative' matters but not so much heads when it came to other more 'professional' ones. These latter phenomena are explored in depth later.

Project Work on Departmental Structure

As we began to work in these three new departments, and later in others, and as we began to discuss with staff from many new authorities the particular organizational structures of their new departments, there began to present themselves to our minds certain general models to which existing departmental structures could be seen to adhere more or less precisely. Later in this chapter two main models of departmental structure, one based primarily

[3] Again, we draw heavily on discussion in conferences.

on organization by function, and one primarily on organization
by place, will be considered in detail.

For a start we will describe some project work from Brent and
from East Sussex which was influential in developing these ideas.

Project work in Brent, which started late in 1971, was not in
the first instance apparently concerned at all with general departmental structure, but with the specific and familiar problem of
proper procedures for finding places for those needing residential care (the project is described more fully from this point of
view in Chapter 8). However, it soon became apparent that ideas
about proper placement procedures were integrally linked with
the assumptions of those involved [4] about the respective roles of
the two main operational divisions within the department (see
Figure 4.1, page 60). Each Area Manager had certain 'liaison' functions in respect of given local establishments. Should the Family
Services Division, through Area Managers, be responsible for
'standards of care' in establishments? After a few months of discussions the broader issue emerged as being whether responsibility
for the total management of establishments should rest with Area
Managers, or whether it should rest with the Residential and Day
Care Division, or whether it should be divided between them in
some way to be clarified.

The third possibility was discarded and after further thought
and consultation the Director and his management team decided
in the summer of 1972 that Area Managers could not in the
prevailing circumstances reasonably take on additional responsibility. Accordingly it was decided to strengthen the existing managerial role of the Residential and Day Care Division and to
underline the full accountability of the Assistant Director for *all*
the work that went on within the establishments. In effect then, the
Department opted for a clear functional organization, as opposed
to a geographic organization or a mixture of functional and geographical organizations – a choice which was to have immediate
practical consequences in selecting the kind of person required
to fill the post of Assistant Director (Residential and Day Care)
which had become vacant in the meantime.

[4] Initial discussions involved the Assistant Director (Family Services) and
the Assistant Director (Residential and Day Care), the Residential Care
Manager, the Senior Administrative Officer, two heads of homes and two
Area Managers, and at a later point, the Director.

At the time of writing, this broader aspect of project work in Brent has moved on to the stage of exploring the intermediate management structure necessary to support the Assistant Director in his task of managing and developing the fifty-six or so establishments concerned.

Project Work in East Sussex

In East Sussex the initial terms of reference for project work, which also started late in 1971, were more obviously related to general departmental structure. The brief was formally as follows:

> To analyse the roles of the Assistant Director (Social Work Services) and Assistant Director (Residential and Supporting Services) with particular reference to:
>
> 1.1 their respective discretion over the allocation of resources and their relationships with Area Directors in this regard;
> 1.2 the development of the two Assistant Director roles as further accountability for the management of operational activities is delegated to Area Directors.

As will be evident from the description at the start of this chapter (see Figure 4.2, page 61), the Department as established had elements of both functional and geographical organization at the first level of division. The existence of the post of Assistant Director (Residential and Supporting Services) gave indications of a functional split. On the other hand, the explicit accountability of the six Area Directors to the Director of Social Services, and their explicit inclusion in the 'managerial group' together with the five Assistant Directors gave counter-indications of a basic geographic orientation. Moreover, there was an explicit intention to shift responsibility for residential care in due course to the Areas, which would in effect bring the Department closer still to a geographical model.

Initial discussions [5] revealed several features of the existing situation which raised questions about general departmental structure (other features which related more specifically to place-

---

[5] Involving the Director, the Assistant Director (Social Work Services) and two of her Executive Assistants, the Assistant Director (Residential and Supporting Services) and one of his Executive Assistants, and three Area Directors.

ment procedures for those needing residential care are again discussed in Chapter 8).

(1) Although Area Directors were explicitly not accountable to
the AD (SWS), the latter tended nevertheless to be seen by them
as carrying the role of 'first among equals'. They tended to rely
heavily on her for advice and guidance. Noticing this tendency,
the Director had already instituted a regular monthly meeting
between each Area Director and himself, in order to strengthen
his direct managerial relationship with them.

(2) There was some tendency for Area Directors to raise problems
about standards of care in residential establishments and even
problems of welfare of residential staff situated in their own
geographical area, with the AD (SWS) rather than the AD
(Res & SS).

(3) A member of the staff of the AD (SWS) dealt with all residential
placements for the elderly, and apart from questions of whether
this might not be better done at Area level, this situation again
raised doubts about how far the AD (Res & SS) was accountable
for all aspects of residential care.

(4) Several Assistant Directors were separately involved in planning
and developing new projects. The AD (Research and Development) had projects in the community work field. The AD (SWS)
had, for example, a specific project to develop 'intermediate
treatment'. The AD (Res & SS) had a specific project to develop
community services for the elderly. Ostensibly the Management
Group meeting was the co-ordinating mechanism for all such
work, but inevitably the question arose whether such development work could not be co-ordinated better with some other
pattern of organization.

(5) The existing division of work left several obvious areas of overlap at Assistant Director level. The AD (SWS) and the AD
(Research and Development) were both inevitably involved in
'liaison work' with other statutory and voluntary bodies. The
job description of the AD (Finance and Administration) referred
to his responsibility for the 'development and maintenance of
operational systems' but the AD (SWS) too would have strong
interests in this area.

These problems were reviewed and analysed in a series of meetings with the full management group in the early spring of 1972.
It was confirmed that the AD (SWS) was not to be held directly
accountable for the operational work. of the Area Directors. It

was agreed that her role should be that of a *staff officer*. This was a type of role that had been identified elsewhere[6] in a number of earlier research projects. Our current definition of the staff officer role in this project reads as follows:

Staff Officer Role

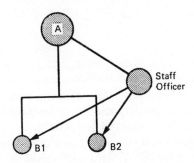

A *staff officer role* arises where a manager A needs assistance in managing the activities of his subordinates (B1, B2) in some particular dimension of work such as personnel and organizational matters or the detailed programming of activities and services.

The staff officer is accountable to A:
- for helping him to formulate policy in the field concerned, taking into account the experience and views of A's other subordinates;
- for seeing that agreed policies in the field concerned are implemented by A's other subordinates: interpreting agreed policy, issuing detailed procedures and programmes, and ensuring adherence to these programmes.

In carrying out these latter activities the staff officer is able to issue instructions. If B1 does not agree with the staff officer's instructions he cannot disregard them, but must take the matter up with A. The staff officer has no authority to make official appraisals of the performance and ability of B1, nor to recommend what the appraisal should be.

However in East Sussex for the time being the continuing operational accountability of the AD (Res & SS) was stressed – not only for 'bricks and mortar' but for the very quality of caring and therapeutic work carried out within establishments. Given this position at least for the interim, the group began to discuss

[6] See Brown (1960), Rowbottom *et al.* (1973).

(as in the case of Brent) what sort of intermediate management structure was necessary between heads of establishments and the Assistant Director to whom they were ultimately accountable. A separate project was mounted to clarify the role of the so-called 'residential and day care officers' (see Chapter 6).

There was also consideration of what should happen to general departmental structure as responsibility for residential and day care was transferred to Area Directors, and some discussion of a full geographical structure started. Would the post of AD (Res & SS) continue after the transfer, changing perhaps to a *staff officer* role complementary to that carried by the AD (SWS)? Or would the AD (SWS) post take over responsibility for *all* operational co-ordination whilst the other post became transformed to one specifically concerned with logistics – capital building programmes, supplies, maintenance, transport, and so on. And if the latter, could it exist on its own, or would it be better combined with the chief administrative post?

At this point it became obvious that no radical changes could be usefully contemplated without taking into account the coming amalgamation of the existing East Sussex with the three county borough authorities in the geographical county. Further work on this broader topic was deferred, but later in 1972 a new project was agreed with all four authorities, to help them plan the general structure of the new department to be established in 1974.

Two Basic Models for the Organization of Operational Activity

Generalizing from this and our conference experience we began to explore in more detail what a fully developed functional and a fully developed geographical model would look like.[7] (As far as the other possible bases of organization described at the start of this chapter are concerned organization according to *kind of client* has lapsed following the Seebohm arguments – although as will be suggested later, this is not quite the end of the matter. Organization according to *kind of worker* does not carry much drive,

---

[7] It may be worth stressing that the organizational 'models' described at this and many other points hereafter are not by any means Weberian 'ideal types'. Far from being the unrealizable extremes of some continuum, they are intended as practical alternatives, capable of complete realization and test.

perhaps because of the relatively insecure and uncertain states of professional specialization within social work; in contrast, say, to health services. Organization according to *method of work* as a prime determinant again carries little drive.[8]) In constructing these

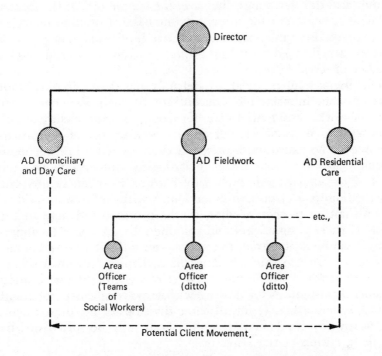

Figure 4.4   Model A – Functional Organization

models we took for granted the assumption discussed in Chapter 2, namely that the *basic* departmental structure was and was likely to remain hierarchical, i.e. compounded of successive managerial relationships; although (as we shall see) other complementary elements of organization needed to be taken into account as well.

As has been stated, the first choice – organization according to function – is the more conventional. Using this basis, we can construct the first model – Model A (Figure 4.4). In this model, the primary divisions of the department are the activities broadly

[8] In contrast, say, to the real choice to be found within industry as to whether to organize workshops according to like-manufacturing methods (*process* or *method*) or according to like-products (*purpose* or *function*).

describable as 'field work', 'domiciliary and day care', and 'residential care'. As pointed out in the previous chapter these terms are not the most precise or most meaningful in which to analyse the work of an SSD. Nevertheless they are functional divisions of a kind; and diffuse though they are, the simple fact of the matter is that they represent the present prime basis of division of activities in many if not most SSDs. At a second level, the organization of field work is divided according to *place* by the establishment of a number of Area Teams.

The obvious *advantage* of Model A is that the various assistant directors can, in principle, concentrate on their own particular fields of work – residential care, for example – and ensure strong management of specialist staff and economical use of specialized resources. The main *disadvantage* is also apparent. The Seebohm principle has not been driven to its logical conclusion. All divisions of the department can easily become involved in any one case (see Figure 4.4), say a problem family with children in residential care and a mother needing psychiatric care and help in the home. If there is significant and sustained disagreement on appropriate treatment or action, the matter can only be resolved at the level of the Director himself, since he is the first 'crossover point'. Worse than this, any question of development or standardization of general procedures for dealing with various categories of client again becomes a matter for all three divisions of the department, and again any fundamental conflicts can only be sorted out by the intervention of the Director.

The obvious alternative to Model A is to create geographical areas or divisions which deal with all work with any one client as in Model B (see Figure 4.5). In effect, this creates a number of mini-departments within the main SSD – at least as far as the *delivery* of service is concerned. In Model A the officer in charge of a particular area is concerned only with field work. In Model B he is concerned with operational work of all kinds. This is a much more responsible position and the title 'Divisional Officer' or 'Divisional Director' may feel more appropriate, although essentially the work is still divided on a geographical basis. (In Figure 4.5 only three Divisional Directors are shown but there could be a larger number.) In larger authorities, it may be necessary to further subdivide field workers thus establishing in effect a layer of 'Area Officers' immediately below Divisional Director.

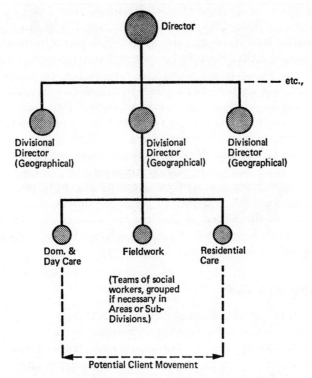

Figure 4.5   Model B – Geographical Organization

Note, however, in this case the difference in conception of Division and Area, not only in terms of level but in terms of functions. 'Division' here implies a comprehensive range of functions including residential care. 'Area' would not necessarily imply this at all, and would be more likely to be limited to field social work, some but not necessarily all domiciliary services, and some administrative support. Below this again might be a 'Team' level concerned only with field social work, and not necessarily self-sufficient in terms of being able to provide a full seven-day, twenty-four hour service.

For the moment our hypothesis is that a full Divisional structure is unlikely to be valid for populations of under 70–100,000; though much would depend here on the intensity and dispersion of social need and on the corresponding size and dispersion of staff and facilities provided. Larger Divisions might support two, three, or even more, Area offices.[9] Residential and day care establishments would be allocated to particular Divisions, though of course there would be certain specialized establishments where control would either have to be retained centrally or given to one particular Division which would be responsible for providing the facility on a service-basis to all other Divisions (see later discussion).

The built-in disadvantage of a functional division are now overcome, or at any rate reduced by relegation to a lower organizational level. In principle each geographical division is now able to respond more freely and flexibly to local needs and circumstances, and to interact with its own 'community' in developing what additional resources it can. By delegating the bulk of continuing operational work in this way to relatively self-contained units at a lower level, the Director and his immediate staff are freed to pursue the development of broader policies. This brings us to the next stage of the exposition.

Supporting Activities

Actually carrying out the operational work is only half the story. No big, complex organizations can continue to run efficiently without considerable support for the 'sharp end'. (Indeed, the tendency to increase the size of the supporting organization at the expense of a reduced but more effective operational organization is characteristic of many modern undertakings, industrial, commercial, and military.) As was suggested in the previous chapter, several distinct kinds of such supporting, non-operational, work can be identified in social services.

For a start there is systematic *research* into needs, and systematic *evaluation* of the effectiveness with which present services are meeting them (the two ride naturally side by side). Then there is what we have called *strategic planning*, the planning of the kinds of services required to meet needs in the long term, together with identification of the kinds and levels of resource needed to sustain them. Then there are more obviously 'supportive' activities – the job of recruiting and training suitable people

[9] It is an interesting thought that the great majority of County Boroughs which at the time of writing run their own self-sufficient SSDs, are within this same order of size, with populations of 70,000 to 150,000.

to man the department (*staffing* and *training*); the job of providing the material resources, buildings, furnishings, transport, materials, etc. which are needed (*logistics*); the job of collating, recording and transmitting data of various kinds, and of physically collecting and disbursing cash (*secretarial and financial work*); and the job of creating and maintaining a good general social environment in which the department may do its work (*public relations*).

Over and above all this there is the job of getting the organization itself to function. The very fact that the work of the department is done by many rather than by one person itself generates work which would otherwise be non-existent. The work comprises matters such as the communication of policies, work programmes and tasks, the allocation of resources, the review of the results of others' performance, the discussion and clarification of mutual problems, the stimulation of new ideas and methods. Such work may be classified broadly as *managerial* and *co-ordinative*. It does not itself result in departmental 'output', and is therefore not operational work, as the term has been defined here. It is work which is spread throughout many parts in the organization, giving rise to relationships which can variously be described as 'managerial', 'supervisory', 'staff', 'collateral', 'co-ordinating', and 'monitoring', each distinct and capable of precise definition (see Appendix A).

One facet of this managerial and co-ordinative work is of particular interest here. In studying the work actually carried out by 'headquarters' staff in several of our client departments, we came across a number of activities that did not readily fit into any of the other categories described above, and yet seemed to imply more attention than could be expected from the Director himself in his straightforward managerial role. These activities included things like:

- discussing various detailed working arrangements and procedures with other statutory or voluntary agencies (as opposed to engaging in discussion with them about long-term plans and financing);
- issuing detailed procedural instructions on various operational matters for use throughout the department; for example, instructions on the detailed implementation of new legislation, or instructions on the recording of case information;
- providing specialist advice and instructions in individual cases, where such was required;

- day-to-day allocation of resources, e.g. places in residential establishments;
- ensuring throughout the department that case work as practised adhered to laid-down policy and observed satisfactory standards.

Now all these activities do in fact broadly conform to the type described above as 'managerial and co-ordinative'. Moreover they are all oriented broadly to day-to-day operations, rather than to long-term planning or systematic provision of resources. Since (anticipating what is to come) they appear to justify in many cases the full-time attention of a senior specialist at headquarters level, it is convenient to have a term to describe them by, and 'operational co-ordination' seems a satisfactory one for the purpose.[10]

Model A Expanded

The next step, then, is to see how the two main models established above need to be elaborated to take account of all this additional but essential supportive and co-ordinative work. Dealing first with Model A, the basic operational framework might be supplemented by the addition of two additional Assistant Director posts and a number of specialist posts, in the way shown in Figure 4.6. Neither of the two additional Assistant Director posts would, of course, carry direct managerial accountability for operational services. And note that although they are shown in Figure 4.6 'higher' than the operational posts, they would not necessarily be more highly graded. Nor would they necessarily be more lowly graded. Each Assistant Director post would be graded according to its assessed work, but all would be at the same general managerial level, i.e. immediately subordinate to the Director. (See the discussion of *grades* and *managerial levels* in Appendix A.)

The Assistant Director (Research and Planning) would be expected to work collaboratively with his four fellow Assistant Directors, as well as with a variety of outside agencies in developing realistic, costed, strategic plans. He would need to establish a strong

---

[10] It is worth stressing the point that *operational co-ordination* is not seen as an activity *additional* to the comprehensive list of departmental functions offered in Chapter 3, but rather a specific part of one of the existing terms on that list, i.e. *managerial and co-ordinative work.*

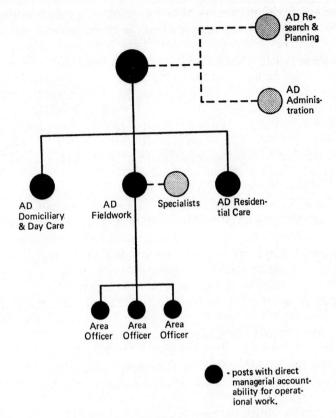

AD Re-
search &
Planning

AD
Adminis-
tration

AD
Domiciliary
& Day Care

AD
Fieldwork

Specialists

AD Residen-
tial Care

Area
Officer

Area
Officer

Area
Officer

- posts with direct
managerial account-
ability for operat-
ional work.

Figure 4.6   Model A – Expanded

link with the medical and other planners in the local Health
Authority, and also with any corporate planning staff employed by
the Local Authority itself. His brief would be established or approved by the Director, and it would terminate with a report to the
Director. Such a report would contain worked out proposals for
action, an analysis of the needs that were to be met, a general specification of the human and physical resources needed, and an
estimate of costs. It would also show alternatives wherever necessary. However, it would not be for the planner to decide which to
adopt – that would be for the Director in conjunction with his
other senior staff, and ultimately for the Local Authority itself.[11]

[11] Acting perhaps through some 'Policy and Resources Committee' following the suggestion of the Bains Report (1972).

Given that the prime job of any systematic research undertaken within the department is to lead to the development and institution of new or improved services, there are strong arguments for placing specialist research staff under the control of this Assistant Director, so adding research to his brief. In this way, the danger is reduced of such research staff being left to operate in a vacuum.

Another advantage of establishing such a specialist planning role is that the danger of unco-ordinated development is minimized. It is only too easy where several divisional heads are concerned for the process of development to take place in a piecemeal fashion – in response to a particular deficiency in service that has suddenly revealed itself here, in response to the various general enthution there, or simply in response to the various general enthusiasms of the individual heads concerned. For no new service can ever be satisfactorily considered in isolation: it usually affects the operation of other existing services in some direct way and always alters the possibility of developing other alternative services by its call on resources. A new scheme for 'intermediate treatment' for children persistently in trouble, for example, affects the quality of case work (basic social work) needed; it affects the load on 'community homes'; and, depending on the scheme, it may affect relations with the local community. Or to take another simple example, the appointment of two new workers for 'community work' means, in the end, the appointment of two less somewhere else.

The second additional post is that of Assistant Director (Administration). Now 'administration' is a term that bears two somewhat conflicting interpretations in everyday use. It can refer to some sort of directing, or more precisely *managerial*, activity (see Appendix A – *managerial role*). Or it can refer to any sort of process which gives aid, support, or service, to some more primary activity. In social services further confusion is added by use of 'administrative' as a collective description for all those individuals in senior positions who do not happen to be professionally qualified in social work. However, since the word administration is in common use, some attempt at clarification is necessary. We suggest that in the context of social services it is best restricted to the second usage, rather than the first or third usages described above; and that in this context 'administration' can usually be employed to stand for some combination of the *financial, logistical,* and *secre-*

tarial, functions discussed in the previous chapter, as well as many of the routine elements of *staffing* work. (It appears that administrative staff may also properly undertake certain defined kinds of operational work, as discussed later in Chapter 7.) In the elaborated Model A structure which we are considering, the Assistant Director (Administration) would be concerned with financial and secretarial work, but the bulk of logistical work would rest with the Assistant Director (Residential Care).

Although much financial work for SSDs is carried out in an associated Treasurer's Department, the Assistant Director (Administration) would have to deal with matters like the collection of parental and other contributions, the preparation of budgets and estimates, and the systematic checking of actual expenditure against agreed budgets as the financial year goes by. Such activities would involve the Assistant Director and his staff in a monitoring role in relation to other divisions in which they carried authority to check the conformity of expenditure to policy (see further discussion in Chapters 5 and 6 of project work in this area).

Certain secretarial work such as the keeping of departmental records and statistics and the provision of centralized typing pools naturally fits, too, with a 'chief administrator' role. At this level the work would not be so much concerned with providing particular statistics or services, as with creating the necessary organization and procedures to provide them. However, it is equally clear that secretarial support must also be provided in local Area Offices. The 'dual influence' situation in which local administrative and clerical staff then find themselves, and possible solutions which have been established in project work, are also discussed in Chapter 5.

As mentioned earlier, however, it is 'operational co-ordination' as defined above that poses the greatest problem in any functionally-organized department. All rests on joint collaboration, and one hallmark of real-life departments organized on the Model A pattern is the frequent occurrence of 'working parties' or 'discussion groups' busily trying to evolve new procedures and systems. In principle, none of the three operational Assistant Directors has any more right to act as co-ordinator of his own and his colleagues' work than another. In practice, the Assistant Director (Field Work) often appears to assume a leading role in such matters. If specialists in various aspects of social work are employed (Figure 4.6) they are frequently put in the Field Work Division. For both these reasons, there is probably some tendency in practice for Model A, which as has been observed was the more common choice at the time of re-organization, to become somewhat lop-sided in operation. All Assistant Directors are equal, in the famous phrase, but the Assistant Director (Field Work) is more equal than the others.

Training officers, too, are likely to be added to the staff of the Assistant Director (Field Work) even though, again, their work is department-wide, so that the same comments apply.

Model B Expanded

In Model B, on the contrary, a separate high-level officer to co-ordinate operations but without managerial accountability for the provision of any one segment of operational work is not only possible but essential (see Figure 4.7).

The role of the Assistant Director (Research and Planning) would be as outlined above in Model A, though now the Divisional Directors would be an important part of the working group with whom he developed plans and schemes. Again, with the agreement of a long-term plan, the Assistant Director (Operational Co-ordination) would be provided with a firm base for action. It would be his role, *as a staff officer and not as a manager of the various Divisional Directors*, to interpret broad plans into operational practice, to arrange implementation and training, and to monitor consequential action. As a staff officer, he could give instructions to the Divisional Directors, provided that they were within the established policy, but he could not himself set or approve new policy, nor would it be proper for him to form official appraisals of the general performance of any Divisional Director. His brief would allow him to range the whole field of operational work in search of integrated and effective procedures, not restricted to case work or 'community' work, but relating to all phases of action with the client and the community. Such work might logically be associated (in larger authorities at least) with specialists of two kinds who could thus be included in his staff:

  (1) those who kept in particular focus the needs of particular client-groups, e.g. the mentally disordered, the deaf or blind, children, etc.;

(2) those who viewed operational activities in terms of particular kinds of services or skills, e.g. specialists in residential care, group work, community development, home help, occupational therapy, etc.

The smaller the department, of course, the less scope there would be for proliferation at this point. Again, it would need to be stressed that such staff did not carry managerial authority with respect to their counterparts or other staff within the operating Divisions. Further, this particular division might be the right place to locate any training staff employed, particularly those concerned with social work training of various kinds. The formu-

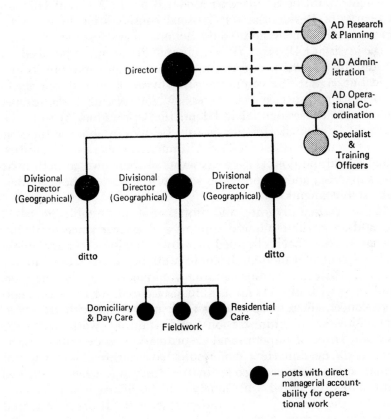

Figure 4.7 Model B – Expanded

lation of training programmes could thus be intimately linked with detailed operational plans. It is an open question how far *staffing* work might also be linked with operational co-ordination. Certainly, as we have noted, it is usual for the more routine aspects of such work – the mechanics of recruitment, the maintenance of staff records, the monitoring of 'establishment' and conditions of service, the provision of welfare facilities, and so on – to be carried out by administrative and clerical staff. But this leaves open the further question of whether such staff should then act in a service-providing capacity from within the main administrative division or whether they should perhaps be attached to the operational co-ordinator's division.

There would be no place in Model B for an Assistant Director in charge of Residential Care. Broad consideration of needs for new residential provision would be an integral part of the work of the Assistant Director (Research and Planning). The need for new establishments would thus be looked at not simply in its own right but as part of a comprehensive survey of what development of operational service was necessary, for example, the proper balance of new residential and domiciliary provision. At the other extreme, Divisional Directors would be accountable for the running of their own residential establishments as operational entities. They would, no doubt, need assistants of their own to help manage, supervise, and support, the work of the staff of these residential establishments.

If the detailed planning and provision of new establishments of all kinds, and their physical support and maintenance thereafter – what has here been classified broadly as 'logistics' – was thought to be a central function, it could well be handed over to the Assistant Director (Administration). Financial monitoring, too, would rest with him. As far as human resources for establishments were concerned, routine staffing work might rest with the Assistant Director (Administration) and training work with the Assistant Director (Operational Co-ordination) as described above.

Thus all headquarters staff would have within their own particular areas of interest co-ordinative functions which extended right across the board, but none would be managerially accountable for the delivery of operational services. It is an essential feature, therefore, of this model that the Divisional Directors would be regarded as immediate subordinates of the Director, and part of his immediate policy-making team. The Assistant Directors might or might not as a group be more highly *graded* than the Divisional Directors, and many would carry authority to issue detailed instructions in interpreting established policy, but they would not, individually or together, constitute a separate policy-making managerial level. It is a moot point whether the Assistant Directors would justify higher grades in view of the extensive responsibilities of the Divisional Directors in this scheme. Indeed Divisional Directors themselves might be at different grades. The main point again is that whatever grades were justified by any particular one of these posts – and some variety might be expected – they would all be regarded as broadly on the same executive level.

Deputy Directors

No mention has been made in either of these models of the possibility of a Deputy Director. In the first instance one must question exactly what this title implies.

The most obvious idea of a deputy is of somebody who stands-in for his chief, when needed. In the absence of the chief there is indeed a strong case for having one designated deputy, although there are those that argue that all the divisional heads can, quite readily, take a little more responsibility for the time being.

However, it is what the deputy does when his chief is there that raises the real problem. Now, if the foregoing analysis is correct and comprehensive, a designated deputy could only carry out one or another of the functions already spelt out whilst his chief was present. In other words, whoever the deputy is, he must carry out one or more of the various supporting roles already described. In Model A, therefore, if a designated deputy were required, the answer would perhaps be to select the most senior of the several Assistant Directors shown, making it clear that his deputizing function only provided authority when the chief is away. In Model B the situation is somewhat different. None of the Divisional Directors would represent a 'natural' deputy to the Director, since none is concerned with total departmental business. Of the remaining senior staff, the Assistant Director (Operational Co-ordination) might, assuming adequate personal experience and seniority, represent an obvious choice given his daily concern with pressing operational matters and problems. Indeed, putting the matter the other way round we are increasingly led to suspect that so-called deputies, where no other duties are specified, spend much of their time in what has been identified as 'operational co-ordination'. They have authority to give instructions in implementing policies, but no authority to set new policies or to make appraisals of personal performance.

Variants of the Two Main Models

Here then are sketches of two different 'models' of departmental structure, each with its own logic given the particular assumption from which it stems. From these two main models, a range of minor variants can easily be derived.

For example, in Model A (functional organization) the functions of domiciliary and day care could easily be split between the two other Assistant Directors if it were felt that three senior posts were not justified. Again, training and operational co-ordination might be combined in two or more sections under one more senior 'deputy' post – see Figure 4.8. Such an arrangement has the clear advantage in Model A departments of finding a location for operational co-ordination outside any of the particular func-

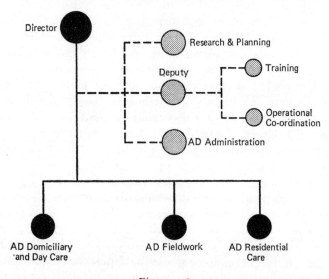

Figure 4.8

tional divisions. As a further alternative, research and planning, training, and operational co-ordination, might all three be combined under one Deputy Director in Model A, or for that matter in Model B.

What is perhaps open to doubt is whether it is desirable to associate training with research as is sometimes done. The usual rationale offered is that both in some sense are 'development' activities. There is an implicit idea that the sort of person who is abreast with the latest thinking in social work practice is also a ready-made trainer. But surely there is a fundamental confusion here. There is a significant difference between keeping up to date with new social work techniques, which an effective trainer would certainly have to do, and producing realistic and costed plans for new services based on systematic assessments of local needs, which is what research should be oriented towards in this context. Were a more realistic research role established, and associated with planning, it is possible that links with training would seem less obvious.

On the other hand, there are perhaps arguments for linking training – the organization of training at any rate – with other aspects of staffing or personnel work. The case is strengthened the more that personnel work is recognized as not just concerned with routine matters like the placing of advertisements for staff and the keeping of personnel records, but also with more complex things like manpower forecasting and the planning of organization and establishment, with which training naturally interlinks. Whether such an integrated personnel role demands a professional social work qualification, or whether it fits with, and starts to give additional substance to, career structure for a separate administrative class is another point.[12]

[12] In effect, the first suggestion gives substance to the role of a separate Assistant Director (Staffing) as suggested in some of our own earlier publications. As far as the second suggestion is concerned personnel work in the broad sense is clearly part of the professional administrator's brief in health organizations, although clinical training for the various health professions would be provided elsewhere – see Management Arrangements for the Reorganized Health Service (DHSS, 1972). At local authority level, the Bains Report gives strong commendation to the establishment of a senior personnel post outside any departmental structure. However this would not necessarily exclude the establishment as well of more specialized personnel posts within each of the major departments such as social services.

The Planning of Specialist Operational Services

One problem which arises in Model B organizations (and in some respects, in Model A organizations too) is how to arrange for the provision of specialist services which do not exist in sufficient quantity to allow each Area or Division to have its own share; for example assessment centres, training centres, specialist adoption services, and (perhaps) occupational therapy.

Two obvious alternatives offer themselves. Such services can be provided by central headquarters, so making the heads of the units or sections concerned directly accountable to headquarters' staff as shown in Figure 4.9 Or they can be placed in an appropriate Area or Division and made the accountability of the Area/Divi-

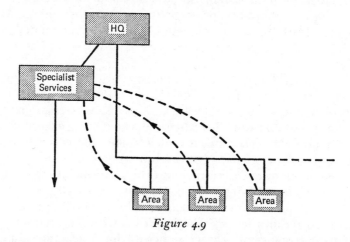

Figure 4.9

sional Officer concerned, but provided on a *service-giving* basis to other Areas or Divisions as shown in Figure 4.10 (using the term *service-giving* as precisely defined in Appendix A). The disadvantage of the first arrangement is that it might be difficult to find a suitable organizational 'home' for fairly minor specialist work. Which Assistant Director, for example, is going to have time to act as an adequate manager in the full sense of the word, for an isolated teacher of the blind or a few occupational therapists? The disadvantage of the second is that, however carefully the arrangement is defined, the tendency is for the Area or Division providing the service to get rather more than their fair share of

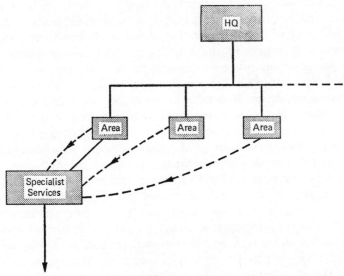

Figure 4.10

the total services available. Nevertheless it may be the better solution on balance.

Multi-dimensional or Matrix Organization

It will now be apparent that to pose the issue of departmental structure in terms of a straight choice of organizing by kind of work, kind of client, place, etc., is to oversimplify. For what emerges from detailed consideration of alternative structures is that each requires a complex set of organizational arrangements if due regard is to be paid to a number of co-existing needs.

Even if at the first level operational work is split according to place or area, at the second level it has to be split by function or type of work. Even if organization according to type of worker is eschewed as a primary principle there is a need to take account of it somewhere. Certain well-defined occupational groups like home helps, occupational therapists, or clerical and administrative staff, will need their own head of service somewhere in the organization attending to the special requirements of the group, such as its recruitment, training, and career structure, though probably through the medium of *staff* or *co-ordinative* roles, rather than *managerial* ones (see Appendix A). Even if division by type of client as an organizing principle has been summarily removed from pride of place in the course of the Seebohm revolution, its presence still lingers in the evident need to have somewhere in the department adequate machinery for considering the adequacy and development of services for the elderly, as a group, or the mentally sub-normal, or the under-five-year-olds. And last but by no means least, even if account is taken of all these considerations, there has still got to be some way of integrating all the work with individual clients in individual cases – a problem which will be explored in some depth in Chapter 8.

What emerges as realistic, then, is the *multi-dimensional* or *matrix* organization already discussed, in which members of departments will at various times find themselves working with various groups of colleagues in many and various orientations.[13] If discussion is needed on the development of new schemes for particular client groups or developments in whole new fields of work, like community work, it may be led perhaps by a senior specialist in the field concerned, who is perhaps on the staff of one of the Assistant Directors. If it concerns the production of long-term plans it may be led by the head of research and planning. If it is on development of working procedures it may be led by the 'operational co-ordinator' or a member of his staff. If it concerns future treatment plans for an individual client, we shall

---

[13] As noted earlier there is an obvious link here with Algie's (1970) notion of 'polyarchic' pattern of organization for social services, although he claims this as an alternative, rather than a supplement, to hierarchy. He advocates the individual worker's membership of many changing 'multi-disciplinary teams' although he appears to avoid the question of which, if any, would involve managerial relationships. His 'sentient groups' would co-ordinate work to meet different client needs. Other groups would co-ordinate the development of specific kinds of work – residential, case work, and so on. He explicitly refers to a 'strategic planning manager' and to an 'operational development manager'.

The links with health services should be noted here too, where the Report on Management Arrangements for the Reorganised Health Service (DHSS, 1972) notes specifically that organization in three dimensions will be required according to 'skills' (i.e. kind of worker), 'needs' (i.e. kind of client), and 'places'. Such hierarchical structure as exists – and hierarchical organization is by no means universal in health organization – will be in the 'skills' dimension, and in the sense that the primary division of organization below District level will be by skill – i.e. type of worker.

suggest later that it may be led by a designated 'case co-ordinator'.

Often these 'leaders' will carry either *staff officer* or *co-ordinative* roles. In these cases, they will have authority to persuade or even to instruct but they will not have authority to re-shape policy or to apply managerial sanctions and control to team members. What is surely crucial in this complex situation is to retain clarity about who (if anybody) carries managerial roles with rights of sanction and with duties to appraise and develop staff. To be a member of many working teams with many different 'leaders' is normal and desirable. To be subject to the managerial control of more than one person is in most circumstances a situation of discomfort and anxiety.[14]

Number of Managerial Levels

This discussion leads naturally to consideration of another general feature of departmental structure. Accepting that the hierarchical structure of managerial relationships in an SSD is only one of the many co-ordinative mechanisms, it is nevertheless obviously an important one. What, one may ask then, is the optimum shape, the optimum height and breadth, of such a structure within the department? If the hierarchy is too high, the Director loses contact with the 'front-line'. If it is too shallow, he may become over-burdened with detail, and he and other managers within the hierarchy become unable to cope with the numbers of staff each has to supervise.

In considering this classical problem, it appears usual not only for management consultants, but for many knowledgeable managers as well, to take as an inevitable and unquestionable starting point the famous 'span of control' principle, which suggests that there is some optimum number of subordinates for any manager to deal with, perhaps seven or eight.[15] The single-minded concern with span of control is a pity, for it removes attention from what is at least as important, the complementary issue of optimum number of managerial levels. The effects on managers of unduly large

---

[14] The *attachment* situation as defined in Appendix A is a possible exception to this principle, though even here the potential for conflict is no doubt high if the definition of the situation is at all unclear.

[15] The original hypothesis by Graicunas (1937) employs an abstract and mathematically-based argument based on the proliferation of interrelations as the size of the group to be supervised increases.

spans of control can often be relieved by judicious use of staff officers or supervisory roles. But the effects of too many, or too few, managerial levels are more insidious and more difficult to overcome.

An important hypothesis offered by Jaques[16] suggests that there is an optimum separation between the general 'capacity' of any manager and that of his subordinates, and hence, in the normal course of things, between their corresponding levels of work. Too close, and subordinates lose respect for their managers as managers. They see them more as senior colleagues, and tend to bypass them for the 'real' boss when needs arise. Too far apart, and subordinates lose touch with their managers, and tend not to want to trouble them with what for the managers concerned (though not for the subordinates) will be minor problems. The thesis goes on to discuss in more detail the possible nature of this executive 'capacity', a quality distinct from professional expertise. Elsewhere evidence is offered of the systematic way in which 'capacity' may develop during the course of a working career through the study of earning progression histories.[17]

Optimum separation between levels means some optimum number of levels for any given executive organization.[18] The important thing is to separate *managerial levels* from what is really quite a different matter, the *grading* structure (see Appendix A). It is certainly not the case that every step in *grade* implies a full managerial relationship.

Thus, returning to SSDs it is not unusual to see pictures of departmental organization employing the various steps shown in Figure 4.11. What is actually depicted is a chart of broad grading structure, and no more. It can be said with some confidence that not all seven above the lowest represent real managerial levels.

How many full managerial levels do SSDs need? (The adjective 'full' is added to emphasize that *supervisory roles* or *staff officer roles* do not in themselves constitute a managerial level as defined

---

[16] See 'Speculations Concerning Level of Capacity' and 'Preliminary Sketch of a General Structure and Executive Strata' (in *Glacier Project Papers*, Brown and Jaques, 1965).

[17] Jaques (1967).

[18] Jaques hypothesizes that even the largest executive organization will need no more than six full-managerial levels – seven executive ranks in all (*Glacier Project Papers*, 1965).

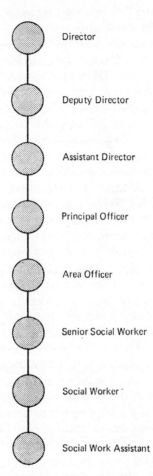

Director

Deputy Director

Assistant Director

Principal Officer

Area Officer

Senior Social Worker

Social Worker

Social Work Assistant

Figure 4.11   SSD Organization as a Hierarchy of Grades

here.) The answer is likely to depend on the size of the department concerned. We do not have hard research data to report, but tentatively we suggest that the answer may be four levels for those in the middle ranges of size, perhaps three for the very smallest, and conceivably, five for the very largest. For a start it seems likely that most Area organizations have need of one full managerial level in relation to (at least) trainees, students, and junior clerical staff, between them and the Area Officer (see Chapter 5). Thus the Area Officer is at least a second level manager. The real question is how many levels exist between the Area Officer and Director on the field work side.

Model A seems to assume that one level is indeed needed in the person of the Assistant Director, making four managerial levels in all including that of the Director. However it is open to some doubt whether the Assistant Director level on the field work side actually *operates* as a full managerial level in very small departments. There is some evidence that the Director tends to establish direct managerial relationships with the Area Officers leaving the Assistant Director in a *staff officer* or *co-ordinating* role. If this is the case, only three real managerial levels exist, including that of the Director, in very small departments.

The answer in Model B depends on how the Divisional Director post is conceived. If in terms of grading it is realistically conceived as equivalent only to a (senior) Area Officer post, and with only 'team leaders' posts below, then the Department is presumably operating with only three managerial levels – the Director, the Divisional Director/Area Officer, and the Team Leader. However it is likely that the size of most Divisions in Model B departments will be such as to create a need for the establishment of a number of separate Area Offices within Divisions in most cases, as suggested above. If this is so, Divisional Director and Area Officer would represent distinct levels, and again four managerial levels, including that of the Director, would exist in the Department.

On the residential and day care side, there can be little doubt that heads of establishments constitute a real managerial level.[19] In the case of more complex establishments like some of the former approved schools, remand homes, or reception centres, it may even be a second managerial level. In many Model A departments, the Assistant Director in charge of residential care clearly carries a managerial role, too. Here the questionable level is that of the groups of staff variously titled 'home advisers', 'residential advisers' or 'executive assistants'. What is in doubt is whether these, or some of them, represent a genuine intermediate management level, or whether their roles are to be explained in a variety of non-managerial terms – *supervisory, staff-officer* or *co-ordinative* (see Appendix A). In very small departments the latter is possibly the case, leaving again only three managerial levels including that of

[19] Detailed discussions with some dozen heads of establishments in project work at various times have all confirmed this view – see Chapter 6.

the Director. In average-sized Model A departments it is, however, very doubtful whether the Assistant Director could sustain an adequate managerial relationship with the heads of, say, thirty to fifty separate establishments. Here an additional managerial level seems to be called for, even if the need has escaped recognition in many departments at the moment (see Chapter 6).

Summarizing then, for the moment our working assumption is that four natural managerial levels, i.e. five organizational levels in all, exist in most departments, leaving aside those in the extremes of the size range, whether of Model A or Model B. The general view shown in 4.12 is expanded in subsequent chapters.

What is certain in all these situations is that unnecessary managerial levels are not only conducive to feelings of anxiety and stress, but simply do not function. In time, work creeps round

LEVEL	MODEL A		MODEL B	
5	Director		Director	
4	Assistant Directors		Assistant Directors and Divisional Directors	
3	Area Officers	*	Area Officers	*
2	Team Leaders & other more senior social workers	Heads of Establishments	Team Leaders & other more senior social workers	Heads of Establishments
1	Trainees, Assistants, etc.	Staff of Establishments	Trainees, Assistants, etc.	Staff of Establishments

* Often a missing level on the residential and day care side.

Figure 4.12   Possible Distribution of Real Managerial Levels in Model A and Model B Departments

them as the sea creeps round sandcastles. But to the extent that
they exist at all they create confusion. They blur clarity as to
who is accountable for assessing operational problems and for
appraising staff, and who is supposed to take decisive action where
such is needed.

Conclusion

By building in the course of project work two separate and sharply
contrasted models of general departmental structure, we have
found it easier to make sense of the wide variety of existing structures, and to orient discussions about possible change and development, both in conference and in project discussions.

Model A is – or was at the time of establishment of the new
departments – the more general pattern, where the prime division
is by type of work and where headquarters staff retained operational responsibility. Model B in effect creates a number of mini-
departments where headquarters staff lose direct responsibility for
operational work, and gain instead various 'across the board'
responsibilities for developing, co-ordinating, or sustaining, the
work of the operational divisions.

Although Model B has many strengths, neither it nor Model A
is being offered as better here. The proper choice no doubt rests
on a variety of factors in which size and geographical dispersion
will be of great importance.[20] And indeed it may well be that
natural evolution in the given conditions of any particular
authority leads appropriately to intermediate forms. At the time
of writing some of the authorities with whom we are in collaborative work on general departmental structure are making a conscious decision to move closer towards a Model A structure as
circumstances allow, and at least one is making a conscious choice
to move towards a Model B structure.

Although the discussion has assumed that the department is
organized around a central hierarchic framework (an assumption

[20] Given the hypothesis mentioned before, that Model B Divisions need
to relate to populations of at minimum 70,000 in order to be viable, it
might be queried whether authorities with populations of less than say
200,000 could realistically contemplate Model B structures, unless they
were prepared to concentrate accountability for all operations in the hands
of only one or two Divisional Directors.

which was critically examined in Chapter 1), it has not been as-sumed that one network of managerial relationships is sufficient to meet all needs. The main managerial structure can only be oriented to one dimension at any point, be it type of work, or place of work. Other dimensions – the particular needs of particular types of clients, the career needs and problems of various types of worker, or the total needs of particular clients themselves – need other kinds of machinery. Here the leaders of various working groups are likely to find themselves in *staff officer* or *co-ordinative* roles, rather than *managerial*.

One crucial factor is the number of levels in the managerial structure, in order to create proper freedom for initiative and judgement for those below, without losing proper control by those above.

Above all, the concern must be to find what combination of hierarchical and other organizational structures best enables the department to respond to the needs of its environment, to deliver services effectively, and to develop them effectively.[21]

[21] There has been a strong tendency in organizational thinking over the past few decades to associate hierarchical structure with inflexibility and inability to respond to a changing environment – the seminal work is probably Burns' and Stalker's (1961) study of 'mechanistic' and 'organic' organizations. Of course all depends on what is meant by 'hierarchy'. Here, as has been said, what is meant is nothing more or less than an extended pattern of managerial relationships. With this definition of hierarchy, we would strongly contest that hierarchical organization is necessarily associated with rigidity or a static outlook, although we would agree that alternatives to hierarchical organization are possible, and in certain situations desirable (see Appendix B).

5 Organization of Field Work

Probe far enough into practically any aching problem in social work practice and sooner or later one comes back to the same deep-rooted tender spot. I am *not* just a local government official – cries the enlightened social worker, the field worker, or the residential worker – I am *not* a species of bureaucrat: I deal with people in a deep and caring way, I am a *professional*! And adds with some despair – why then am I not regarded as are other professionals who deal with people, as doctors or lawyers are regarded: why do *I* find myself singled out for supervision and bureaucratic control?

Leaving aside the unduly contemptuous view of the 'bureaucrat' implied in such utterances on the one hand, and the overly-idealistic assumption that other 'professionals' are all as free as birds on the wing on the other (these broader issues we return to later) a large part of this chapter is concerned with studying in some detail just how the conflict between organizational control and the freedom of the practitioner manifests and regulates itself at field work level.

Now it has already been suggested that 'field work' is a term of no great precision. The 'field' can stretch from the home to the school, the hospital, the foster home, the private home, and even (for some kinds of work) to the residential establishment. The 'work' can stretch from social case work in its most esoteric sense, to the provision of a full range of services, material and other, to those living in the community; and indeed to the provision of all this plus many elements of work at the community level itself.

What in effect we shall be doing in this chapter is to study the work and organization of a particular group of people who are commonly described as field workers – Area Officers, senior social workers, social workers, social work trainees, and assistants. We shall also be looking at their interactions with the clerical and administrative staff, particularly those who support them in the field. The work of certain others who might also in a general sense claim to be field workers – like occupational therapists, home helps, and deliverers of meals to the home – is considered in Chapter 6.

The discussion is restricted by and large to issues which have spontaneously arisen in various of our projects. These include work in the present Community Services division in Wandsworth; work in the field work divisions of the former Children's, Mental Health, and Welfare Departments in Wandsworth; and work in two Area Teams in the former Children's Department in Essex. As always, many of the ideas have received elaboration and refinement as a result of discussion within the conference programme, which now brings us in close contact with senior field work staff from many SSDs throughout the country.

The main issues which have repeatedly called attention to themselves in the projects in which we have so far become involved can be summarized in three groups as follows.

(1) What is the proper role of the senior social workers or other supervisors of social workers? Are they just 'enablers', or are they complete managers? How can they best observe the balance between professional freedom and departmental control? (And more recently) How can senior social workers cope with the 'generic' problem i.e. providing adequate support and supervision across the whole range of social work situations?

(2) What is the proper relation of administrative sections to social workers? Is *their* role fundamentally to enable, or to control? Are clerical and administrative staff, who work alongside social workers, primarily there to help the latter, or should they be regarded as outposts of central administration?

(3) Increasingly situations arise where social workers employed by local authorities are working alongside other professionals in a variety of institutions concerned primarily with matters other than social work – in clinics, schools, hospitals, etc. They are often referred to as 'attached'. What exactly does this mean in terms of organizational relationships, and must it always mean the same thing in every situation?

In addition project work has brought us into contact with certain other issues, which will also be explored as far as our experience allows.

(4) Is it possible to establish genuine consultancy roles in social work? What room is there for the employment of specialists? Is it possible to establish a career path which allows certain kinds of people to advance whilst continuing in direct work with clients, and without having to assume significant managerial responsibilities?

(5) How far should field work teams extend beyond 'case work' into the various kinds of work that are generally subsumed under the title 'community work'?

Problems of Supervision

One of the main questions to emerge from the various projects described above was the proper role of senior social workers, team leaders, or other senior officers, in relation to the worker whom they were supposed to supervise. In successive early projects in two Area Teams in the Essex Children's Department, this question arose naturally out of the terms of reference which were to make a general review of organizational arrangements.[1] About the same time a project was launched in the Wandsworth Children's Department specifically to review and clarify the role of the seven Senior Child Care Officers (SCCOs), each of whom was in charge of a 'sector'.[2] Subsequent projects arose in Wandsworth with social workers in the Mental Health and Welfare Departments in 1970-71 to help clarify and understand the particular characteristics of their work and organization in preparation for the amalgamation

[1] The first project involved in individual discussions the Area Children's Officer, four child care officers, and a Principal Child Care Officer associated with the Area, and started in late 1969. A project in a second Area involved in individual discussions the Area Children's Officer, a senior child care officer, five child care officers, a senior administrative assistant, and a clerk within the Area, and started in the spring of 1970. At a later stage, all the staff of the Area joined in group discussions.

[2] Individual discussions with the seven SCCOs started late in 1969 and led to a number of discussions with the whole group in the early summer of 1970.

with the Children's Department shortly to come.[3] These subsequent projects, like the earlier ones, revealed difficulties and doubt about the supervisory role and process. Nor, needless to say, were all these problems immediately resolved in the new Department. Discussions with practically every department with which we have contact suggests continuing uncertainty about the supervisory role, specifically at the 'team leader' level. Explicit project work in this field continues in Wandsworth, where at the time of writing a deliberate attempt is being made to introduce throughout the Department, and to test over a measured period, a particular specification of the role of team leader.

Some idea of how social workers and their supervisors regard this issue can perhaps be communicated by quoting extracts from a few reports of individual discussions.[4]

A report based on discussions with one Child Care Officer (CCO) in an Area Team in Essex contained the following passages.

Review of case work by designated supervisor
The CCO feels that this activity tends to be dictated by what she wants i.e. that she raises for discussion with her supervisor the cases on which she requires help and advice.... The supervisor's style is to initiate discussion with the CCO and provide a framework in which the CCO can formulate her own tasks which are implicitly acceptable to the supervisor. The supervisor does not prescribe frequency of visiting, or firmly formulate specific tasks. In other than routine decisions the CCO would be referred by her supervisor to the Area Children's Officer as the extent of the supervisor's discretion to make decisions is unclear. It feels appropriate to the CCO, considering her own stage of professional development, that she should have more direction of her work particularly in formulating treatment plans in the more complex cases.

[3] The Mental Health Department Project started late in 1970 and involved the Principal Social Worker, the Deputy and Assistant Principals, and four other mental health social workers. The Welfare Department Project started at the same time and involved the Principal Social Worker, one Area Team Leader, a social worker with the blind, a social worker with the deaf, and two social workers with the homeless.
[4] The extracts do not necessarily represent verbatim quotations of what the individual concerned said. Reports usually contain a mixture of description, discussion, and analysis. They are drafted by the researcher concerned, and then offered for approval to the individual or group concerned – see Appendix C, Sample Reports.

A CCO in another Area Team was the designated supervisor of two other CCOs in the same sub-area, and as such she carried a slightly higher grade than they. In the course of discussions she stated that she certainly did not feel accountable for the totality of work of the two other CCOs but only for routine checking, in so far as matters were brought to her attention by events or by either of the CCOs concerned. Were she and either of her supervisees to experience any significant disagreement on what was to be done in a particular case she would simply pass the matter to the Area Children's Officer to deal with. The report of discussions with her adds some further interesting sidelights on the situation:

> Apart from the unclarity implicit in the foregoing regarding accountability and authority in the supervisor role, there are two further problems associated with supervisory work as far as the CCO is con-concerned:
>
> (1) Her own acknowledged lack of interest in being a supervisor. This arises from her wish to work directly with clients, and her feeling that given the workload of cases for which she is accountable she does not have sufficient time to do both satisfactorily. The result of negotiating between the two demands is, she feels, that both suffer at the expense of each, i.e. that in neither area of work does she achieve a level of performance which is satisfying to her.
>
> (2) The physical circumstances of accommodation mean that the CCO is too available to her supervisees, and also as other people are present when 'supervision' is taking place their presence affects the style she adopts, as she is conscious of how they might experience her comments and she tries to be sensitive to their feelings. Coupling this with the lack of clarity about her authority it means that she errs on the side of being less directive than more so....

It is significant perhaps that a third CCO, an untrained and relatively inexperienced officer who was also attached to this higher graded CCO for a specific period of induction complained in discussion of the need for 'more positive support' and regretted the absence of direction and the lack of assumption of authority in her role.

The report of discussions with one of the Senior Child Care Officers (SCCO) in Wandsworth raised many of the same issues.

The problem for the SCCO is to know how best to check every one of the cases for which he is accountable. The SCCO uses in-coming post and the administrative change reports to pick up points from cases. He expects the CCOs to summarize their work every two to three months or three to four visits, handing in their reports or bringing them for discussion with him. He holds weekly discussion sessions with each CCO in which to find out what they are doing and to enable them to reach the appropriate decisions. Before it has gone too far he might take up a case which looked troublesome.

Another problem facing the SCCO is the conflict between stepping-in to re-direct a case for which he is accountable and allowing the CCO concerned to proceed in the interests of her own professional development. As a case worker the SCCO is inclined to adopt the non-directive approach with such a CCO. The tendency is to see himself in a helping relationship to the CCO as well as in authority over her. The absence of departmental directives on the extent of supervision increases the reliance on case work principles.

The weekly discussion sessions are seen both as an opportunity for case work consultation and as a means of control. The SCCOs aim in these sessions is to find out how the CCOs want to use him. At the same time it is his responsibility to see that the work allocated to them is done satisfactorily.

And again from discussions with another Senior Child Care Officer in the same project:

In allocating cases to particular CCOs and in commenting on their work, the SCCO has uncertain views as to her ultimate authority in the matter. CCOs consult the SCCO about existing cases at their own discretion. The subsequent discussion appears to the SCCO as one in which, in effect, she is commenting on the way the CCO is applying her own discretion in a case, the methods she is using and the priorities she is setting and from whence the CCO makes her independent decisions about subsequent action.

Considering this and other similar material two fundamental questions continually thrust themselves forward.

- Does the supervisor have any right to prescribe, that is, to give firm instructions, or can in the end only the social worker who is in direct contact with the client know what is best?
- Even if the supervisor does have such a right, can the prescriptive role possibly be combined with an enabling one, without intoler-able conflict?

Both questions have been explored many times now, in various project discussions, with individuals and groups described above, and in conference discussions. Our own analysis, and therefore in effect our own answer to each is now discussed in turn.

Professional Freedom and Delegated Discretion

The trouble about attempting to deal with the question of the professional freedom of the social worker is that one is apparently offered a choice between complete autonomy on the one hand, and complete, rigid, bureaucratic control on the other. As pointed out in Chapter 2, this is an unreal choice.

If it is firmly accepted that *all* work allows the worker some greater or lesser degree of freedom – that no realizable job could be devised that could not be demonstrated to require some degree of discretion in its performance – then the real issue is laid bare. The issue is not whether the social worker should be, or even is, allowed a degree of discretion. The issue is whether the discretion allowed is *delegated* by those who are accountable for how it is then exercised, or whether the discretion allowed is within some defined and inviolate area which is the professional worker's own by right. In other words the issue can be summarized as: *delegated discretion* or *professional autonomy*?

Now the situation of genuine professional autonomy is neither unknown in practice, nor unthinkable in social work in particular.[5] However it must be recorded that, virtually without exception, all staff from social services of whatever grade with whom we have seriously discussed this issue over the past four years have unhesitatingly concluded after due consideration that the situation of social workers in SSDs is one of exercising delegated discretion rather than professional autonomy, and is likely to remain so. When the issue is posed in this fashion, it is universally accepted that present-day Directors of departments are accountable to their employing authorities (and hence ultimately to the communities

---

[5] The existing professional autonomy of certain (but not all) doctors in British Health Services is described in Rowbottom *et al.* (1973). Appendix B examines how far an analogous situation might be possible in SSDs.

who elect them) for all the work that is done within departments, and for how it is done.[6]

With this accepted, it seems clear that the right of the Director to prescribe what work shall be done (and if needs be how it is done), his right to appraise performance, and his ultimate right to sanction, must be granted too. That is, the presence of a potential *managerial hierarchy* must be granted.

However this does not dispose of many associated issues. Does the Director necessarily delegate all these functions to each so-called social work supervisor? Does each social work supervisor delegate appropriate discretion to each professionally qualified social worker to allow him to make due use of his professional skills and to have due room to express his professional values? What is more to the point, does every supervisor have the personal capability to carry a managerial or quasi-managerial role? As we shall see later there is some evidence from our research to suggest that the question of whether or not so-called social work supervisors play an effective role is often bound up with whether they are, and are seen as, sufficiently greater in capability than those whom they supervise. In a time of rapid expansion it is likely that some social workers are promoted prematurely to supervisory positions. It may well be that overt appeals to the principle of professional autonomy in some cases mask the real source of friction, which is much more specific and personal.

The Idea of 'Task' in Social Work

There can be little doubt, then, of the right somewhere in existing departments to give firm prescriptions to social work staff, and there appears no reason in principle why such authority could not be delegated to those with supervisory roles, provided that they possess sufficient personal capacity. Before the other central issue identified above can be tackled, the issue of how far 'controlling' and 'enabling' can ever peacefully coexist in any such supervisory role, it is essential to be clear on certain points about the nature

[6] It is interesting to note that the Working Party on Professional Integrity in the Child Care Service set up by the former Association of Child Care Officers (1969) reached virtually the same conclusion. They rejected the reality of 'individual professional responsibility' and stressed the ultimate accountability of the chief officer of the department.

of the ultimate activity to which both processes are directed. The problem might be stated thus: what exactly is it in the social work process that would be capable of control, and what is it that would be capable of being enabled?

As a starting point it must be stated again as axiomatic that the nature of social work, as all work, involves exercising judgement or choice in situations of uncertainty.[7] It is immediately apparent that any question of specification or control of work is not a question of total *removal* of the discretion from work but of how and how far to limit or delimit it.

One distinction of practical importance here is between these limits or prescriptions which apply indefinitely until modified or withdrawn, and those which set specific goals to be achieved if possible within specific periods of time. The latter we shall call *tasks*. Lists of *duties*, those for example given in job descriptions or in legislation, are by contrast prescriptions of the first kind: they refer to activities to be pursued for an indefinite period. As defined then, *duties* and *tasks* are not independent conceptions, as it is not possible to perform duties without first establishing specific tasks to be pursued – otherwise work would be shapeless and endless. However, tasks are not necessarily externally prescribed: the worker frequently establishes tasks at his own discretion in response to his given duties and his own reading of specific situations.

Thus it will often be the case that two workers, pursuing the same given *duties,* establish in fact quite different *tasks*.

To illustrate this latter point, consider the various ways in which social workers might carry out the following duties in respect of children placed with families with a view to adoption:

(1) satisfying themselves as to the well-being of the infant;
(2) assessing the potential of the applicants as adoptive parents.

The duties incumbent on each social worker will be the same in the general terms described in relation to each adoptive case, but each worker must exercise his discretion in each case to decide just how he will fulfil his duties. Will he restrict himself to noting

[7] See Jaques 'The Mental Processes in Work' (in *Glacier Project Papers,* Brown and Jaques, 1965) and Jaques (1967) *Equitable Payment,* Chapter IV.

on each visit that the baby is well and kicking, and that the child's activity produced doting smiles on the faces of the adoptive parents; and then conclude that he has fulfilled his duties? Or will he additionally explore various aspects of the family's functioning and attitudes, and isolate areas for further exploration and discussion, according to his assessment of need and the applicants' ability and willingness to co-operate?

In the first formulation he is setting himself a simple task of checking on the infant's current well-being and the applicants' current response to the baby. The task will arise on each visit and will be repeated several times during the supervisory period.

In the second, he is setting himself a complex programme of work which may well take the whole of the supervision period of three to four months to complete. He will have to exercise discretion as to how to generate and follow through discussion on adoptive parenthood. If he identifies any problems he must decide what to do about them, and how to involve the applicants in recognizing them and working with him on these problems; and he will have to programme his visits in such a way as to allow himself sufficient time and opportunity to accomplish all this work. Thus it is only when duties have been broken down into tasks in this way that work becomes evident and concrete.

In responding to this idea of task, social workers with whom we have worked have sometimes suggested that in the nature of social work, with its complex emotional interactions between workers and clients, the purpose of intervention is to meet and work with these interactions on an *ad hoc* basis, as it were situationally – visit to visit, interview to interview – and that the notion of task can hardly apply. Case planning in this context is thought to be a matter of determining general objectives or hoped-for results which do not necessarily have an implicit or explicit time-scale attached. These objectives serve rather to condition the responses that workers might be expected to make to situations as they arise, rather than as specific tasks, i.e. specific end-points which require programmes of active intervention to achieve.

It has to be reasserted however that all work is in fact carried out in task form, whether wittingly or unwittingly. Those workers believing in situational responses only, are seeing in fact short

tasks; whilst those working through on a programme of intervention see longer ones.[8]

In discussing these matters with social workers it has been our
experience that practical activities such as arranging for the adaptation of premises, or for provision of home helps, or for admission to establishments, tend to be more readily recognized by social
workers as analysable in terms of task.

Obviously too, all social workers have a lot of short tasks which
are easy to identify; for example:

- to phone another agency on a specific subject (matter of days)
- to make a specific referral (one day)
- to produce a social history report for court (a matter of up to
  four weeks).

In some cases a number of tasks may be in hand simultaneously.
For example, in a large family with multiple problems, where
both parents were deaf and without speech, one worker saw the
general duty of supporting the family as giving rise to the following
tasks at various times, some concurrently with others:

- to provide an escort (matter of hours)
- to act as an interpreter, for example at court (matter of hours)
- to obtain a grant for school uniform (one month)
- to obtain reconnection of electricity supply (two months)
- to get two-year-old boy placed in a nursery school (six months)
- to supplement parental role, in providing sex education (six
  months)
- to help mother to be able to undertake part-time employment
  (nine months).

[8] Is there perhaps some relationship between the inability to perceive
longer tasks and the felt lack of a special area of competence and an
exclusive body of social work knowledge (Wilensky and Lebeaux, 1965)
either in the individual social worker, or in the profession as a whole?
Goldberg in her experimental study of help for the aged notes the 'vague-
ness of the descriptions of what social workers actually do' and comments
on the 'pompous and complex language' that social workers often use in
trying to describe what they do (p. 23). She agrees the enormous difficulties
of establishing measurable criteria for ultimate goals but (p. 26) one of
the findings which the study demonstrates is that it *is* possible to set some
limited goals capable of definition and assessment. These 'middle-range
goals' (p. 200) are, we suggest, with appropriate time scales added, precisely
the *tasks* that are being identified here.

Most social workers who have been able to describe their work in task-terms beyond the one-visit, situation-response, type of task mentioned previously, have been able to identify some tasks in the time range three to six months; a smaller number in the six to twelve months range; and a smaller number still in the range of one to two years. (It should be noted that we are referring here only to tasks being carried out directly with clients and not to managerial development, or training tasks, which may well have quite different time scales.)

Some actual examples of longer social work tasks described to us by social workers, together with the time-scale within which they saw themselves working, are as follows:

- to ensure that a boy in care in his last year at school was settled in work and accommodation at the point of leaving school (nine months)
- to help a client newly suffering from blindness to make a primary adjustment to his changed condition by a combination of material aid, teaching of new skills, arranging for training, and discussion of emotional and social problems (one year)
- to establish an unmarried mother and her child as a self-supporting unit in the community (one year)
- to clarify interpersonal relationships with clients as part of an assessment process aimed at determining the suitability or otherwise of the clients to obtain legal guardianship of an infant in their care (one year)
- in the case of a young married woman with a history of chronic depression, to help her establish her identity and separate herself from neurotic dependence on her mother (one year to eighteen months)
- in the case of a racially mixed marriage, following the wife's attempt at suicide, to help the couple to clarify and understand the strengths in their relationship and to gain insight into the dynamics of their behaviour (eighteen months to two years).

In each of the above cases the workers were able to describe the activities in which they were engaged and the programme they were working through consistently in order to secure the results they specified to us. None had explicitly identified a time-scale when embarking on these tasks, but each, when asked in discussion, felt that the desired results could not feasibly be achieved in less than the time stated, and felt strongly that if there were not observable results by the end of the times they assigned, they would (at least intuitively) have been reconstructing their tasks with these clients.

Thus social work, no less we suggest than any other work, on analysis reveals itself as structured more or less consciously in terms of various sequences or combinations of tasks. And one might add – where no specific task can possibly be discerned, it becomes impossible to believe that effective work is being done.

This approach offers new possibilities for the mechanics of 'control' and 'enabling' and their combination. Instead of control as a process of constriction and denial, and enabling as a process of profligate advice-giving, it offers, through task-specification moulded to individual capability, a process which weds the two.

In other words, for any social worker, but particularly for those in training, or those qualified but still relatively inexperienced, the explicit definition of task may provide a means both of adjusting work to the particular level of capability of the individual, and of helping that capability to become more fully realized. In discussing tasks to be carried out, the individual social worker can see clearly what is being expected of him or her, can comment on the feasibility of the expectations, and can participate in the exact formulation of the task. At the end of the day, the existence of a specific task to which the social worker has committed himself or herself makes an objective standard against which the worker's actual performance can be judged (taking due account of unexpected difficulties encountered *en route*). This can help to move the assessment interview out of the morass of psychological comment and on to the firm ground of discussion of effective or ineffective methods of work.[9]

The Content of the Supervisory Role

Let us summarize how all this contributes to the question of what supervision in social work properly involves.

[9] This whole process is of course a central feature of the 'management by objectives' approach pioneered by Drucker and McGregor in the U.S.A. and by Humble (1970) amongst others in this country. The process of assignment and assessment of work in a more general context has been analysed by Newman and Rowbottom (1968).

First, we have pointed out that there is no question but that supervisors have rights to intervene and direct, given the present setting in which social work is practised in local authority SSDs. Second, we have established that although the individual social worker does not enjoy professional autonomy, he must enjoy considerable freedom to exercise professional judgements if he is to do effective work. The assumption is that there will be for each worker some optimum degree of freedom suited to his particular capability at his particular stage of development. Conversely there will be some optimum degree of support and direction. For a relatively experienced and capable social worker, in respect of case work as such, it may be little and rare. (The availability of informal consultation with colleagues is of course another matter.) Striking the proper balance between prescribing on the one hand, and leaving freedom for the worker to stretch and develop his capabilities on the other, will be a large part of what is generally called 'enabling' and may be achieved through the specification and approval of appropriate tasks.

Third, given again the existing chain of accountability of social workers in SSDs, not only must supervision imply help and specification, but it must also imply *review*. As a result of the review the supervisor may modify or add to the previous specification.

Inevitably too, as a result of successive reviews, the supervisor will begin to form some general opinion of the capability of the worker concerned and his or her rate of development. Growing from this it will be natural to form judgements about more fundamental responses needed. Perhaps the worker is ready to take on some new or extended role, or perhaps is ready for a new range of experience or a new kind of training. Sometimes on the contrary the appraisal must be that the worker's role should be more restricted, both in his or her own interests, and in the interests of the department. Occasionally the regretful judgement will be that all having been tried, the person concerned is simply unsuited for the kind of work concerned, so that action to initiate some transfer or change of job must be considered.

Gathering together these various elements of supervisory activity, the result begins to look as follows. The duty of the supervisor includes:

  - assigning work according to his assessment of the capability of the supervisee
  - helping the supervisee to deal with work problems, as they arise
  - reviewing the work actually being carried out by the supervisee and in consequence modifying the specifications of particular existing or future tasks
  - as appropriate, acting or recommending action to enhance or reduce the role of the worker, to provide additional experience or training, or (in extreme cases) to report that alternative employment is necessary.[10]

At this point in thinking we in the research team were inevitably searching in our minds for relationships between this role and other types of role which had been identified in previous project work in the Social Services, the Health Services, and the industrial field. Two immediate comparisons offered themselves: with the *managerial role* and with the *supervisory role*.[11] The most recent versions of the gradually-evolving definition of these terms are shown in Appendix A. The notion of the *managerial role* as defined has now considerable status, for not only has it

[10] The foregoing description has much in common with the perceptive and highly realized description of the supervisor's role presented by Pettes (1967). She argues that the three elements of 'administration', 'teaching', and 'helping' are inseparable. The supervisor is in a social agency and must be able to assign work, to set standards and limits, and to know, and be able to report on, the quality of work achieved. She points out that hesitancy about adopting a positive supervisory role often stems from the supervisors themselves rather than the staff being supervised (pp. 147-148). Her comments on the supervisor's duty to provide formal evaluation of performance and staff development indicate a view of the role as fully *managerial* (see below).

The more conventional sociological view that the educational and administrative functions are in basic conflict in supervision is presented by Toren (1969 – pp. 169-184). As she shrewdly observes, an authoritative relationship removes the possibility of friendliness and intimacy (but is the teaching relationship *really* any different?). She also draws attention to the special character of supervision in social work which is necessarily concerned to some degree with the worker's own psychology because of its impact on the psychological and personal problems of his clients.

[11] The overlap between the term *supervisory* as used here and its more general use in social work is unfortunate since the nomenclature seems at first sight to beg the question. However, *supervisory role* was already well established both in our thinking and in our own publications as a technical term with its own precise definition and we have been reluctant to retitle it.

been agreed and adopted in many industrial and health settings, but by and large it has proved acceptable as a working tool for most of those with whom we have had discussions over the past four years in social services. The notion of the *supervisory role* is perhaps somewhat less well established, though clear enough examples exist in 'charge-hand', 'leading-hand', and 'senior clerk' types of roles in a variety of manual-work and clerical-work settings.

At any rate the important thing for the moment is to establish clearly the differences between the two types of role in order to find out whether supervision in social work as it has emerged from the discussion above is identical with either.

In the fully-conceived *managerial role*, the manager is concerned not only with the allocation of work to the worker concerned, and with helping him to deal with working problems, but is also concerned in the selection of the worker in the first place, and (at the other end of the cycle) in deciding in effect what action is necessary to enhance the worker's development or, to modify his role. In extreme cases it is part of his role to decide whether the particular person is suitable for the work at all. As was suggested in the previous chapter, such functions presuppose some considerable capacity differential between the manager and his subordinate – or in more colloquial terms, that the manager knows what he is about and possesses a degree of judgement that can be respected by his subordinate and others.

On the other hand, the *supervisory role* in the technical sense used here does not imply such a marked degree of difference in capacity. The emphasis is on the supervisor's role being to *help* the manager in the exercise of his managerial functions. But crucial decisions on such things as selection, appropriate level of work, and sanction or reward, rest firmly with the manager. Typically, help in the form of supervisors is needed at lower levels of the organization where managers often find themselves looking after relatively large groups of staff subject to high turnover. In such situations there is a constant stream of routine management to be provided – new staff to be inducted, specific jobs to be assigned, frequent personnel and work problems to be dealt with.

The question is, which (if either) of these two models most closely represents the needs of a well-structured 'supervisory' role in social work? Is anything like either of them, or both of them, already to be found in actual settings? Let us consider relevant findings from project work.

Project Findings on the Location and Nature of Supervisory Roles

The applicability of these two models to the 'supervisory' role was specifically explored in one of the Area Team projects in the Essex Children's Department with the Area Children's Officer, a senior social worker, and five social workers (one of whom became a senior during the project). Two of the social workers in the interviewed group were officially 'supervised' (in the conventional sense) by the senior social worker, and three by the Area Officer. In terms of *managerial* and *supervisory* roles a situation of some confusion emerged.

The Area Officer felt accountable for the totality of the work of all the staff (though recognizing some interference with this accountability from headquarters' staff) and saw herself in *managerial* relationship to all the social workers including the senior social worker. She perceived the latter as playing not a *managerial*, but perhaps a *supervisory*, relationship (as defined above) to her own 'supervisees'. However, the senior social worker saw the situation differently. She did feel fully accountable for the work of the social workers she supervised and in a full managerial relationship to them. The two social workers interviewed were split on this question. One saw the senior social worker as her 'boss', the other the Area Officer.

Whilst none of this confusion (and there was much in other working relationships too) appeared to present insuperable obstacles, the group confirmed collectively that uncertainties about the extent of the supervisory role contributed to a number of misunderstandings and frictions.

It was impossible not to suspect that variations in individual capacity were a factor in this situation, and discussions with individuals and the main group confirmed this. Senior social workers felt more comfortable about the notion of being held accountable (in the managerial sense) for the work of some workers than others. They agreed that this reflected their recognition that some more skilled social workers might be nearly as competent as they were themselves, or might become so within a relatively short period of time. In this event the relationship, using the terms under consideration here, would shift from a *managerial* to a *supervisory* one. But where this happened, the group felt that such movement needed to be made specific so that all three involved in each case – the manager, the supervisor, and the subordinate – might redefine their situation and behave appropriately. For example, the Area Officer might respond by undertaking direct supervision herself, or alternatively, by drawing on her own direct assessment of the social worker's performance in order to redefine the supervisory tasks required of the senior social worker. In turn the social worker would be aware that the supervisory sessions with the senior social worker which took place were within a general setting established by, and under the control of, her manager.

A somewhat similar confusion revealed itself in the project in the Welfare Department in Wandsworth where the two Team Leaders with whom we worked both assumed that they were in a *managerial* relationship to members of their respective teams, whereas the social workers concerned tended to see the Principal Social Worker in charge of the Department as their manager, and the Team Leaders either in a *supervisory* relationship, or (in one case) as simply a colleague! Again it was interesting that although there was a lack of clarity about the Team Leaders' authority it was unanimously recognized that the Principal had authority to review, prescribe, veto or sanction work.

However it must be stated that, as they stood, all these findings turned on the reality of this distinction between *managerial* and *supervisory* roles as applied to the social work supervision situation. As we shall see this apparent choice of role came under severe doubt at a later point.

Alternative Organizations for Area Field Work Teams

Generalizing, as the situation seemed at this point in project work there appeared to be several identifiable alternatives for the organization of an Area Office. We considered a typical group consisting of an Area Officer, a small number of senior social workers, a larger number of basic grade social workers (some qualified, some not; some well experienced, some not), some social work assistants, and a small number of trainees and attached students.[12] There might perhaps be anything between fifteen and thirty social work staff in all. Almost certainly the staff would be organized in a small number of separate teams for various administrative purposes, each headed by one of the senior social workers.

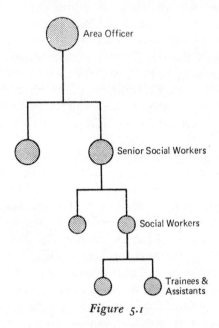

Figure 5.1

The first possibility to explore was that every difference in grade should be accompanied by a full *managerial* relationship. Assuming senior social worker grades, basic social worker grades, and social work assistant (or similar) grades, this would result in a

[12] Seebohm talked of a typical team of at least ten to twelve social workers in an Area Office, serving a population of some 50,000–100,000 in towns (para. 590). Considerably larger teams are now in existence, or envisaged as resources increase in many of the authorities with whom we have links (and indeed there were comments at the time the report was produced that the suggested ratio of workers to population was too low, particularly for urban areas). There is a growing tendency too, hastened by shortage of trained social workers, to employ more unqualified assistants, and growing realization of the large volume of work which is quite suitable for such workers to undertake – see for example the survey carried out in Scotland on this topic by the Royal Institute of Public Administration (1971).

structure with three managerial tiers and no supervisory relationships, as shown in Figure 5.1. Evidence of the kind quoted, page
112, however, threw and still throws very great doubt on the reality
of this proposal. Where such charts appear (as was noted in the
previous chapter) they are really telling nothing more than the
fact that a hierarchy of grades exists.

Going to the other extreme, we then considered the possibility
that all members of the Area social work staff, at whatever stage
of development, might be considered direct subordinates of the
Area Officer, with senior social workers playing only a *supervisory*
role (Figure 5.2). This seemed a more likely possibility but for
evidence from project work that so-called 'supervisors' usually saw

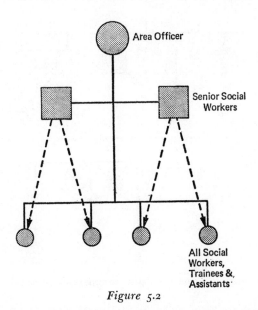

Area Officer

Senior Social
Workers

All Social
Workers,
Trainees &,
Assistants·

Figure 5.2

themselves as fully accountable for the work of trainees or students
allocated to them as well as in some cases seeing themselves as
fully accountable also for the work of certain more junior or inexperienced social workers.

In order to see the situation clearly it was obviously necessary to
step out of the framework of existing grades for the moment and
attempt to see the variety of workers in any area not in terms of
particular skills (psychiatric work, work with the blind, etc.) but,

for the purposes of the exercise, in terms of a spectrum of capacity-levels. Perhaps the workers could be classified in three broad levels as shown in Figure 5.3, where the differences of capacity between the adjacent levels were just such as to promote an easy managerial relationship. Thus all workers in Level 2 would look upon the worker in Level 3 (the Area Officer) as a 'natural' manager. On the other hand, the workers within Level 1 would naturally look for managers in the band above, in Level 2 that is.[13]

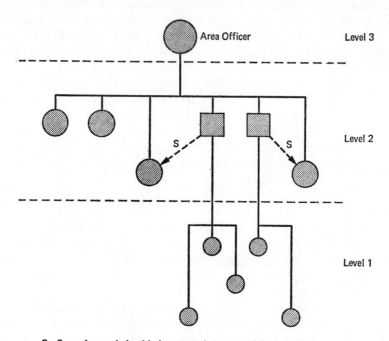

S = Supervisory relationship (as opposed to managerial relationship)

Figure 5.3

Still retaining the possibility of *supervisory* as opposed to *managerial* relationships, some of the higher capacity workers in Level 2 might well be given a *supervisory* role in relation to some of the workers at the bottom of Level 2. To the extent that these supervisors, or other workers at the top of Level 2 themselves needed

[13] 'Capacity' is used here again, as in Chapter 4, in the sense suggested by Jaques (Brown and Jaques, 1965).

case-supervision or support, they would, however, look for it directly to the Area Officer.

Returning to existing grades, one might assume that most senior social workers were in the top of Level 2 whether or not they carried supervisory roles. However, all the workers in Level 2, in this model, would be in a direct managerial relationship with the Area Officer. Most basic grade workers would no doubt fall in the lower half of Level 2; but some, newly-qualified, unqualified, or less capable, might be judged again as coming within Level 1. Level 1 would contain trainees, students, and welfare assistants, who would thus not just be 'supervised' but in fact 'managed' by senior workers at the top of Level 2. Needless to say, as workers developed, their position in these bands would change, and of course it would be very much the job of those with managerial responsibilities to be alive to these developments, and do their best to restructure the situation accordingly.

However, both this possibility and the previous one include a feature that increasingly gave rise to most serious doubts as our project work then moved on. Both models placed many workers in a position where *supervision* on one hand and *management* on the other emanated from different sources. The question had to be faced: could the supervisory process in social work as analysed and described above ever really be separated from those capable of carrying a full managerial role in all its parts, and equipped with full managerial authority? If it could not, then one was forced to think of a further possibility which allows for all the following features:

(1) the assumption that where genuine processes of social work supervision were required, however intermittently, a full *managerial* relationship should be defined and adopted;

(2) the recognition, however, that every step in *grade* did not necessarily constitute such a managerial relationship;

(3) the assumption that workers would need to be grouped into teams for various administrative purposes (office accommodation, provision of secretarial support, duty rosters, allocation of cases, etc.);

(4) the assumption that all workers as they advanced in experience and capability would not necessarily wish to assume the managerial and administrative work associated with the role of the Team Leader.

A further model which meets all these points is shown in Figure 5.4 and is currently the one we assume to be most realistic and useful. Certain but not all senior workers in Level 2 would be designated as Team Leaders. These Team Leaders would act in managerial relationships to all the workers in Level 1, but in relation to certain other more experienced workers who were assigned to their teams (workers in Level 2) they would quite explicitly not play a managerial role. The relationship here would be a *co-ordinative* one, in effect to ensure within established policy that incoming work was allocated and that things ran smoothly

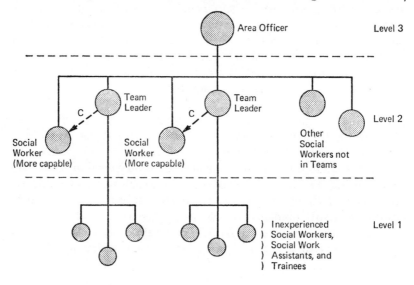

C = Co-ordinative relationship

Figure 5.4

thereafter. They would not be expected to provide case work supervision for these workers though naturally they would supply informal consultations. Such supervision and formal consultation as was needed by such workers (which would be little) they would receive directly from the Area Officer. The Team Leaders would have no authority to apply or initiate sanctions in respect of those senior workers, and would not be expected to provide appraisals of their ability or performance. Some of these more senior workers might carry the same grade as Team Leaders (i.e. 'senior social worker') without detriment to the co-ordinative relationship. Other social workers, for example specialists in community work or group work, might not be assigned to teams at all, or at least, not for purposes of work allocation. Many if not most of these, latter workers might be expected to be operating at Level 2 and to be graded accordingly.

As we say, some such model seems inevitable if the four assumptions above are accepted, and at the time of writing we are now actively exploring its validity in several of our field projects. The implications of this model for training and career development in social work are discussed in Chapter 9.

Relations with Central Administration

Let us move now to the second topic to be considered in this chapter, the relation of field workers to administrative sections.

Ask social workers to practice free association on the word 'administration' and they respond with such things as 'planning', 'control', 'finance', 'restriction', (and even) 'frustration'. The problem, as has been noted earlier, is that the very word 'administration' is double-edged. On the one hand it implies by its own etymology the act of giving service – of ministering. On the other it also carries a clear connotation of regulation. At the extreme, it can simply stand as a synonym for 'management', i.e. the activities associated with a *managerial* role.

This fundamental ambiguity is evident in practice in social services. In the project in the Welfare Department in Wandsworth, for example, some of the social workers concerned with homeless families commented that the Senior Administrative Officer of the Department would sometimes give them direct instructions not only on obvious 'administrative' matters but also on what work to carry out with families. On occasion his assistants would use their own judgement in deciding how to respond to preliminary applications from homeless clients. Where other social workers in the Welfare Department made requests for the supply of aids to the disabled, or for the adaptation of their homes, administrative sections would frequently question the validity of the need, or offer suggested alternatives like soliciting help from voluntary agencies. Moreover such instances might arise even where budgeted money was available.

Conference discussions suggest that such direct control of operational work by staff from administrative sections is by no means unknown in the new SSDs. (The particularly unclear relationship of administrative sections to heads of residential establishments is considered in the next chapter.) Such situations of full administrative control are regarded as unsatisfactory when brought to light. However, to go to the other extreme in identifying the proper role of central administration simply as one of 'service-giving' is probably unrealistic, and ignores certain manifest needs and realities. True, there are certain activities in which administrative sections can be seen to be playing what can be technically described as a *service-giving* role, i.e. genuinely providing services on demand, when and only when they are required (see Appendix A). Staff recruitment, maintenance of premises, or provision of transport is often dealt with in this way. But there are certain other areas of activities where administrative sections properly take a much more active part. They keep a keen eye open, they intervene, they raise doubts, they block – and all this is appropriate. The central question is how and under what conditions such administrative control activity can be carried out without conflicting with the other channels of control that we have already identified, the main chain of supervisory or managerial roles. The answer is, by use of the *monitoring role*.

Now it is an essential part of the managerial role to review work of subordinate staff in all respects. But there are many situations in which there is need for a detailed check of some proposed action against regulation, or against established policy, or against financial budget. Often it is convenient for the manager to rely on some specialist section to carry out the work, as it were, on his behalf. In a *monitoring role* (see Appendix A) the administrator concerned has the job of checking the social worker's activities in some defined respect – perhaps its financial or legal implications, or perhaps its conformity to policy on personnel or purchasing. His job is essentially to check some proposed action against established policy, if such exists. If the action proposed is clearly outside policy, he must inform the worker concerned, who if he still wishes to proceed must then take up the matter with his own immediate superior. If the action is within policy, but of doubtful validity, there is no reason why the monitor should not comment, but his response is of quite a different status and certainly should not carry the force of instruction. Moreover, his comments are appropriately applied only to the special aspect he is supposed to be monitoring: it is certainly not his job to make a total review of the adequacy of judgement of the worker in the case concerned, let alone to comment on his total performance (that rests with his own superior, if with anyone).

For example, in the case where a social worker was applying for a costly adaptation to the home of a physically disabled person he, the administrator, might in certain situations say in effect 'you need the approval of a more senior officer for this work' or 'we are already overspent on this budget, and I cannot therefore agree to proceed without further authority'. In both these situations some clear policy-bar is apparent. In other cases his response might be in effect 'I note your application for certain adaptations. I will provide them if you wish, but are you aware that many of your colleagues are specifying such-and-such things, which are cheaper?' What, however, would be clearly inappropriate would be to say in effect 'having studied the case details I suggest that you have in fact applied bad judgement – other clients' needs are greater' (or) – 'this client should surely be in residential care,' etc. If such reviews of discretion are necessary, they rest appropriately with the superior of the case worker concerned.

Relations with Administrative Staff in the Area

The other related situation in which project work has revealed serious ambiguity in organizational relationships is where clerical and administrative staff are posted to work in support of Area Teams of social workers, in close geographical and physical proximity to them. On the one hand it is natural for strong links to be built up with the social work team, and for the latter to look for some degree of control over work that is mainly for their benefit. On the other, we have always found also, strong links with central administrative sections in such situations.[14] In one of the Area Offices in the Essex Children's Department, for example, the work of attached clerical staff – four clerks and three copy-typists – was

[14] The situation has been explored specifically in project work in relation to two Area Offices in the Essex Children's Departments, and in relation to all the Area Offices in Wandsworth SSD. It has also arisen for discussion many times within conferences.

largely determined by the needs of the Area Officer and his staff. But the Area Officer complained that he had no control over the appointment of clerical staff, and no control over their hours of work or holidays, which they arranged directly with the Administrative Officer, sometimes at highly inconvenient times. In effect, he felt accountable for the 'output' without having any control of the 'input'.

	Area Officer	Central Admin.	Both
Who selects?			0
Who inducts, and defines duties?			0
Who prescribes day-to-day tasks, programmes and priorities?	0		
Who defines procedures?			0
Who provides working resources?			0
Who deals with questions of pay, hours, leave etc?	0		
Who monitors works done?			0
Who monitors adherence to prescribed procedures?			0
Who monitors discipline?	0		
Who assesses personal performance?			0
Who arranges formal training?		0	
Who provides ongoing staff development?		0	
Who has authority to initiate transfer or dismissal?			0

Table 5.1   *Proposed Division of Managerial Functions in Relation to Area Administrative Staff, Wandsworth SSD*

Discussions in Wandsworth SSD [15] tracked down a whole list of detailed questions which required answer as to who ought to control or support the work of the area clerical staff at various points. Table 5.1 shows this list and also the allocation of responsibilities between the Area Officer and Central Administration proposed by senior staff in Wandsworth. The resulting profile

[15] Including discussions with the Director and three Assistant Directors, and at a later point discussions with Area Officers, senior social workers, and various heads of central administrative sections, in a seminar setting.

corresponds to what in project work we have called an *attachment* situation (see Appendix A). This can be thought of as one possible solution of the general situation where a worker is subject to organizational influence from two separate sources, both of which are or might be managerial. In effect *attachment* meets the situation where it is required to leave a clear-cut line of operational accountability and control with the Area Officer, whilst at the same time building a strong managerial link with central administration for the professional staff concerned.

'Attachment' and 'Secondment' of Social Workers to Clinics, Schools Etc.

There are a significant and increasing number of local authority social workers who are based for some or all of their time in institutions such as hospitals, clinics, or schools, whose primary function is not the provision of social work but where the need for some social work provision nevertheless arises.[16] Such workers are colloquially referred to as 'attached', or (particularly if some transfer of money is concerned to offset salary costs) 'seconded'. Like the administrative staff in Area Offices discussed above, their situation can immediately be recognized as a 'dual-influence' one in which they are potentially at any rate subject to managerial control from two distinct sources and thus potentially in some situation of conflict (see Figure 5.5). If, for example, they work in

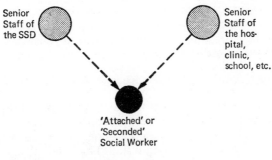

Senior Staff of the SSD

Senior Staff of the hospital, clinic, school, etc.

'Attached' or 'Seconded' Social Worker

Figure 5.5

[16] See the arguments in the Seebohm Report for 'attachment' (sic) of social workers to schools, health centres, hospitals, courts, housing departments, etc. (para. 222 et seq., para. 413, para. 523).

a psychiatric hospital does this mean that they are under the control of a psychiatrist or a senior administrator of the hospital? Does being 'attached' to a general medical practice mean being subject to instructions from the doctor concerned? Or is the Area Officer alone still accountable for, and in control of, their work in all such situations? Or do they, in contrast to all these possibilities, float free, exercising professional judgements as they think best, and subject to no external control?

If the word *attachment* is used in the precise way established above in the example of area administrative staff it cannot in fact apply here. For the attachment situation as defined is a system of shared co-management which rests on and relies absolutely upon the concept of some ultimate 'cross-over' manager who can establish policy binding on both the co-managers concerned (see Appendix A). Where one is talking of separate control by two independent agencies, for example a local authority and a health authority, such a 'cross-over' manager just does not exist.

This appears to leave three possibilities in principle, which we have called respectively *outposting*, *secondment*, and *functional monitoring* and *co-ordinating*. Extended definitions of these various situations have been gradually established in this and previous project work in the industrial and health field.[17] and are shown in Appendix A. In essence the differences are these.

Outposting

The social worker works in a physically remote site, but the managerial links with his or her original superior (be it Team Leader or Area Officer) remain intact. Inevitably he or she also becomes part of some local team[18] and as such, subject to the *co-ordinating* role of some natural team leader – a medical consultant for example. However the co-ordinator does not carry any elements of managerial authority.

Secondment

The social worker not only works in some physically remote site, but managerial control and accountability is transferred completely and *en bloc* to some new superior – perhaps a senior social worker or a senior doctor on the same site. The original manager (say the

[17] For the industrial field see Brown (1960). Later work on this topic in the health field is reported in Rowbottom *et al.* (1973).

[18] This then provides a clear example of the *multi-dimensional* organization described in previous chapters.

Area Officer) retains accountability for the long-term career development of the social worker concerned.

Functional Monitoring and Co-ordinating
Here managerial control passes to some new superior on the new
site, but the original manager (say, the Area Officer) retains not only
accountability for career development but also the job of co-ordinating the development of professional practices and the monitoring
of professional standards.

Most of our first-hand project experience of such situations has
arisen from work in the Mental Health Department in Wandsworth. Here we discovered situations in which different mental
health social workers spent regular working sessions in a psychiatric hostel run by a Hospital Management Committee, in two
day-hospitals for psychiatric patients, in a group general medical
practice, and in a child guidance clinic run by the education
authority. In the last situation part of the salary of the social
worker concerned was paid for by the education authority.

In attempting to analyse these various situations the Principal
Mental Health Social Worker (the head of the Mental Health
Department) was clear that workers in nearly all of them were
simply *outposted*, as the term has just been described. She did
not regard them as subordinate to any of the doctors or members
of any other health profession in the various institutions concerned,
but saw them as there to accept referrals at their own discretion
from these other professionals, either for the provision of psycho-
social diagnoses, or sometimes for continuing active social work.
In the situation of the child guidance clinic, however, she regarded
the social worker concerned as *seconded*, again in the sense defined
above. Discussion with the particular social worker confirmed this
view, and confirmed too that she saw the Director of the Clinic,
a psychiatrist, as her manager during the regular periods of time
that she worked at the clinic. Discussion with the social worker
attached to the group practice confirmed that she saw herself as
outposted.

Elsewhere we have had little or no discussion with staff directly
involved in such situations. However, certain general trends are
surely predictable.

First, we suggest that the presence of social workers employed
by local authorities is increasingly likely to be looked for in a

wide variety of settings other than Area Offices – in hospitals, prisons, schools, and so on – as the nature of their work and potential contribution becomes more generally known.[19]

Second, as social work becomes more sure in its own particular knowledge and contribution it is increasingly likely that whatever supervision or management of practising social workers is necessary will be seen as most properly provided in most circumstances by a more senior fellow-professional rather than by, say, a doctor or a senior administrator.

If these predictions are correct then they suggest that *outposting* will indeed be the predominant organizational form in the sorts of situations considered here.

All the main managerial links will be to the appropriate level within the SSD. Local control will amount to two things. On the one hand, the social worker concerned will be subject to some form of *monitoring* to ensure his adherence to the 'house rules' as it were of the site concerned. On the other he will probably be subject to the *co-ordinating* influence of whoever is the natural leader of the multidisciplinary team who happen to be concerned with any case.[20]

'Consultant' or 'Specialist' Roles in Social Work

Another issue that has often been posed to us in connection with field work organization is how far it is possible and desirable to

[19] The proposal that the social workers employed at present by various hospital authorities should be transferred to SSDs has now been officially adopted. This proposal has generated great controversy. Perhaps some of the anxieties would be removed if the various possibilities of 'dual influence' situations were better understood. For after all, the proposal does not necessarily imply that hospital social workers would be totally swallowed, socially, administratively, and in terms of siting, in one universal and amorphous social work team! (See further discussion on this point in Chapter 9.)

[20] Perhaps psychiatrists more than any others might wish to query the generality of this picture. A report on mental health services produced by a Tripartite Committee established by the B.M.A., the Royal College of Psychiatrists, and the Society of Medical Officers of Health (British Medical Association *et al.*, 1972) for example suggests strongly in child psychiatry, that social workers should be 'seconded' to units or clinics for long periods, and that the clinic director should always be involved in their selection. The inevitable inference here is indeed *secondment* as defined above, with the clinic director carrying a managerial role.

make use of the expert and sometimes specialized skills of certain senior social workers in so-called 'consultant' roles. The subject has arisen on a number of occasions in conferences, although our direct experience of the issue from project work is somewhat limited.

In the first place it is taken as axiomatic that any question of consultant roles cannot possibly be looked at adequately in isolation from that of the basic supervisory machinery to be established. For if normal supervisory machinery appropriate to the particular stage of development of the social worker concerned is already provided the correct starting point must be to ask: what is still missing?

There might be three answers. First there might be a need for work in a particular case which called for the services of a worker expert in some special field. The situation then would be one of arranging transfer of the case to this worker or of arranging for continuing collaboration. However, if the situation were simply this the specialist worker would no doubt be referred to as such, rather than as a 'consultant'. No question of consultancy pure and simple would arise.

A second answer might be that any worker, in addition to having formally available the support of some designated supervisor, might want at various times to draw informally on the support, guidance, particular knowledge, and accumulated experience, of a large number of colleagues. If this is what is meant by 'consultancy', then it raises no great organizational problem. It would raise no problem provided, that is, that there was general understanding that such informal 'consultations' were initiated at the discretion of the worker concerned and that any advice given was not binding on him; and provided that it was understood that it was therefore up to him to decide what use to make of the advice, unless he wished to refer the issue to his designated supervisor. Indeed, far from raising problems one would have expected that such systems of informal support and consultation amongst colleagues were to be strongly encouraged. But in a sense this still evades the issue, since there is still no question here of any worker carrying an additional and special role as a consultant.

This brings us to the third possibility. In addition to some or all of the arrangements described above, the department might well recognize the need to bring to bear high-level specialist advice more generally throughout its work – perhaps in relatively new fields, or those where in terms of existing staff the department as a whole was felt to be weak. Here, indeed, the possibility of a specialist consultant role would arise, but certain questions would require answer. Would those who fill such a role really act in a purely consultant, i.e. advisory capacity? Could the 'advice' always be freely taken, or freely left? Supposing the social worker who was seeking consultation showed every sign of ignoring some piece of advice which the consultant regarded as absolutely critical in the particular case concerned, what would the consultant then do?

In project discussions with one Principal Social Worker who tended to be seen in a consultant role,[21] she felt that in such situations, if the matter was important enough in the end she would be bound to raise it directly with somebody who *did* have authority – the immediate supervisor of the social worker concerned. But perhaps this would only amount to drawing attention to intolerable situations – to a breakdown in the normal supervisory machine. It is certainly true that giving the 'consultant' authority to instruct in normal circumstances in case discussions must undermine the main channels of managerial accountability for work.[22]

There are other issues apart from the genuineness of the consultancy relationship. If a department has workers of such specialist knowledge is it not likely to need to harness their skills more systematically than in merely providing a resource to be used at will in individual case work? Will not such specialists be required to act more positively: to produce various schemes and

[21] A Principal Social Worker in the Children's Department in Essex.

[22] Caplan (1970) produces an admirable analysis of genuine consultant roles, in contrast to supervisory, teaching, therapeutic, and collaborative, roles, based on many years of practical experience of acting as a consultant in the field of mental health. He emphasizes that the genuine consultant accepts no direct responsibility for action with the client (p. 19) and that the person making the approach is free to accept or reject all or part of the help offered (p. 20). But he points out that the consultant usually comes into the agency from 'outside' – he is not a member of its 'regular staff' (p. 22). He also analyses two components of the consultant's work – 'client-centred' consultations and 'consultee-centred' consultations, the latter aimed at increasing the capacity of the person making the approach to deal with cases in general.

plans in regard to their own specialist field, to lead various working parties, to carry out positive checks on general standards in their field, and the like?

In recent project work in this field we have moved tentatively to the idea of two distinct roles for specialists of this kind. As *specialist practitioners* the persons concerned would have cases of their own, and thus be in a position to refresh continually their experience of field problems. Generalist workers could refer cases to them either for the benefit of their advice, or for their active collaboration, or even with a view to transferring the case where appropriate. In the first instance the specialist would act in a genuine consultant role – much as does a medical specialist who has cases referred to him by a general practitioner or another specialist, for an opinion. As *specialist co-ordinators* the persons concerned would be concerned with promoting developments generally in the field concerned – initiating new ideas for new services, contributing to long-term planning, providing specialist training, and so forth. However, the use of the term 'co-ordination' would emphasize that they did not carry managerial authority in carrying out this work. What they might do would include things like calling and chairing meetings, issuing and progressing detailed programmes for agreed projects, preparing new plans and policies. What they might not do would be to set or sanction new policies on their own authority, to make personal appraisals of their colleagues (other than any assistants to whom they might stand explicitly in a managerial role) or to issue overriding instructions in situations of conflict. (See *co-ordinating role*, Appendix A.)

Clearly the two roles might be combined; and it is possible to speculate that more junior specialists might have a larger proportion of 'specialist practitioner' than 'specialist co-ordinator' work, whilst the reverse might hold for more senior specialists.

In the previous chapter it was assumed in Model B structures that the Operational Co-ordinator's staff might include a whole range of specialist co-ordinators. As was mentioned, specialism might be established in a number of dimensions – in terms of client types (children's work, the mentally subnormal etc.), or methods (group work, methods of community work, methods in groups (home helps, occupational therapists etc.).

One could perhaps then begin to see more clearly a definite residential care etc.) or even in terms of certain occupational career path for the worker who wished to progress in depth of social work technique, rather than in increasing managerial responsibility. In terms of Figure 5.4 the trainee at the bottom of Level 1 would first progress to the 'generic' or general purpose at the top of Level 1, but still supervised by the Team Leader. With growing experience the worker might eventually move into Level 2, where supervision from the Team Leader was recognized as no longer necessary or appropriate. With the development of special interests, and desirably too the acquisition of specialist training, the worker might then move to a recognized specialist post outside the team structure altogether, perhaps with a grade similar to that of team leader ('senior social worker' grade for example).[23] Here, he or she would act largely as a specialist practitioner, though some general co-ordinating work of the kind described above might arise too. Further progression might well be to a specialist post on the staff of the appropriate Assistant Director (the Operational Co-ordinator in Model B, the Head of Field Work in Model A). By this time the person concerned might carry a grade equivalent to that of an Area Officer. Here the bulk of the work would be concerned with general co-ordination in the field concerned, though there might still be some limited possibility of continuing to act as a specialist practitioner too. (See further discussion of the general topic of career development in social work in Chapter 9.)

Extension into Work at the Community Level

Up to this point most of the discussion of the field worker's role has been in terms of what might broadly be referred to as case

[23] It is often assumed that the Seebohm Report advocated that all social workers without exception should be general purpose, or in the current jargon 'generic'. Actually their precise concern in this respect was that 'a family or individual in need of social care should, as far as is possible, be served by a single social worker' (para. 516). It is true that they stressed the need for generic training and for social workers to be able to deal with many types of problems, but in fact they by no means ruled out the possibility of employing specialist workers (paras. 519, 524). However, their proposed career structure arguably underplays the possibility raised above of specialization from a relatively early stage (para. 576). Of course the *chief* Seebohm concern was to see all social workers in one administrative structure. Now that this has been largely achieved, we hear many senior staff who argue that the 'generic team' is more important and practicable than the 'generic worker'.

work, or rather more precisely social work with individuals and families in actual or potential distress. Before concluding the discussion it would be as well to stress that field workers in Area teams are likely to be significantly concerned with many elements of what we referred to in Chapter 3 as 'operational work at the community level' as well. Such extensions can perhaps enrich the role of the field worker, and help to avoid the often complained-of effects of an exclusive concentration on work with people who are already social casualties in contrast to the more positive work which may prevent their becoming such.[24]

Moreover, Area teams will probably wish also to become associated in some way with the tasks of ascertaining total needs within their own geographical area, and of planning how new or better services can be established to meet them. In other words, in the language of Chapter 3 (Table 3.1) they will wish to be involved to some extent in *research and evaluation* functions and in *strategic planning* functions.

The following were agreed in a series of cross-departmental discussions in Wandsworth SSD[25] to be essential items to add to any specification of the functions to be carried out by their newly-established Area teams as they developed:

- ascertainment of the extent and nature of social distress in the Area, and evaluation of the adequacy of existing services carried out by Area teams to meet such needs
- planning and improving ways of meeting such needs within the Area
- stimulating, and monitoring at a local level, work to meet social distress undertaken by private and voluntary agencies and associations operating within the Area
- creating public knowledge within the Area of services available from the Department, and of rights to them.

(The premise was added that, as in all other things, Area teams were subject to the constraints of Departmental policy in pursuing these activities.)

[24] The Seebohm Report was quite emphatic that Area teams, as well as certain specialist officers at headquarters level, should be concerned with community work (paras. 504-507).
[25] The discussions involved at an early stage the Director and three Assistant Directors, and at a later stage in two two-day seminar events about seventy senior field work, residential, and administrative staff.

Further discussions in depth with one Area Officer added the useful point that an important element in planning at Area level would be the establishment of appropriate priorities as to how social workers deployed their time and skills, including appropriate discrimination between what they should do and what should be left for other statutory and voluntary agencies, or for volunteers.

Conclusion

As was indicated at the start of this chapter, in our experience the chief problems of field work organization all cluster around one central area of doubt – the relation of the field work practitioner to his or her personal supervisor. Has anyone the right in the end to dictate to the social worker how to deal with his or her own client? If so, exactly who should carry this critical role?

In answer to the first question we have argued that once it is accepted that whatever the system the individual field worker must properly be left with considerable freedom or discretion in dealing with his clients, it is easier to accept the undoubted fact that he does not possess professional autonomy in the local authority setting. He is ultimately accountable for all he does to the Director, and through him to the local authority and then to the electorate. And he is subject to normal managerial rights to instruct, appraise, and if needs be sanction.

Through the idea of *task* it can be seen how discretion can be measured out, as it were, according to the various capacities and capabilities of various workers, and in a positive fashion. If the supervisory role is defined around this idea, the supposed conflict between 'control' and 'enabling' evaporates.

One of the difficult issues that remains, however, is exactly who is to carry the supervisory role in relation to a number of workers not all equal by any means, but ranging along a scale from the most inexperienced trainee to the most highly expert, and perhaps specialized, practitioner. In this situation the capacity of the supervisor too becomes of critical importance.

Having considered alternative definitions of the supervisory roles in social work it seems increasingly likely that only one which stresses its full *managerial* content (as defined) will be adequate. Given this and certain other criteria a particular model (Figure

5.4) of organization for the Area Office has been discussed, in which heavy stress is placed on the wide range of capabilities to be supported and managed. In this model the Team Leader role implies a full *managerial* relation in regard to certain staff – inexperienced social workers, social work assistants, and trainees – but a *co-ordinating* relationship only to other very experienced workers. With this clear conception of supervision it becomes possible to throw new light on other current organizational problems in field work – the roles of specialists of various kinds, the situation of so-called 'attached' social workers, and the proper combined *monitoring* and *service-giving* role of central administrative sections.

6 Organization of Residential Care

Moving from field work to residential work one comes to an area that feels itself to be, and is often represented as, the poor relation. It is perhaps significant that a great deal of our work over the last three and a half years has been (by invitation) concerned with residential work and its organization. During this time we have conducted discussions in depth in various projects with fourteen heads of residential establishments, and with some nineteen other senior staff with residential responsibilities – assistant directors, executive officers, homes advisers, etc. We have so far done little work with staff of establishments other than heads.

Since these staff were drawn from five different local authorities and the heads were drawn from a wide variety of establishments, it might have been supposed that project work would have revealed a correspondingly wide range of organizational problems. Strikingly, however, the same two major problems have presented themselves in nearly all these settings.

The first is the absence of strong and straightforward organizational anchorages of residential establishments to the main management structure of the department. This does not mean to say that heads of establishments are without contacts with the rest of the department (though the manifestation of these contacts in actual visits may not be as great as many heads might desire). They may be in contact at various times with a very wide variety of staff. Moreover, many of these they may see as carrying some degree of authority. They may be contacted or visited by Area Officers, senior social workers, and other social workers. They may be visited by a 'homes adviser' or a 'residential officer'. They will frequently be in contact with a 'homes management' or 'homes administration' section in the Administrative Division at headquarters. Occasionally they may see the Assistant Director in charge of residential care, though he or she is likely to have many dozens of other establishments to visit. Once a year the Director himself may find time in his busy itinerary to make a flying visit – perhaps to join some special social event for the residents. Any or all of these staff may freely unburden themselves of comment, advice, and what indeed may often seem to be outright instructions. But which, if any, carries direct responsibility for what goes on in the establishment, and for what goes on twenty-four hours per day, seven days per week, is often quite unclear.

The second main problem which we have regularly encountered is the uncertainty amongst residential staff as to exactly how their work should interlink with that of field work staff. If, for instance, the head of a children's home is experiencing problems with parents is it the job of the field worker 'in charge of the case' to deal with them? If a field worker does not agree with the head of a children's home about a particular child's returning home for occasional week-end visits, whose view should prevail? In homes for the elderly, is it right that field workers should so rarely visit their erstwhile clients? Whose task is it to make arrangements for permanent transfers of the elderly from the home to hospital, where these become necessary? And so on.

The combined effect of these two problems is to produce in many establishments a feeling of isolation, even of alienation, from the rest of the department. Indeed the phrase 'rest of the department' here is almost misleading in this context. Here is the Home geographically contained and with its own busy institutional life embracing both residents and staff in continuing and close interaction. Out there somewhere is the Department; a large but ill-defined group of vaguely authoritative figures some of whom are better known than others, all of whom must be wooed, placated, or resisted, as appropriate, in order that the Home and its way of life may be protected.

So much for a statement of the general problem. Within it we shall be describing various pieces of project work in more detail, and various attempts by departments to do something to alleviate it. Before doing so, however, and by way of preparation, it is necessary to consider in some detail exactly what is trying to be achieved in residential establishments. As always we take it for granted that there can be no useful discussion of organization without prior clarification of the basic functions to be carried out.

Analysis of Work in the Residential Setting

An early opportunity arose to analyse the nature of residential work in a project in the Wandsworth Children's Department involving eight heads of residential establishments.[1] In each of the discussions we explored with the head of the establishment concerned how he saw his work in terms of the *functions* he understood the establishment as existing to perform. As work continued in various other projects described below concerned with residential care in this and other local authorities, we were able to generalize our findings. Conference discussions provided a chance to test emerging generalizations.

Gradually, we were able to build a coherent analysis of work in the residential setting which now stands as shown in Table 6.1.[2]

[1] Including a reception-observation centre, three long-stay homes of medium size, two long-stay 'family-group' homes. a short-stay home, and a short-stay residential nursery.

[2] This statement and the following discussion may be compared with two other substantial analyses of the nature of residential work. The Castle Priory Report on the Residential Task in Child Care (Residential Child Care Association *et al.*, 1969) expands an analysis in terms of *direct nurture, indirect nurture,* and *remedial care*; making the important point that all children in care are by the nature of their separation from normal family life in some need of remedial treatment. Ignoring Righton's (1971) rather unwieldy distinctions between 'objectives' and 'task', the various items he discusses – assembling relevant information, identification of tasks to be met and problems to be solved, clarification of actual work to be done, provision of means to stay alive, provision of 'basic maintenance services', provision of opportunities for personal growth, execution of care/treatment plans, linking the unit to the community etc., strike some obvious parallels with the analysis presented here. A third published source which might have been expected to throw light on this subject, the Williams Report (1967) on staffing residential homes, is disappointing in this respect. Although one of the first chapters is called 'The Nature of the Job' there is little hard analysis of residential functions and a tendency to pose vague aims such as 'to create a harmonious group ...' 'to help him (the child in care) to develop his own personality and capacity in whatever direction they may lead'. A recent Discussion Document on Residential Training issued by the

TABLE 6.1
ANALYSIS OF FUNCTIONS TO BE CARRIED OUT IN THE RESIDENTIAL SETTING

Operational Work

basic social work (all residential establishments)
- making or contributing to assessments of need and of appropriate response
- providing information and advice
- monitoring and supervision of residents
- helping individual residents to maintain and develop personal capacity for adequate social functioning
- arranging provision of other appropriate services for residents

basic services (all residential establishments)
- providing clothing, other goods, and money
- providing meals
- providing accommodation
- providing help in daily living (including help with personal hygiene, dressing, moving, looking after personal property, etc.)
- providing recreation, social, and cultural life (including the fostering of links with the local community)

supplementary services (provided as needed, and varying from establishment to establishment)
- providing aids for the physically handicapped
- providing medical or paramedical treatment
- providing formal education, etc.

Staffing and Training Work
- recruitment of domestic and other staff
- student training
- dealing with welfare problems of all staff

Managerial and Co-ordinative Work
- selection or sharing in selection of domestic staff and care staff
- induction of new staff and prescription of work
- personal appraisal and development of staff
- dealing with problems of staff, and of staff interaction
- (in some cases) co-ordination of work of non-residential staff in relation to needs of particular residents

Central Council for Education and Training in Social Work (1973) contains an analysis of residential functions which has been drawn in part from our own work.

Logistics, Finance, and Secretarial Work
  - ordering of supplies, replacements, and repairs
  - collection and banking of incoming money
  - control of petty cash
  - local fund raising
  - maintenance of various records and preparation of various reports
  - care and security of stock and premises.

The link, indeed the exact parallels, between this statement and the broader statement of departmental functions shown in Table 3.1 in Chapter 3 will be at once apparent, and of course the connection is not accidental. An explicit aim in this study was to see the various strands of residential care not simply in their own right, but always in relation to the broad loom of departmental activity. And conversely, the statement of total departmental activity was woven from many more specific statements from various particular fields of exploration. Again, as in relation to the broader statement of departmental functions, certain reservations must be emphasized.

First, this is a list of functions which are carried out in a particular setting, not a list of functions carried out by any one particular occupational group. Many of the functions described will, of course, be carried out by residential care staff, but medical care, for example, will be provided by doctors or nurses, and formal education by teachers. The provision of meals (as opposed to the provision of help in eating them) will be the duty of domestic staff rather than residential care staff. Certain functions in the *basic social work* area, for example helping individual residents to maintain and develop personal capacity for adequate social functioning, may perhaps be shared between two occupational groups, namely residential care staff and field workers (this question is discussed more fully below). However it does seem to be the case that heads of establishments at least have direct managerial accountability for certain main blocks of activity in Table 6.1 – for some if not all *basic social work*, for all *basic services*, and for all the various supporting activities like *staffing*, *logistics*, *finance*, and *secretarial* work.

The point must be made again too that this particular analysis is concerned only with the *kind* of activities to be carried out, and eschews other questions of the *quality* of activity, the *standards* of care, the *attitudes* brought to bear, the '*atmosphere*' created, and so forth. We do not for a moment dispute the importance of these things, but the point must be reiterated that attending only to attitudes and standards and atmosphere can never take one far into issues of how to structure departments, or what sort of occupational groups to establish and train in the first place.[3]

Specific Tasks in Residential Care

Before proceeding to consider various ways in which these various kinds of work in the residential setting may best be organized and managed, it is appropriate at this point to describe project work which has in fact moved at least one step closer to the question of specific quality of care or treatment. In the course of the project with heads of children's homes in Wandsworth, mentioned above, we systematically explored with each head not only what *functions*, i.e. what kinds of work, he saw as necessary, but also how he saw his work in terms of specific *tasks* to be undertaken with residents. Clearly the way in which work is constructed in terms of specific tasks affects the quality of result.

Here our work led us into territory alongside that explored in our discussions about tasks with field workers described in the previous chapter, and we found many of the same hesitations and un-

[3] Many studies of residential care take these factors of *style, attitude*, and *standard*, as their main concern. To take one example, the recent major study by King, Raynes, and Tizard, (1971) of the care of mentally-handicapped children in a number of hospitals and homes, establishes measures of what is called 'child management practice' along a scale from 'institutionally-oriented' at one end to 'child-centred' at the other. The measures were explicitly about *quality*, but exactly what functions this 'quality' related to, i.e. what functions the establishments saw themselves as carrying out, remained unexamined, the researchers no doubt making their own implicit assumptions. The Discussion Document on Residential Training of the Central Council for Education and Training in Social Work (1973) is unusual in making an explicit exploration of both necessary attitudes (Chapter 3) and functions to be carried out (Chapter 4).

certainties as in those discussions. Again, as for field workers, many more concrete tasks were easy to identify and agree – arranging holidays for children in care, recruitment and induction of staff, buying clothes, arranging meals, co-ordinating and collating the provision of assessment reports, and so on. In other areas perceptions were much more varied. On the question of how to meet the complex emotional needs and problems of children, for example, opinion fell broadly into two schools. The first did see the possibility of establishing specific therapeutic tasks for specific children, and, indeed, were able to offer examples. The second did not, and thought that such problems were helped primarily by work designed to establish a general therapeutic environment, and by inculcating certain general attitudes and orientations in their own staff. (What are referred to here and below as 'therapeutic tasks' are what we would now locate more precisely as attempts to 'develop or maintain personal capacity for adequate social functioning' – see Table 6.1, page 135.)

The following extract from a report of individual discussions with one particular Head in a home for twenty maladjusted children elaborates the second view:

It is difficult to identify any specific long-term tasks which follow a systematic programme of therapy, to be carried out by the Superintendent or his staff. (Whether such exist for the psychiatrist or the psycho-therapist, is of course another matter.) It seems likely that the real nature of the therapeutic work carried out by Homes staff is as follows. As a result of case discussions, say with the psychiatrist, a particular *treatment strategy* is agreed for a particular child. This may require considerable skill in carrying out, but does not in itself constitute a task or series of tasks as here defined. Rather, the 'strategy' (for example a strategy of planned regression) amounts to a policy which shapes the way *existing* tasks are to be carried out with children, e.g. putting them to bed, telling them stories, providing recreational and social opportunities for them, carrying out formal-education tasks, dealing with emotional crises, and so on.

If this is so, such therapeutic tasks, though requiring high skill, are themselves of short time-span (i.e. mostly of hours or days). In contrast, the *concern* is long-term; the *strategy* may be expected to be long-term in its effects, and the *prognosis* may be long-term. Again, many of these tasks are carried out by houseparents and other staff, but some are carried out or participated in, by the Superintendent on occasion.

Support for the first view was provided by the following examples (amongst others) of specific therapeutic tasks identified by the Superintendent of a long-stay home for about sixteen children:

(1) In the case of an asthmatic teenager the Superintendent embarked on a programme of treating the causes rather than the effects, and judged that it would take her a minimum of *one year* to achieve any lasting improvement. Work undertaken to achieve the object was:
  – reorientating staff attitude to the attacks;
  – encouraging the girl to reflect on what circumstances induced attacks and why;
  – as the frequency of attacks began to decrease, acknowledging the girl's own part in this and strengthening her motivation to gain control.

(2) Preparing a 15-year-old for employment by reality testing of fixed interest in working with animals, visits to Youth Employment Officer, provision of information, i.e. duties and prospects in a number of different occupations, arranging attendance at school leavers' course at Agricultural College, programme of discussion aimed at ventilating and clarifying girls' perceptions – *one year*.

(3) Helping the same 15-year-old to establish a sense of identity, and to articulate feelings by words rather than self-induced fits and loss of speech. Exploration of available history and other information and the involvement of the Child Care Officer. Helping the girl to make contact with her old home and her grandmother. Creating the climate within which the girl could choose to visit her mother in psychiatric hospital. Discussing problems of colour and sexual behaviour – *one year*.

The housemother in charge of another smaller long-stay home for about eight children gave many additional examples of what she saw as specific therapeutic tasks, amongst them the following:

(1) In the case of siblings aged three and four years, the Housemother implicitly allowed *four to five months* to herself and the staff to help the children to settle in and to judge whether or not through the general régime of the home, and particular activity with these two children, they were progressing. (At the end of this period it was recognized that there had been virtually no progress in terms of their general development, including such factors

as vocabulary recognition, toilet training, muscular co-ordination or understanding of cause and effect. The Housemother has now referred the children, through agreement with the relevant Child Care Officer, for specialist assessment, and will now acquire the task of taking them for appointments and contributing to the Assessment Centre team's diagnosis.)

(2)   In the case of a six-year-old who manifested insecurity through stealing, following a number of changes of staff and children, a task to relieve his insecurity through:
- raising bed-time
- giving him special status by little jobs to do with younger children
- gaining the co-operation of his teacher
- allocating the assistant housemother to give him extra attention
  – *six months.*

(This task has been successfully worked through – had there been no progress at the end of this period of time, though not before, the Housemother would have sought referral to the Child Guidance Clinic.)

(3)   In the case of a fat, sullen, and unkempt thirteen-year-old girl, a task to improve her self image and sense of feminine identity by:
- (things like) offering her help in setting her hair and creating opportunity for discussion with her focused in this area
- involving the doctor in encouraging the girl to diet
- encouraging the skills that the girl has, e.g. cooking, and seeing that she was rewarded for her efforts by unofficial aunt
- motivating her to stick to diet by encouraging interest in more 'trendy' clothing (new items to be bought every time she registered a loss of five pounds)
- encouraging other staff and housemothers' husbands to reinforce girl's efforts by complimenting her when a realistic improvement was achieved – *six months.*

(4)   In the case of an eleven-year-old girl placed for four months, to enable her to mourn over her mother's death and reorientate to fostering with aunt who tended to shut off feelings of grief, a task shared by the Housemother and the Child Care Officer, who both used opportunity to help girl to express feelings and to encourage her to talk about mother – *four months.*

A number of further examples of such treatment tasks were identified by heads of other establishments.

Existing Confusion in Managerial Structure

Now whether each of these therapeutic task formulations strikes the reader as equally realistic or convincing is one thing. (Unfortunately further discussion and test of this particular project material was not able to be continued, for a variety of reasons.) What they surely do indicate, however, if indeed it were in any doubt, is the possible existence of real work over and above the provision of *basic services* in residential establishments, in what we have called the *basic social work* area. More specifically, much of this would be work concerned with the 'helping individual residents to maintain and develop personal capacity for adequate social functioning' to use the language suggested in Table 6.1 above.

This may seem an unremarkable point to make, but the fact is that the more conventional description of the residential situation in terms of these all-too-easy terms 'care' and 'case work' tends to obscure this issue and in doing so leads to severe problems. Generalizing from project work in at least three departments, reinforced by many conference discussions, the trouble is as follows. Where residential work is conceived in terms of 'care' and 'case work' there is a *tendency* for the latter to be wholly associated with 'professional' staff whilst the former becomes associated with 'administrative' staff. In effect everything that concerns the treatment of the individual client in care then tends to be seen as the ultimate concern of field workers. The rest – the provision of bricks and mortar, of decent environment and material provision, and perhaps even the provision of a 'therapeutic atmosphere' – becomes the concern of an 'administrative' rather than a 'professional' background. And in the middle stands the poor head of establishment, caught in an impossible attempt to split apart 'professional' control from 'administrative' control, and 'case work' from 'general care'. Nor does the matter stop here. The 'residential adviser' (or 'homes adviser' or 'residential officer') becomes a victim of the same myth. Given the notion that the staff of the establishment are not, nor could be, concerned with positive focused intervention in respect of individual residents, and that such concern would rest exclusively with field workers, the residential adviser is relegated to being a provider of materials, a recipient of complaints, and a monitor of administrative procedures. Hardly ever is he seen as a positive manager accountable for helping the residential head to provide and develop a full and effective range of service and intervention on behalf of his residents. Nor, often, is there any identified person who does carry such a role.

Illustrations of the absence of clear-cut managerial roles with accountability for all aspects of residential work abound in our project experience. In the project described above with heads of residential establishments in the Wandsworth Children's Department, for instance, the Children's Officer, the Assistant Children's Officer (Homes), the Case Work Supervisor, the Senior Child Care Officer (Homes), and the senior administrator in the Homes Management Section, were all seen as possible contenders for a managerial role. Different heads varied in their ideas of exactly what degree of authority each of these people carried. Two thought that only the Children's Officer himself represented a full manager, five tended to identify the Assistant Children's Officer as their manager, and one just did not know. Some saw the Senior Child Care Officer (Homes) as having *supervisory* authority. Some saw him as having *monitoring* authority, and three thought that possibly he carried no authority in relation to them. The staff of the significantly-titled 'Homes Management Section' (a section of the administrative division) were seen not just as monitoring adherence to regulation and policy, but as playing a much more positive role in deciding what material support was appropriate. Indeed, two heads even thought that they might share in managerial functions – selection, definition of work, appraisal of performance, and so on. In this particular case there was little doubt that the senior residential staff – the Assistant Children's Officer (Homes) and the Senior Child Care Officer (Homes) – were seen as wearing a professional mantle, but neither one nor the other was seen fully and unequivocally in a straightforward managerial relationship. Subsequent project discussion with these two latter people confirmed these uncertainties from their point of view as well.

In Brent too, ambiguity about residential management arose, as was noted in Chapter 4, but here it was in a different form. According to the published charts the Assistant Director (Residential and Day Care) was in direct and straightforward control of all establishments. However, discussions with one Area Manager produced the following statements:

> The Area Manager sees his role as that of giving social work support and advice to the staff of the residential homes. It is not clear to him what the precise form of this advice is, whether it carries authority, or whether it is 'take it or leave it advice'. The Area Manager is of the opinion that matrons see Area Managers as powerful figures who can 'put things right'.
>
> More precisely, the Area Manager would define his present role as:
> - making joint decisions with client and residential staff concerning immediate client problems
> - educative, preparing Heads for changes as far as social work practice is concerned
> - monitoring general standards of 'bricks and mortar' which affect the client.

In initial discussions at least, the Assistant Director (Residential and Day Care) was inclined to see the Area Manager as 'the manager of the establishment head in all matters concerning client-staff relationships'.

A very similar situation was evident in East Sussex. In the initial project there, which was concerned with field-residential relationships, one Area Director observed that although the Residential Division was manifestly concerned with all aspects of residential care, in practice he himself tended to make a mental split between what he called 'welfare' matters and 'building management and maintenance'. Unresolved welfare problems he would refer to the Assistant Director (Social Work Services) rather than the residential division. Another Area Director said that many of the Residential and Day Care Officers (equivalent to 'residential advisers') projected an image as being concerned for the most part with 'nuts and bolts and general hotel keeping'. Reinforcing this view, a report of discussions with the Executive Assistant in the Residential Division included the comment:

> The R & DCOs currently in role are not qualified social workers and lack confidence and expertise in supervising the total operations of establishments. This is reflected in some unwillingness to get involved in case reviews which would provide opportunity to develop their skills and enable them to be real bridges between estab-

lishments and Area staffs by following through on treatment plans made.

The Executive Assistant added that she perceived herself to be in managerial relationships with all heads of establishments, though she noted that some, e.g. the Head of one of the Approved Schools, probably did not regard her in this light, nor would some of the heads of establishments who were not originally part of the Children's Department from which she had come.

Later work in East Sussex in a project[4] specifically designed to reach an agreed definition of the role of the Residential and Day Care Officer threw up much more evidence of the uncertainty about accountability for residential work.

As the head of one establishment experienced it, there was no one individual in the Department between herself at the one extreme and the Assistant Director at the other who carried a clear-cut twenty-four hours a day, seven days a week, responsibility for the Home and its problems. And it was taken for granted that the Assistant Director could not himself be directly approached with all the problems with which the Head could not cope.

Another Head commented that whilst the role of the R & DCO was still evolving, it was at the moment largely concerned with problems of material provision. But she was quick to add that it was impossible to separate problems of material provision from quality of care on the one hand, or indeed from the many pressing problems of staff and staff relations on the other. She noted that there were a number of people in the Department who were very ready to comment on the quality of care provided for residents (including for example many visiting social workers) but no one person who then seemed disposed to take responsibility for doing anything constructive about it.

Coming to the two R & DCOs who were themselves involved in the project, the report of work with one summarized his own view of the position as follows.

---

[4] The project started in July 1972 and involved the Assistant Director (Residential and Supporting Services), the Executive Assistant referred to above, two Residential and Day Care Officers, two Area Directors, and the heads of a home for the elderly, a hostel for the mentally sub-normal, an adult training centre, and a children's home.

Generally, your role is unsatisfactory in practice, at the moment. On the one hand you are seen as 'matron's friend and advocate' – words like advice, support, help, guide, tend to be used. On the other you are seen as an agent of County Hall. These two aspects feel inconsistent. Put another way, you feel that you carry responsibility without authority.

The report fed back to the other R & DCO commented in a more analytic vein:

You believe that the R & DCO does not carry the authority of a fully fledged manager, but does carry authority. Although the style of discussions might be advisory, you believe that any indications you give are necessarily prescriptive and that you must accept responsibility for the advice given. Perhaps the nature of the role is a general supervisory one.

Residential and day care staff are subject to authoritative influence from other quarters, e.g. they have been told that they are part of the geographical area and it is clear that an Area Director is in charge of an area.

One of the Area Directors involved in the project observed that the present role of the R & DCO was ill-defined as far as she was concerned, and this made for difficulties in working relationships. She noted that matrons of homes sometimes approached her with problems, not only about individual clients, but even on occasions about staff.

Alternative Clarifications

Well, how might all this be put right?[5] First, surely the nettle must be grasped. That is, the fact must be accepted that residential work, by residential staff, is an activity which aims to provide not only what we have called *basic services* (provision of food, accommodation, recreation, etc. in an appropriate 'caring' manner) but also the systematic provision of what we have called

[5] There appears to be little or no literature which goes beyond discussion of general approach and standards in residential care to the harder and more abstract issues of organizational structure for optimum support and control. A significant exception is an article by Hodder (1968), which examines from a practitioner's viewpoint the need for a stronger and clearer management structure.

basic social work. Moreover, the two are integrally and indissolubly linked in the residential setting. For if this fact is grasped, the corollary is that *any management structure (as opposed to monitoring structure or service structure) for residential care must be concerned with* BOTH *these aspects of work.*

Moreover, given the fact that the practice of all social work in a local authority setting is subject to managerial assessment and control in present circumstances, then such a managerial link is unavoidable. Staff of homes do not in reality exist in a separate organizational structure, however close-knit the texture of institutional life, and seemingly loose the links with the rest of the department.[6] In the end, if no other officer is accountable for what goes on in any establishment, then the Director at least certainly is: and his employing authority are likely to leave him in no doubt of the matter if the case is serious enough.

Acceptance, however, of the need for a clear managerial link with establishments still leaves open the question of where it might best be located in the main departmental structure.

In Model A departments (Chapter 4) the general managerial line will, of course, flow down the main functional strand under the Assistant Director in charge of residential care. The main question will be the exact form of structure between the establishment and the Assistant Director. The sheer number of establishments to be managed in departments of medium or large size (of the order say of thirty to sixty[7]) suggests that in these departments the Assistant Director cannot manage them all unaided. This supposition is reinforced by the existence already in most departments of a whole range of residential advisers, executive

[6] Although it might be important to recognize here the distinction (and impingement) of two social systems – the organizational structure of the department as an executive entity and the more comprehensive social system of all those staff or residents who share much of their life together within the walls of one institution. To analyse, for example, husband and wife teams in a small family group home *only* in terms of departmental organization would no doubt be to miss much of importance. However trends like these described and advocated in the Williams Report (1967) towards the professionalization of residential staff – the trend for example for more staff to 'live out' – may tend to strengthen the distinction between occupational and other roles in the total-life situation of such staff.

[7] That is thirty to sixty *residential* establishments. If an organization is contemplated which involves day-care establishments as well, the number will be significantly increased.

officers, etc., of intermediate grade, albeit often in ill-defined relationship to establishment heads, as indicated above.

All the evidence points to the need to create in departments of medium or large size new posts under some such titles as 'residential group manager' or perhaps 'residential manager' (see Figure 6.1) to fill what we have come to call the *missing level in residential management*.

In terms of general managerial level, though not necessarily in terms of precise grade, such staff might equate with Area Officers – Level 3 in Figure 6.1. This is on the assumption that heads of most establishments operate in Level 2 (the first managerial level) – equivalent, say, to Team Leaders or experienced

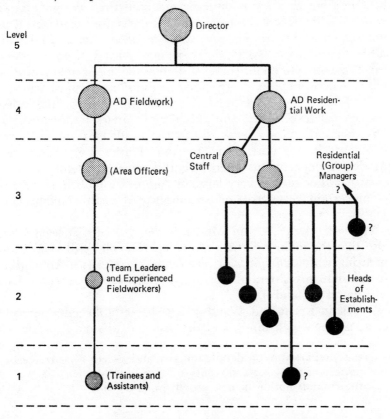

Figure 6.1 Developed Management Structure for Residential Care – Model A

field workers. However, it may be that certain heads of very large or very complex establishments, perhaps for example heads of those community homes which were formerly approved schools, must be recognized as not only higher in grade than the general run of heads, but operating at a managerial level higher by one step (Level 3). If so, one would predict that the only comfortable managerial relationship in most Model A departments for these heads would be directly with the Assistant Director, though the appropriate Residential Manager might conceivably carry a *co-ordinating role* in relation to them with regard, say, to development of standard practices and procedures. Again, the heads of certain very small or uncomplicated establishments might perhaps be operating at a level lower by one step than the general run, which could suggest the need for an intervening managerial post not shown in Figure 6.1, one or more 'group heads' in Level 2. This might apply particularly if one moved from residential establishments to establishments such as day nurseries or luncheon clubs, where these were organized in the same main division.

In Model B departments the same problem of the missing managerial level arises, but this time it arises between any one Divisional Director (Level 4) and the heads of residential establishments in his particular Division (Figure 6.2). Again, as in Model A departments there are the same problems of how to treat heads of certain very large or complex establishments (Level 3) or certain very small or uncomplicated establishments (Level 1).

In both Model A and Model B departments, it seems likely also that the main structure of managerial roles will need supplementing with *staff-officer* or *service-giving* roles (see Appendix A) in relation to residential work – the posts shown as 'central staff' in Figures 6.1 and 6.2.

Work in Brent and Wandsworth[8] has established a whole list of activities which might well be assigned to such support staff:

- the preparation of detailed plans and briefs for architects, in respect of new establishments
- the commissioning of new establishments

---

[8] With a 'Residential Manager' in Brent and the head of the 'Residential Services' Section in Wandsworth.

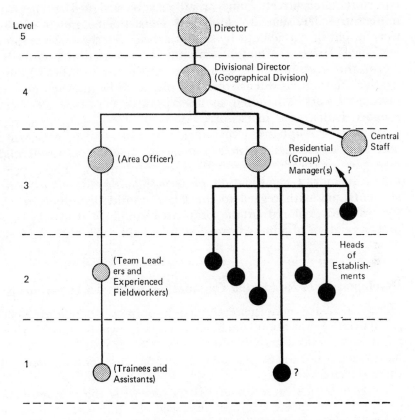

Figure 6.2 Developed Management Structure for Residential Care – Model B

- the provision of food, supplies, and equipment, for establishments
- the maintenance and repair of establishments
- the provision of transport
- the maintenance of central records and statistics
- the preparation and monitoring of budgets, etc.

Such work clearly falls into the 'non-operational' categories described in Chapter 3, and particularly into the fields of *logistical*, *secretarial*, and *financial* work. In Model A Departments such work may be carried out by central staff attached to the Assistant

Director. Alternatively some or all may be assigned to the Administrative Division. In Model B Departments much of the work might be carried out by staff attached directly to the various Divisional Directors, though some might be carried out centrally. Again, this work might be seen as part of the work of the Administrative Division, as discussed in Chapter 4. (The question of how placement work is handled, another possible field for staff-officer support, is discussed in Chapter 8.)

It must be emphasized that such administrative or other support staff would not be in a *managerial* relation to residential managers or heads of individual establishments. Their roles would include a combination of *service-giving* and *monitoring* elements and with regard to the latter, would be subject to all the provisos explored in the previous chapter in discussing the proper relation of administrative staff to field work staff.

Developments in Residential Organization in Project Departments

Here, then, are some general models or pictures of developed residential organization. Such ideas have grown from, and then in turn influenced actual developments in, project departments, particularly in East Sussex and Brent. Let us describe some of these developments.

In East Sussex, a series of discussions with the management group[9] in the spring of 1972 produced the following report on the subject of residential management.

Present Organization
It was agreed that presently the Assistant Director (Residential and Supporting Services) is accountable to the Director for the totality of residential work activity:
  – hotel keeping and maintenance of premises
  – environment – general social and recreational opportunities and the régime of the establishment which enhances or detracts from the individual's good life experience
  – individual therapy – planned and focused treatment physical, social or emotional.

[9] See page 61.

There are more than fifty (residential and day care establishments) and it seemed to the group unlikely that the Assistant Director could or should be in a direct manager/subordinate relationship with each Head of establishment, i.e. that he would require assistance in managing establishments.

Manifestly there are six Residential and Day Care Officers and one Executive Assistant 'between' the Assistant Director and Heads. The nature of the role relationships between these people and Heads is open to alternative interpretations.

The report went on to emphasize the general need to distinguish grade from managerial level, and continued more specifically as follows:

The salary grades of Heads range from approximately £1,100–£3,500 per annum, the majority falling in the range £1,800–£2,000 which is roughly the same grade as that paid to general social workers. Residential and Day Care Officers are paid one grade above some Heads and less than others. If it is assumed that salary grade in some rough way reflects the felt level of work, it can be assumed that a large proportion of Heads could not be managed by Residential and Day Care Officers.

The situation is made somewhat more complex by the fact that only one Residential and Day Care Officer in post is qualified. Therefore the ability to act 'across the board' which is expected of managers or supervisors is limited. However it was agreed that these facts should not limit the generation of requisite alternatives; these alternatives might well carry implications for future recruitment and remuneration and for staff development activity in the here and now.

The report went on further to record the views of the group on which of various organizational alternatives that had been considered, appeared to them to be the most viable, noting, however, the problems that this particular choice brought in its stead.

The following diagram suggests the organization structure of choice which the group settled on after considerable discussion. The weakness of the structure is that the Executive Assistant is expected to be in a staff role to the Assistant Director, helping him to coordinate on general policy implementation and at the same time manage some establishments and the team of Residential and Day Care Officers.

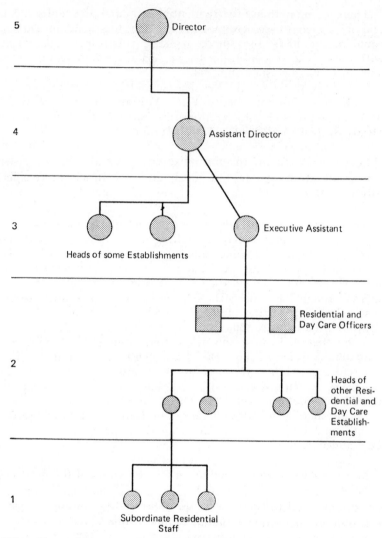

The discussion moved on to consider organizational implications of a further change which had been contemplated for some
time, i.e. the transfer of control of residential and day establishments to Areas. Even though the problem of managing heads of
establishments would be reduced by dividing establishments out
amongst the Areas, it was considered that Area Directors would
still need some help in this respect. Could senior social workers

combine supervision of heads of establishments with supervision of social workers? The group thought not. Probably separate supervision was necessary, using some form of staff like the present Residential and Day Care·Officers. However, the need for special treatment for the 'high level' establishments would remain. Heads of these would, no doubt, have to be managed directly by Area Directors.

Following this discussion a further project was mounted to establish a more precise specification of the role of Residential and Day Care Officers, on the assumption that they would be more closely integrated with individual Areas. The project still continues at the time of writing, some of the initial discussions with various members of the department having been drawn on above in illustrating the precise degree of unclarity about such roles. A draft job description which has been produced identifies the R & DCO as clearly accountable to the Area Director and (for the time at any rate) with a *supervisory* role rather than a *managerial* one, in relation to all heads of establishments, except some designated ones whose heads would be both managed and supervised by the Area Director. The R & DCO would deal with all aspects of work in establishments: general levels of care, the treatment of specific cases, staffing, training, financial, and logistical matters. He would also act in a co-ordinating role in:

- allocating vacancies, including in consideration the availability and use of residential accommodation in private and voluntary establishments
- arranging and attending case reviews according to established policy for those in care
- progressing agreed programmes between collaborating workers (either in respect of individuals or as general facilities for residents).

In the field of voluntary or private establishments he would deal with applications for registration, carry out regular visits of inspection, and give advice as required.

With regard to project work in Brent it has already been noted how discussion of the problem posed initially – that of placement procedures for those needing residential care – inevitably broadened to consideration of total residential organization. After a number of discussions with various individuals, two discussions were held in the summer of 1972 with a whole group of senior staff concerned with the project, including in the second discussion some heads of residential establishments. The report of the second discussion is reproduced in full in Appendix C. It describes how the group rejected the viability of any 'split' management of residential care, and began to pay serious consideration to the alternative pros and cons of Model A or Model B organizations.

For various local reasons a departmental decision was made in August 1972 to opt for the time being explicitly for a Model A structure. Since that time project work has proceeded in Brent in a detailed examination of present intermediate management structure between the Assistant Director and heads of establishments, and possible ways of strengthening and clarifying it. One of the issues under consideration is the possibility of grouping residential establishments according to three main client types – children, the elderly, and the mentally and physically handicapped.

Relations Between Field and Residential Workers

The other main problem in the area of residential care described at the start of the chapter is the uncertain relationship between field and residential workers – specifically between heads of establishments and the particular field worker concerned at various points with the individual residents. The uncertainty is partly about how much authority the field worker carries *vis-à-vis* the residential worker in their vaious dealings, and partly about where the work of one ends and the other begins.

Approaching these questions in discussion with field workers one notes the tendency, at any rate initially, for them to bend over backwards in emphasizing the desirability of field work and residential staff operating as 'equal partners'. But the point is then usually made that due account must be taken of the general disparity in level of training between field workers and residential staff.[10] Coupling this with the evident weakness described above in the managerial structure of residential care it is not surprising

[10] As already observed less than 4% of residential staff have training for residential work (Central Council for Education and Training in Social Work, 1973, para 6). About 40% of main grade field workers have a professional qualification of some sort, ignoring trainees and assistants (Department of Employment, 1972).

that many departments explicitly assign a special role to field workers to 'liaise with' or 'support' establishments in their particular geographical area.

In East Sussex the statement of the supportive role that one Area Director saw herself as expected to play in respect of residential staff has already been quoted earlier in this chapter. So, too, has a statement of the 'liaison responsibilities' of Area Managers in Brent as seen by one of them.

In the Children's Department in Essex we had a chance to explore in some depth with a group of Child Care Officers and one Senior Child Care Officer a situation where each individual field worker had an explicit 'liaison role' in relation to a given establishment.[11] Below are some quotations from the way some of them analysed this liaison role in conjunction with the researchers. Looked at together a number of different elements will be seen to be battling for position. Clear elements of a *monitoring relationship* are discernible where reference is made to checking standards of residential work. At other points *co-ordinating* elements are indicated in relation to work on particular cases. At other points again, hints of *supervisory* or even *managerial* functions begin to appear, particularly with reference to support and training, even though, as will be seen, none of the field workers concerned believed that they had clear authority to instruct, let alone to provide official appraisals of personal performance.

(1) ... it is (the duty of the CCO) to know the Home, to be able to gauge the total feel, to provide support for the residential staff, and to be discerning enough to pass on to the appropriate senior staff information which is relevant to them, having knowledge of the establishment and being able to ensure that the Home is generally being run within the policy of the Department. The CCO is specifically not concerned with administrative or staffing matters, i.e. all she can do about problems in these areas where she judges them to be having an adverse effect on the care of the children, either directly or indirectly, is to bring the problem to the attention of someone with authority to act (usually the Deputy Children's Officer). The CCO is concerned with the professional child care practices of the Home, and feels that she is expected to provide positive support to the staff in handling child care problems and to interpret departmental policy to them.

[11] The question was explored with six field workers from one Area Team and seven field workers from another.

(2)   The duty of the liaison officer is:
- To co-ordinate the treatment plans for children as between the residential officer and the child's CCO, in order to ensure continuity and efficiency of service to each child.
- To support and advise residential staff on the day to day care of the children.
- To provide a ready reference point for any queries of the residential officer.

(3)   ... the CCO has a duty to maintain sufficiently good contact with the establishment to be able to form relationships with the staff within which they are able to discuss any problems and difficulties with the feeling that they are not inferior to the CCO but working *with* him on the problem. Whilst adopting a style which he considers consistent with his perception of the duties described above, he believes that in an extreme case he would have a duty to inform a senior officer of any matter arising in the Home which he felt could be of concern.

(4)   The SCCOs duty is to co-ordinate information from the field and residential staff. This involves visiting the Home regularly, reading the files of all children in the Home, including up to date reports and letters, contacting the CCO concerned if the housemother has a problem with the child, arranging with the housemother for the case worker to use facilities in the Home if necessary – for instance for meeting the parents of a child – informing herself about any case due for review and attending the review when it occurs, ensuring that the CCO concerned is aware of any action arising from the review, and later checking that it has been carried out, and the Deputy Children's Officer informed. The SCCO does not see her duty as liaison with the housemother over problems concerned with the physical welfare of a particular child, nor as checking on conditions and statutory requirements in the Home. These are the prerogative of the Homes Staff at Head Office.

(5) – participating in all formal reviews of children within the Home
- acting as a field case worker as the necessity arises with all cases where children in residence are not already associated with a particular field worker
- helping to solve, or reporting to the Deputy Children's Officer (who has a special responsibility for homes), staffing, administrative or other more general problems arising at the Homes.

(6) The CCO has no absolute authority to give instructions to the staff of the two establishments, but she is expected to check on how the establishment is run, i.e. in ways consistent with good child care practice; to advise and support the staff in their handling of the children; to negotiate for improvement, and to report to senior staff where improvement is not effected.

Clearly a complete analysis of such liaison roles could never be satisfactorily driven home without consideration of the kind of roles to be played by senior staff of the residential division, and such did not happen in this case.[12] However, it is reasonable to enquire which (if any) of these relationships might remain in departments where all *managerial* and *monitoring* functions are firmly assigned to the residential division.

We had another opportunity to test the nature of the relationships of field work to residential staff, this time from the residential point of view, in the project with residential heads from the Wandsworth Children's Department described above. In this particular situation there was no question of field work staff having any special liaison functions, and we explored their relationships as follows. Basically, we asked, was the relation of the social worker in a case to that of a residential worker like that of a doctor to a nurse? Should the former be regarded as having an authority to *prescribe* specific treatments or courses of action to be carried out by the latter?[13] Or should the two properly be regarded as equal and co-operating parties, in *collateral* relationship, with neither having authority over the other (see Appendix A)? The group of heads were unanimous in their choice: the answer must be *collateral*. And so too has practically every other social worker, field or residential, with whom we have discussed this particular issue subsequently, either in project work or in conference.

Given this general view, there is of course a powerful corollary, that in the long term training should be aiming to provide a central cadre of residential staff (though not necessarily all) who

[12] Project work in Essex ceased in fact with the abolition of the Children's Department in 1971, but all existing material was released by the Department for general report.

[13] What in hospital studies has been identified as an organizational relationship in its own right a *prescribing* or *treatment-prescribing* relationship (Rowbottom *et al.*, 1973).

are able to interact on equal terms with trained field staff at an
equal level of professional competence.[14]

However, this is not quite the end of the matter. For a start,
it appears that there is a need for some one person in a case at any
time to play a *co-ordinating* role (see Appendix A) in respect to
other staff involved from other disciplines. At any point this might
be the field worker or the residential head, and such a role with
its own specific functions and authority would clearly have to be
taken into account as well as the basic collateral relationship. (This
issue is discussed further in Chapter 8.) Secondly, there is still the
possibility of some kind of *liaison* role, as we shall now discuss.

Division of Work Between Field and Residential Worker

Even the recognition of a *collateral* relationship (with or without
a *co-ordinating* 'overlay') still leaves the issue of how work is to
be shared between field and residential workers. For if, as we
have suggested above, there is no essential difference in the common thread of *basic social work* with which each is involved, this
leaves wide open the question of which parts of it are best done
from a residential base, as it were, and which from a field work
base.

There can be little doubt that the establishment of a clear and
proper division of role is a real and present problem. Heads of
establishments have frequently complained to us of what they
call (revealingly perhaps) the 'lack of social work support'. In the
words of a report of work with one Head from East Sussex:

> It is often difficult to get hold of social workers from other Areas
> in order to discuss a particular child – you go next to the social
> workers' senior and in their absence to your local Area Director or
> to the Executive Assistant. This lack of contact is specially difficult
> in respect of new children when neither side knows the other –
> this is the time when the children are most likely to be a problem,
> because you do not know them either. It is more usually the case
> that you need help with problems to do with the parents of the
> children rather than the children themselves. By their nature those
> are most likely to occur out of regular office hours – it is highly

[14] A view strongly advocated by the National Working Party on Residential Training (Central Council for Education and Training in Social
Work, 1973) who press for joint training programmes, common qualifications,
and common career structures for residential and field staff.

unlikely that you can contact the family social worker and the duty social worker is not familiar with the case details.

Although there are many cases where a client in care has a firm and continuing relationship with a field social worker in addition to his relationship with residential staff, there are many cases where such a relationship is faltering or does not exist, and its weakness or absence is felt. The field worker who originally arranged the placement may have left the department; or he may simply be too pressed to fit in the necessary visit and other work to maintain an effective relationship. Again, the client may have been taken direct from a subnormality or geriatric hospital without involvement of a specific field worker from the department.

On the other hand, the view has often been expressed to us that accountability for certain types of client might be transferred completely to residential staff, who would then need direct access to all case records. This might apply, for example, to certain elderly or subnormal clients who were expected to need residential care for an indefinite period.

Logically there would seem to be three possibilities to consider:

(1) that the field worker who arranges the placement remains firmly responsible for continuing work with that client, or that another field worker is appointed to continue work with the particular client concerned, i.e. one field worker per client in care;

(2) that one or more 'liaison' field workers are appointed to carry out continuing work with all (or most) of the clients in any one establishment, i.e. one or more field workers per establishment; or

(3) that for some clients in care it is assumed that continuing field work support will not be necessary, and that therefore accountability for all continuing case work rests with the head of the establishment concerned, i.e. no field work support.

The three possibilities could all of course coexist in respect of different groups of clients. Which of the three tactics was most appropriate for a particular client could be made an act of deliberate choice at any case conference or case review (see further discussion in the next chapter).

Where 'liaison' roles were established certain clarifications would be necessary. Presumably it would be part of the job of the liaison social worker:

- to pick up case work in the field as required, for any client in the establishment who had not already been assigned to another case worker;
- to provide the head of the establishment with a general appreciation of the work, staff, outlook, and developments, in the local Area Office;
- to provide staff of the Area Office with a general appreciation of corresponding features in the establishment.

However, even with such a liaison role established it would be clearly understood that all monitoring, supervision, or management, of residential heads rested with the residential division, and not with field workers. The *basic* relation of field and residential staff would still be collateral.

Internal Organization of Establishments – Varieties of Occupational Groups

Finally a word must be said about the internal organization of establishments, if only to acknowledge the importance of the subject. Unfortunately project work as it has naturally unfolded has provided us with very little experience in this area, but what we have learned or surmised is as follows.

Discussion with the various heads of establishments mentioned above – fourteen in all – has strongly suggested that they, and only they, play full *managerial* roles in their establishments.[15] A preliminary exploration in one establishment[16] suggested that below this level only *supervisory* relationships arose, though exactly who supervised whom and with what degree of authority was not always as clear as those concerned would have liked.

The other point about internal management that warrants emphasis is that not one homogeneous group of staff but a number of separate sub-groups in terms of functions and in terms of skills must surely be recognized in residential work. For most purposes it is as

[15] It might be noted that no discussions have taken place with heads of really large establishments, former approved schools, or remand homes, where one might guess that a real internal managerial level would reveal itself *below* the head (as suggested by implication in Figures 6.1 and 6.2 where certain heads are shown in Level 3).

[16] A home for the elderly with ninety places. Discussions were held with the Matron, Deputy Matron, Assistant Matron, and Senior Attendant.

inappropriate to lump together heads of establishments, 'professional' care staff, 'non-professional' care attendants (for example in old people's homes), and domestic staff, in one portmanteau category of 'residential worker' as it is to lump together all grades of field workers from senior specialists to welfare assistants. These various sub-groups cannot be expected to carry out identical work, they do not require identical training, and they will not necessarily be recruited from the same kind of people. It should not be assumed that they are able or potentially able to work at the same level. Developing this theme, we are now beginning to consider such questions (in the language of Table 6.1) in project work as:

- which *basic services* in residential establishments are provided by so-called domestic staff, and which by 'care attendants'?
- is the work of 'care attendants' purely in the *basic services* area, or are they expected to become involved in any *basic social work* too?
- what specific elements of *basic social work* can be expected of 'professional' care staff below heads of establishments, at various stages of their career?

Again our assumption is that the recruitment, training, and formation, of identifiable occupational groups should rationally proceed from analysis of the functions to be performed, and not vice versa.

Conclusion

The most important point made in this chapter is the inadequacy and unreality of the commonplace split between 'case work' and 'care'. Demonstrably, many heads of residential establishments are involved in *basic social work* to an extent which differs in no fundamental respect (apart from the setting) from the involvement of field workers. If this fact is accepted and welcomed, then the implications for organizational structure are profound. No longer can administrative or quasi-administrative sections be unthinkingly assigned managerial accountability for the 'caring' aspects of residential work, leaving the 'case work' aspects to the field work division or sub-division. Residential management means management of the full range of work with clients in establishments, and if better qualified or experienced residential managers are needed than at present available, then they will have to be found or grown. Almost certainly a whole new layer of residential managers will have to be developed to fill the 'missing level' above establishment head which exists in most departments.

The second implication is that residential staff, or a central core of them at any rate, are social workers just as are field workers. Field workers are social workers who work with clients at home, or in foster home or in hospital: residential workers are social workers who work with clients in residential care, who then have additional functions in connection with the organization and delivery of *basic services*. Level for level the two are natural colleagues, needing a large degree of common outlook and common skill. Their natural organizational relationship is not that of manager and subordinate, supervisor and supervisee, prescriber and prescription-filler. In the language of this project it is basically a *collateral* relationship: though it seems that either party might at various moments of time carry an additional co-ordinative relationship with respect to work on a particular case. (Such findings lead naturally to general considerations of occupational development and career structure within social work. These topics are pursued in Chapter 9.)

7 Organization of Day Care and Domiciliary Services

The shortness of the chapter that follows simply reflects the slightness of our own direct project experience in day care and domiciliary services. Apart from some brief work in three day care establishments[1] and brief discussions with two heads of central sections concerned with administration of day care, the material which we have to present rests on fairly speculative formulation tested only in conference discussions. However, it is important at least to peg out the area concerned for further exploration, and to draw attention to some of the major problems that can already be discerned.

Nature of Day Care and Domiciliary Services and the Occupations Involved in Them

The phrase 'day care and domiciliary services' is a conventional complement to 'field work' and 'residential care' but, as was pointed out in Chapter 3, it does not seem any more capable of precise definition than the other two. The following broad equivalence was suggested in terms of certain more precise language offered in the same chapter.

Domiciliary and Day Care
  – provision of various *basic services* and *supplementary services* for those living at home, in lodgings, in foster homes, (and occasionally

[1] One adult training centre for the mentally and physically handicapped, one day centre for the elderly, and one day centre for the handicapped.

also for those in residential care, as in the provision of day centres for those who live in local authority homes); and occasionally also the provision of *basic social work* for those who attend day centres.

Again the point must be made that this by no means portrays a clearly identifiable or clearly bounded area of work. Moreover, the title does not apparently carry exactly the same meaning in every department which employs it. Looking for guidance to the general statement of *basic services* and *supplementary services* made in Chapter 3 (Table 3.1) it appears, however, that 'day care and domiciliary services' is usually taken to include most if not all of the following activities:

Basic Services
  - direct provision of money and goods, for example concessionary travel for the elderly, goods at concessionary rates for the elderly, direct financial aid to families in financial trouble
  - provision of meals direct to homes ('meals on wheels') or in luncheon clubs and day centres
  - provision of accommodation, for example temporary accommodation for homeless families
  - provision of help in daily living, for example by the provision of 'home helps'
  - provision of transport for the disabled
  - provision of recreation, social, and cultural life, for example within day centres, or through direct provision of outings and holidays

Supplementary Services
  - provision of aids for the disabled, and adaptations to their homes
  - provision of communication and mobility training, for the blind, deaf, or disabled, living in their own homes
  - provision of occupational training and sheltered employment for the disabled in day centres
  - where necessary, managing the property of clients who are in hospital or residential care
  - provision of paramedical treatment in the form of occupational therapy for those at home or in day centres[2]

[2] Bearing in mind that responsibility for the employment of occupational therapists as such, seems likely to be transferred to health authorities – see later comment.

In addition, there may be some unknown quantity of *basic social work* to be taken into account, for example in some of the work with the mentally and physically handicapped within training centres.

The *occupational groups* involved in the delivery of these services are many and various – occupational therapists, craft instructors, qualified social workers, specialist workers with the blind and deaf, social work assistants, home helps, volunteers, and general administrators. One of the significant features is the uncertain professional status of many of those involved in this work. Are, for example, wardens of day centres for the elderly an occupational group in their own right needing special recruitment and training? Are wardens of homeless family units? Are 'administrative' staff who arrange holidays, or provide meals, or organize transport?

Linked to this is the question which groups of workers in the day care and domiciliary service field are required or qualified to carry out *basic social work*, as this has been defined (Chapter 3). To what extent for example, should occupational therapists or home teachers of the blind be involved in general assessments and general 'treatment', apart from assessments and consequent actions in their own specialized fields? Should heads of day centres be providing any general social work, as it were, or should their role be more specifically prescribed?

In discussion with a warden in charge of a day centre for the elderly he reported the following activities as clearly within his brief:

(1) providing subsidized lunches and refreshments;
(2) providing recreation within the centre;
(3) providing outings and theatre visits;
(4) selling goods at concessionary prices;
(5) building-up and using appropriately a general 'amenities' fund.

His main uncertainties were how far he should extend beyond the Centre itself in attracting clients in the first instance and visiting them in their own homes thereafter. In establishing a membership of the Centre should he take whoever presented themselves (the majority) even if he felt that their need was not great, or should he only take those who were referred by field social workers (the minority)? He referred in discussion to those who came in 'just for a cheap meal' and regarded the place 'just as a café'. (Although

it might be argued of course, that such attitudes were quite legitimate!) Would he have any duty to look around for those whose
need was pressing, but were unaware of the availability of the
service? He certainly regarded himself as accountable for the well-
being of members during the time they were physically present
in the Centre. If members stopped coming he and his staff did try
to visit and see what help was needed, but the whole thing was
very informal and unsystematic at this point.

Another issue is the extent to which any of these services should
be provided by designated administrative sections. As was pointed
out in Chapter 3, the basic definition of 'administration', at least as
it applies in SSDs, includes the following elements:

(1) *Logistics*
  – provision of premises and equipment, materials, and other
    supporting services to enable operational and other work to
    be performed
(2) *Finance*
  – collection and disbursement of cash, accounting, budgeting,
    and budgetary control
(3) *Secretarial*
  – recording and communicating of decisions, actions, and events
(4) *Staffing Work* (some elements)
  – recruitment services, welfare, maintenance of staff records,
    monitoring of establishments, and conditions of service.

None of these activities demands professional social work training
(here is the main point) none is operational, i.e. none results in
direct departmental 'output'.

Now all the day care and domiciliary services listed above are,
by definition, *operational*. However, some, though not all, do not
demand high professional social or therapeutic work skills in their
organization or delivery, and it is certainly worth considering which
can be suitably dealt with by administrative staff over and above
their basic supporting and monitoring activities.

The answer would seem to be that there are no bars in principle
to administrative staff carrying out operational activities provided
one condition is met. This is that other (professional) staff are able
to specify the quantity and quality of output required in such a
way as to leave the administrator little or no discretion on *output*,
though he may be called to exercise considerable discretion in

engineering the required output in the most efficient way. Indeed, work which can be specified in this way is just the kind to which general administrative skills might best be applied. Such work would seem to include the provision to clients of many material goods and services: the provision of meals, transport, money, groceries, laundry, etc. Moreover such things often fit naturally with the existing 'logistics' element of administration identified above.

What is excluded by this criterion is any operational activity in which significant discretion in respect to interpretation of needs has to be exercised by those who have actually to deliver the service. If it is required to mobilize services of these latter kind, there is an implication that the prime actor (e.g. a social worker) can do no more than *refer* the case to the second actor. And it is further implied that this second actor then has special training or capability to make an independent or supplementary estimate of the client's real needs. In other and more precise words it seems that administrative staff can appropriately become involved in operational activities where they can be in a *service relationship* to social work or other professional or therapeutic staff, but not where a *collateral* relationship is necessary.[3]

The Organization of Day Care and Domiciliary Services

With these considerations in mind one may begin to sketch at any rate the main alternatives for placing day care and domiciliary services within a departmental structure. For simplicity one may consider Model A, or functionally organized departments, bearing in mind that in Model B, or geographically organized departments, the same issues arise almost point for point in the functional structure below the level of the main geographical Division.

There are, then, two main alternatives. On the one hand a Day Care and Domiciliary Division or Sub-division may be established which is separate from either Field Work or Residential Care (Figure 7.1).

In this situation it is unlikely that the Administrative Division will undertake any operational activities, but will probably be con-

[3] A more subtle question is whether the request for a *service* might not be so strong in some cases as to amount to a binding *prescription* – see *service-giving* and *prescribing relationships*, Appendix A.

cerned wholly with support and monitoring activities: secretarial, logistical, financial, and staffing work.

On the other hand no separate Day Care and Domiciliary Division may be established (Figure 7.2). In this case Day Care is likely

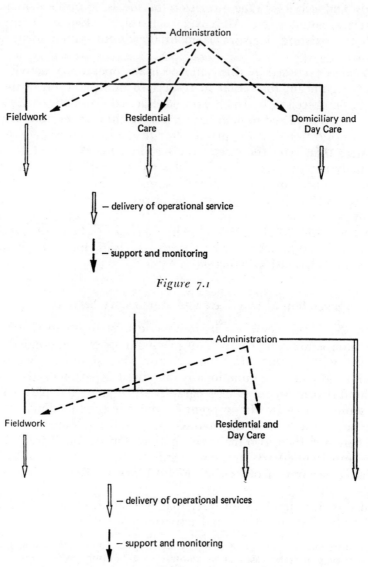

Figure 7.1

Figure 7.2

to be combined with Residential Care. Domiciliary services are likely to be split. Some (the more professional) will be included in an expanded concept of field work. Provision of the more concrete or material domiciliary services is then likely to become the responsibility of the Administrative Division, in the way discussed above.

What seems likely, however, from our own research, is that in both these cases the organization of two particular occupational groups, the home helps and the occupational therapists, will present special and rather complex organizational problems. The two will be examined in turn.

The Organization of Home Helps

The first thing to emphasize in discussing home helps is the sheer size of the problem. A typical medium-sized department may employ many hundreds or even over a thousand home helps. Most of these will, of course, be working part-time, and none are likely to wish to travel very far to their places of work. (Although the phenomenon of 'bussing' home helps from one part of a city to another, to cover poorly-provided areas, has been described to us in conference discussions.) Given these facts, some considerable degree of decentralization is likely in either Model A or Model B departments, so that each Area Team (of field workers) has its own associated group of home helps under one or more Home Help Organizers. The question is, what is the organizational significance of 'decentralization' in this context?

At one extreme it could mean that home helps become a full and straightforward part of each Area Team, managed (through the Home Help Organizer) by the Area Officer and by him alone (Figure 7.3). No central organization of home helps would exist.

However, none of the departments with whom we have discussed this issue seems to feel that the home help service could operate satisfactorily without some central organization. A Borough or County Home Help Organizer (or Divisional Home Help Organizer in Model B departments) seems to be required for such things as:

– recruiting and training Home Help Organizers

– co-ordinating recruitment and training programmes for home helps throughout the division (or department)
– standing in for Home Help Organizers in their absence.

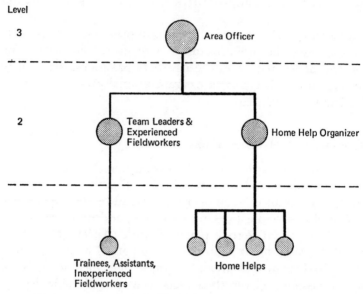

Figure 7.3

Moreover, some departments consider that responsibility for other services like 'meals on wheels' can be usefully combined with this work, to make a broader post under such a title as 'Domiciliary Services Organizer'.

Inevitably then, the simple structure of Figure 7.3 must be modified by some 'line' (i.e. organizational relationship) between the local Area Home Help Organizer and the Departmental (or Divisional) Home Help Organizer or Domiciliary Services Organizer. This is the classic 'dual influence' situation (see Appendix A) where possibilities of some degree of managerial control now exist in either or both of two 'lines' (Figure 7.4).

It is in fact the same situation as identified for area administrative staff in Chapter 5, and as in that case there seem to be in principle four different possibilities – *outposting, attachment, functional monitoring and co-ordinating*, and *secondment*.

A full description of each of these forms is included in Appendix A. In effect they represent a range of different shares of control. In *outposting* at one extreme, the Departmental (or Divisional) Home Help Organizer would carry a full managerial role, and provide home help services on a local basis to Area Teams, through local home help teams. In *attachment*, the management would be

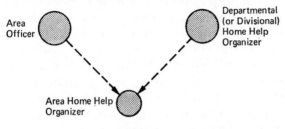

Area
Officer

Departmental
(or Divisional)
Home Help
Organizer

Area Home Help
Organizer

Figure 7.4

shared: operational control resting with the Area Officer, and 'professional' control with the Divisional (or Departmental) Home Help Organizer. In *functional monitoring and co-ordinating*, the Area Home Help Organizer would be accountable only to the Area Officer, the Divisional Home Help Organizer retaining (as the title suggests) a monitoring and co-ordinating role only. (*Secondment*, where workers are temporarily allocated to the full control of another manager is a theoretical possibility, but seems unlikely on two grounds. First, Area Home Help Organizers will presumably wish to work permanently in one Area. Second, the Departmental Home Help Organizer will be required to carry out continuous co-ordination. *Secondment*, as defined here, does not allow for either of these features.)

We have not as yet been able to follow this analysis fully through in any actual field projects, but many discussions in conferences have confirmed the prevalence of the dual influence situation in most departments. Over and above this they have suggested that organizational practice already veers to *functional monitoring and co-ordinating*, or *attachment*, rather than *outposting*.

Organization of Occupational Therapists

One of the problems of discussing the organization of occupational therapists is to know which to include and which to exclude for the purposes of discussion. The presence or absence of a *quali-fication* is a clear enough matter, but the kinds of work which possessors of a qualification in occupational therapy currently carry out within SSDs are somewhat varied. Some are concerned with providing aids for the disabled and with teaching them how to use them; and also with advising on the desirable adaptations of premises for these people. Some in addition carry out more regular therapeutic work with clients in their own homes. Some work in, or are in charge of, day centres of various kinds for the mentally and physically handicapped.

For those who are employed in domiciliary work, various dis-cussions have suggested that the same organizational issue arises as for home helps. Although the number of occupational therapists employed in departments is far fewer than the number of home helps employed (a typical departmental strength may be well under a dozen) they too have usually been felt to be best employed 'attached' in some way to Area Teams.

As the number of occupational therapists employed in a depart-ment has increased some departments have employed a 'Head Occupational Therapist' to co-ordinate professional practice and development. Is the individual occupational therapist practising in an Area then accountable to the Area Officer, or to the Head Occupational Therapist (Figure 7.5)? Again the presence of a dual-influence situation is evident.

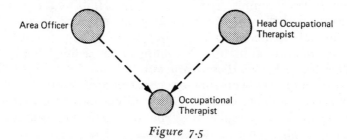

Figure 7.5

However, a new factor arises here which presumably does not in the case of home helps. Would an Area Officer with normal social work qualifications and experience *be capable* of managing the work of an occupational therapist? The issue is not, of course, whether he could *do* all the work of the occupational therapist. It is whether he could be expected to appreciate enough of the technicalities of occupational therapy to be able to provide a reasonable appraisal of personal performance, to be able to help the occupational therapist in dealing with work-problems which might well have a technical content, and so on.

Again we have no opportunity for full-scale testing of the organizational problems and possibilities here. Such discussion as we have conducted with Area Officers in field projects and in conferences reveals considerable doubt in their minds as to their own unaided competence to manage occupational therapists. If this is realistic it suggests *outposting* or perhaps *attachment* as the most appropriate forms in this particular dual-influence situation.[4]

Conclusion

'Day care and domiciliary services' forms a convenient portmanteau phrase with which to discuss the present organization of certain aspects of SSDs but has no fundamental significance in terms of specific method, occupational group, or field of work. Even more than with 'field work' or 'residential care' use of the phrase suggests a definite entity, which turns out on closer inspection to have no clear identity or clear outlines.

The important thing to stress again is the need to regard departmental organization for work with individuals and families in terms of a number of kinds of provision – provision of food, recreation, help in personal development, monitoring, paramedical services, etc. – which can be linked in a variety of combinations to provide more or less comprehensive intervention on behalf of clients in a number of different settings.

The two key questions are, who is accountable for what specific groups of staff, and by what mechanisms the work of these various groups can be co-ordinated at ground-level in the interests of individual clients. This later thought leads on to the next chapter.

[4] There are indications that all occupational therapists will in future be employed by health authorities, and deployed to provide services in SSDs as they are required. An important practical issue will arise as to which occupational therapists are involved, for this purpose: for example, the principle will presumably not apply to staff of day centres who have this qualification. For those occupational therapists affected by this change, the appropriate organization is perhaps likely to be *outposting*, managerial accountability resting with some senior occupational therapist employed by the Area Health Authority -- the mirror-image of the new situation for hospital social workers, described in Chapter 5.

8 Co-ordination and Control of Work with Individuals and Families

The trouble with conventional descriptions of social service activities, whether in terms of particular methods like 'case work' or 'group work', or in terms of the activities of particular workers like 'social work', 'occupational therapy', or 'home help', or in terms of particular settings like 'field work' or 'day care', is that they all tend to obscure a clear view of the totality of activities undertaken with any one particular client or client-family.

Consider, for instance, a problem family with a mentally disturbed mother and children neglected and running wild. A whole complex of activities may arise, involving workers from all branches of the department and from other agencies as well. A social worker may be carrying out 'case work' with the mother and father, and perhaps with the children. Home helps may visit the home. Some of the children may need to be 'in care' for a period, which will bring foster parents or residential staff into the picture. If any of the children are greatly disturbed, psychologists and psychotherapists may be involved. Almost certainly their school teacher will be involved. If the mother is receiving hospital treatment, a psychiatrist will be involved and perhaps another social worker.

Such complexity may not be frequent, but it is far from unknown. Somehow the work of a large group of workers, some within and some without the department, must be co-ordinated to the benefit of the client-family concerned in a way that is not immediately obvious from the main outlines of administrative structure. Given that SSDs and other agencies could not conceivably be organized so that one worker or one section provides all possible services for any one client, there have to be (and are) mechanisms brought to play other than that of the managerial hierarchy.

The general problem addressed in the chapter that follows is exactly this: how the totality of work with the individual client gets adequate co-ordination and control. More specifically four questions are addressed:

(1) How are new referrals or applications dealt with, and how is an assessment made of adequate response (*reception, duty, and intake systems*)?

(2) How do cases get allocated to specific social workers and how is their work subsequently reviewed (*case allocation and supervisory review*)?

(3) How are placements in residential care arranged (*placements*)?

(4) How is continuing work with clients – particularly those in care – adequately co-ordinated (*case co-ordination*)?

Each topic is examined in turn. In each instance, the main pieces of project work from which our ideas have grown are described, and then a more general analytical framework is offered.

Reception, Duty, and Intake Systems – Initial Work in Wandsworth

One of the most crucial problems facing any department is how to deal with the continuing bombardment of new demands for services. On the one hand, the reception and intake point can be viewed as the department's only defence against the ravenous attack of all too many legitimate claimants on the department's all too few resources. On the other, an unsympathetic or unskilled first response may fail to allow those in deep and genuine need to establish contact, and may repel those with apparently minor problems only to see their inevitable return at a later point when the problems have multiplied unchecked.

Our own thinking in this area is strongly coloured by a series of projects in Wandsworth, starting in early work in the Children's Department and extending into the new SSD. In the Children's

Department we had the good fortune to be involved in examination of the working of a specialist intake section – good fortune because the presence of a specialist intake system in addition to a normal 'duty' system provided a chance to examine, as it were, the most complex case first. Initially the problems posed were those of transferring cases from intake to 'long-term' sections. Later, consideration shifted to how the intake section could be better used to control the workload on the department as a whole. Later still a variety of different practices for duty and intake were examined in the five Area Teams of the new integrated department, as a result of which it was possible to construct a general analysis of the situation which might be applicable to all departments.

The intake section in the Children's Department (known as the 'Applications Sector') handled all new work presented by would-be clients in person, all new work coming by telephone, and also referrals of rent arrears cases by letter. Where long-term work was seen to be necessary, cases were passed to six 'long-term' Sectors, which were organized on a geographical basis (Figure 8.1). (Certain types of referral by letter went direct to the long-term Sectors.) Each of the seven Sectors was headed by a Senior Child Care Officer (SCCO) and manned by a number of Child Care Officers (CCOs) with supporting clerical staff.

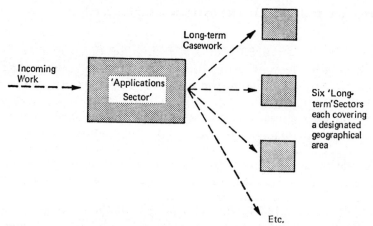

Figure 8.1 Organization of Intake Work – Wandsworth Children's Department

Work over six months with the SCCO and four CCOs of the Applications Sector produced a final report [1] which started with a brief outline of the present system and how it was supposed to work:

Each CCO has her own 'patch' and handles approximately twenty new referrals each month. The CCOs agree that a substantial majority of referrals are dealt with fairly rapidly and without transfer, after an initial interview and one or two home visits. The remaining cases take longer to assess and deal with, and produce further work, for example through the reception into care of children on either a short- or long-term basis or through the need for ongoing case work.

The Children's Officer's policy statement with regard to transfer reads 'the responsibility of Applications is to assess new cases ... and determine which are likely to need long-term (i.e. more than three months) work. It should retain short-term and transfer long-term cases ... Cases should be passed immediately after assessment by the SCCO (Application Sector) to the SCCO of the (long-term) Sector concerned.

The report went on to record some of the detailed problems revealed by project discussion:

Discussion showed that it is not believed to be possible to make an exact and invariable prescription of the point at which transfers should take place. Discretion must be exercised in each case. The SCCO prefers to let her more experienced CCOs judge for themselves when transfer is appropriate, but reserves the right to confirm or veto that judgement in discussion. In fact, more experienced CCOs do on occasion make preliminary approaches to long-term Sectors about prospective transfers with their SCCO's agreement, and it may be that members of a long-term Sector have discussed a transfer case in one of their own allocation meetings before the case file is submitted to the SCCO (Applications) for formal consent. However, all are agreed that the SCCO has the right to make all final decisions as far as the Applications Sector is concerned.

The policy statement quoted above seemed to imply that those in the Applications Sector had authority to insist on transfer of a case to a long-term Sector. However, reality turned out to be more complex.

[1] Based on individual discussions with each of the five, followed by two discussions with all the social work staff of the Sector as a group.

CCOs have distinct feelings of difficulty in effecting transfer of cases. It feels to them that long-term Sectors in some way blame Applications Sector for the influx of work to them which is more than their resources allow them to undertake comfortably. (However, Applications CCOs estimate that only 10–12 cases per month are transferred. This figure, if accurate, means that only 10% of all referrals handled by the Applications Sector lead to long-term work.)

Those cases ultimately coming forward for transfer are likely · to be those more complex ones where the assessment process has been more lengthy and less definitive, and where the continued contact of the Applications CCO with the client has at least mitigated some of the presenting problems so that the need for ongoing service is less apparent to the long-term Sector. Again, where an Applications CCO is trying to transfer a case, her own assessment is being subjected to the scrutiny of others, and a lack of clarity as to who has authority to accept or reject transfer in these cases does not help the situation. Altogether it is not surprising that there feels to the Group to be factors inhibiting them bringing forward cases for transfer.

Finally the report proceeded to a more general analysis of some of the problems and to a description of some of the changes which the group were proposing in order to alleviate the situation:

It became apparent in discussion that transfer is a process rather than a single act, and that confusion arises about who is accountable for a case which is in the process of being transferred. Two decisive points can be extracted, firstly the decision that a case should be transferred and secondly the point at which accountability for that case actually passes from the Applications Sector to the long-term Sector.

It is felt that Applications CCOs attending allocations meetings (in long-term Sectors) should not be there to sell a case but by outlining the case, enable allocation to an appropriate officer. This implies that the decision to transfer has already been made and accepted.

When the transfer of a case has been agreed the group felt that it should be decided at the same time whether personal introduction of new worker to client is appropriate.

Where personal introduction is not indicated accountability should pass as soon as the new worker is named, and that a name should be available in not more than a week.

Where personal introduction is indicated the group recognized that a longer period of time may be needed (though not more than two to three weeks) before the named officer could be introduced to the client. Accountability would remain with Applications Sector and transfer on the day of introduction.

It was noted that where indications for transfer are clear the Applications CCO should initiate transfer procedure two to three weeks ahead, knowing that this amount of time will be needed. During this time she can prepare the client, round off her work and, hopefully not get involved in more complex tasks which might make transfer inappropriate.

In addition to the assessment work and short-term case work it is accepted that Applications CCOs should carry a small ongoing case-load. The notion is that this allows them to develop other skills and keeps them in touch with the general work of the agency. The consensus of the group was that six or seven cases was the maximum to be consistent with the aim of development and the demands of the other work.

Concurrently with this project, another had been established to discuss more generally with the seven SCCOs their role in the Department. Inevitably, the question of transfer arose in these discussions too, and work with the long-term Sector SCCOs revealed some sharply divergent perceptions of how the transfer and re-allocation process should operate:

Individual discussions revealed considerable uncertainty about mechanisms for transferring cases from Applications Sector to long-term Sectors. One SCCO of a long-term Sector perceived herself as having discretion to decide when to accept or resist the transfer of cases. Two mentioned discussion prior to transfer and the possibility of clarification leading to a return of cases. Another SCCO stated that it is the group itself which, in the interests of staff development, is allowed to make the decision to accept or reject cases. One SCCO maintained that seniors have no choice in the matter, and that the Applications SCCO has the authority to insist on cases being passed. The Applications Senior herself took a similar view, suggesting that once cases have been diagnosed as long-term there should be no difficulty in passing them.

Following three discussions, the group of SCCOs reached the view that the SCCO (Applications) should indeed make final decisions on transfer and should not concern herself with the implications for workload on the long-term Sectors. It was also agreed that, whilst the process of transfer is not an instantaneous matter, a definite point could be established in each case at which accountability shifts from one worker to another.

In fact, a distinction was being made here between two rather different processes – the process of *referral* and that of actual *transfer*. Having made the distinction it appeared to have a very wide validity. What is generally called 'referral' not only arises between intake and long-term Sectors, but in many other situations as well. It arises, for example, wherever it is judged that the help of a specialist worker is needed, or the help of another agency. If there is any question of transferring the case, the same uncertainty about the exact moment of the shift of accountability may well arise in these situations too. However, the referral may well not be aimed at transfer: it may just as well be aimed at getting supporting services of some kind, or collaborative help (the technical distribution here would be between a *service-giving* relationship and a *collateral* one – see Appendix A). A general definition of referral might therefore read as follows:

Case Referral
  – the process of passing details of cases or potential cases to the department or from one person or section of the department to another, or to another agency for
  (a) proposed transfer, or
  (b) proposed collaboration, or
  (c) prescribed treatment or services.

By implication referral always requires an answer. And even if it is aimed at transfer, the main point is that referral does not *automatically* imply the simultaneous transfer of accountability. Even if the proposal is that the case should be transferred, accountability for the case stays with the originator of the proposal until it is accepted by the recipient of the proposal.

In keeping with these ideas, relevant definitions of *case transfer* and *case collaboration* were constructed as follows:

Case Transfer
  – the agreed transfer of accountability for a case at a given moment of time from one person or section of the department to another person, section, or agency (i.e. from the head of the section concerned to the head of another section or agency)

Case Collaboration
- the agreement to divide accountability for future work on a case, from a given moment of time, amongst two or more parties (individuals, sections, agencies). It may also be agreed in this situation that one of the parties acts as *case co-ordinator*.

Further Work on Intake in Wandsworth

The analysis had, then, clarified one problem, but it had exposed a larger one. How was the Department to control its total workload, and how far could the intake section be used to this end? A few months later a further project was mounted to explore this question with members of the Applications Sector. More particularly, it was required to see how far it was practicable to establish specific policies or prescriptions for appropriate response to various types of client, which could be changed as available resources changed in order to maintain control of total Departmental workload.

In fact, further discussions with staff of the Sector [2] failed to reveal any confidence that such policies could be constructed in principle, let alone any concrete suggestion as to how clients might be categorized. On the contrary all were at pains to emphasize the highly discretionary nature of the work, which threw so much on the judgement and skills of the individual intake worker and also on the adequacy of the supervisory support available to each. In the words of one CCO:

> The best control mechanism for intake is a highly-skilled intake officer with particular personality and assessment skills that are different from those for long-term case workers. Administrative skills, ability to organize several concurrent tasks, an ability to cope with anxiety, and strong supportive control from a senior are the necessary ingredients for intake assessment. [3]

Given this feeling, a number of ways were suggested by participants in which the judgement of the worker might be guided and

[2] The SCCO and six CCOs.
[3] It is interesting to note in passing that several CCOs again emphasized the need also for some long-term caseload. One suggested that protracted short-term work could result in increasingly faulty assessment. Another emphasized the special satisfaction derived from long-term relationships.

supported so that good work would be done, and moreover work which took due account of the problems of total workload. It was considered by the project group that any systems established must allow intake workers:

- to have a constant flow of information about the current state of the department's resources, including details of caseload size and vacancies in homes;
- to have as extensive a knowledge as possible of community and local resources, particularly information about voluntary and other agencies that could provide alternative services to those offered by the department;
- to have available specialist consultation and discussion of cases and assessment technique;
- to receive regular feedback from long-term groups concerning action taken on cases referred to them in order to highlight any inconsistencies in the assessments of intake and long-term workers;
- to receive detailed information about what had happened to cases which intake had not accepted in the past.

Case Assessment, Short-term and Long-term Case Work

In connection with the first point – the need for intake workers to be aware of the state of availability of departmental resources at any time – an interesting issue had come to light. Discussions with some of the workers revealed that they were much concerned about the desirability of what they called a 'pure' assessment. A 'pure' or proper assessment would be one which was oriented wholly to the needs of the client, without, as it were, contamination by considering the constraints of what the Department might realistically provide. But if intake workers saw their job only in this way, evidently they would be exceedingly liable to create a workload which the Department was unable to meet. The point was discussed with this group, and later more generally,[4] and the following definition of the assessment process was eventually agreed:

Case Assessment
   – the process at any stage of a case of
     (a) considering the needs of the case,

[4] With the management group and later in two two-day seminars with in total about seventy senior social work and administrative staff.

    (b) considering the resources available in the department and the priority of the case, and

    (c) deciding or recommending whether to continue with the case and if so what action to take.

In other words, it was agreed that any process of assessment was incomplete if it did not, as well as considering the needs of the client, also discuss possibilities for action in the light of the existing state of workload and availability of resources. At the same time two other things were becoming clear. The first was that intake work involved more than just *assessment* as defined here. The converse point was that the assessment process did not only take place within intake work – as acknowledged in the definition finally arrived at. For although the main function of the intake section tended to be described loosely as that of 'assessment', thought and discussion soon demonstrated the inadequacy of trying to break off a part of the case work (i.e. *basic social work*) process in this way. Assessment as a reflection on the progress of any case and its possible outcome is an inextricable counterpart of action. It is likely to be undertaken in an informal way by the worker involved at any stage in a case according to a spontaneously-perceived need for some sort of reappraisal. Even a departmental or statutory demand for a formalized and duly-recorded assessment might be likely to arise at many separate points along the road. What was often referred to loosely as 'assessment' was no doubt intended to relate to one specific moment in a case – the first stage at which it was possible to make a deliberate and formal assessment of whether active work or support was going to be necessary over a prolonged period, and if so, of what kind. Moreover, a process of pure assessment that does not also in some way interact on the client is unthinkable. The very act of posing questions, for example, expresses some attitude. It begins to imply 'advice' to consider this aspect of things, or 'guidance' to ignore another.[5]

Having confirmed the unreality of describing the early and later parts of case work simply as an 'assessment' phase and an 'action' phase, it was still necessary to find some way of distinguish-

[5] One is reminded of the famous Heisenberg Uncertainty Principle in physics which (roughly) indicates that no observer can make a measurement of any phenomenon which does not in some degree affect the very phenomenon to be measured.

ing the two. In fact, the crucial distinctions seemed to be the *time scale* in which assessment and consequent action was conceived, and around this criterion the following definitions were constructed, discussed, and agreed within the Department:

Short-term Case Work
 – the process of *basic social work* in new cases up to the point where *case assessment* produces
  (a) the need for *long-term case work*, or
  (b) a decision to close the case, or
  (c) a decision to proceed only by future provision of certain *basic or supplementary services*.
(This process is expected to be within a defined short term of X days or weeks.)

Long-term Case Work
 – further *basic social work* in a case which is expected to be needed for some period significantly longer than that allowed for *short-term case work*.

Wandsworth Children's Department had already set a value of three months for 'X', as indicated in the report quoted above. At a later stage, in an effort to concentrate the skills of the intake teams even more on the initial stages of case work, they shortened the figure to one month. More generally, any duty team which deals with all intake is in effect setting out to do short-term case work within the defined span of the duty period, one day, one week, or whatever it may be. As to what is the *optimum* time period in which to try to deal satisfactorily with incoming cases, or to hand them over for long-term intensive work, we have at this stage no findings to offer: we assume that it is related to various theories of the efficacy of brief case work and crisis intervention.[6]

Towards a General Model of Intake Processes

At about this time (the summer of 1971) the whole situation in this particular project changed radically with the coming to an end of the Children's Department in Wandsworth and the setting up of the new integrated Social Services Department. Five Area Teams were established and each, as a deliberate policy, was allowed

[6] See, for example, Reid and Shyne (1969); Rapoport (1970).

considerable freedom in what arrangements it made in dealing with intake and duty work. After a minimum settling-down period, with the agreement of the Area Teams we began to explore with them exactly how the new intake and duty systems were working, and found in fact a wide variation in practice.

All Areas, at least initially, had duty teams which changed daily. Some employed intake specialists and some did not. In some Areas, a whole team went on duty together, so that the Duty Team Leader was the normal team leader of the team concerned, and in others the Duty Team Leader and other team members were assembled at random according to the working of individual rotas. In some Areas, duty workers other than intake specialists automatically transferred any cases which were incompleted at the end of the duty period. In others individual duty workers retained them if only a limited amount of further work was considered necessary.

In this considerable complexity it was not only difficult for researchers such as ourselves to understand what was going on, but it was difficult even for the Department to know clearly what was happening, and thus to start comparison of the comparative merits of the various approaches. We turned our attention to the question of providing a more precise descriptive framework. What for example did 'duty work' mean exactly? What was the distinction between 'duty work' and 'intake work'? In how many ways did new cases arrive in the department, and what indeed was a 'case'? Where did 'reception' come into the picture?

Work was undertaken with the staff of one particular Area to help clarify the intake and case allocation arrangements. The daily duty team in this Area was composed of the following: a Duty Senior drawn from a roster which included a designated 'Intake Specialist Senior' and the Area Officer; one or two basic grade social workers also designated as intake specialists; and two basic grade social workers drawn from a separate roster.

Considerable uncertainty was experienced by the staff of this Area on the respective roles of duty workers and so-called 'intake' specialists. It was not clear, for example, how far intake specialists could make their own decision on whether or not to take on a case themselves for sustained work, and whether or when to initiate transfer for long-term work. An attempt was made to define a special role for intake workers in terms of co-ordinating intake processes, analysing the effectiveness of the system, and co-ordinating the training of other workers in intake and duty work. Following discussion along the lines of the general analysis presented below this particular Area eventually opted for a more straightforward duty system, although registering their desire to move to a fully-fledged specialist intake system as the availability of resources allowed, in the future.

Gradually, from this and other work we constructed a general model, of which the outlines are shown in Figure 8.2. We built into it the ideas of *short-term case work*, and *long-term case work* that had already been developed. The major missing element that needed to be added was that of the initial screening process.

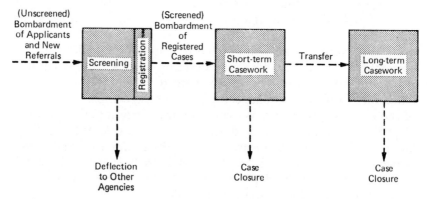

Figure 8.2   A Flow Chart of Case Work with Individuals and Families

Definitions of 'Screening', 'Case', and 'Client'

New cases arrive in a department in a variety of ways. Sometimes individuals or families arrive in the department to present their problems in person, having come of their own accord or having been referred by a doctor, a teacher, or some public official. Sometimes the same people present their case by telephone or letter rather than in person. Sometimes cases are referred in writing or over the telephone by third parties – the police, courts, housing departments, and so on.

In a minority of these situations the referral cannot be refused, for example where courts refer cases of young offenders for a statutory social report. But in the vast majority of cases the *first* job of the department, before any significant short-term case work is embarked upon is to make the primary decision as to whether the applicant or referral represents a proper case at all for a SSD. Sometimes applicants may simply have wanted another department and have come to the wrong door. In other cases applicants may be turned away (rightly or wrongly) because the person who first meets them himself judges their problems to be inappropriate to the department – too trivial perhaps, or more suitably deflected to housing or education or social security, for them to deal with.[7]

This decision as to whether the applicant or referral represents a proper case is what we mean by *screening*. For applicants arriving in person it is usually carried out by receptionists (who will not usually, of course, have any social work training). For those who telephone, the department's telephonist will inevitably be carrying a minor screening role. Sometimes, as in the case of written applications or referrals, screening may be carried out by the social worker who first examines the opened letter. Particularly in the latter situation it may seem hard to know where *screening* ends and initial *case assessment* begins. Here we suggest it is useful to employ the precise criterion of *registration*, and this in turn is tied up with the definition of *case*, and ultimately of *client*.

What broadly is meant by the 'client'? From one point of view the clients of a social services department are all people in the locality to be served who suffer from need of the particular kind describable as 'social distress'. (Put another way: all those whose social functioning falls below what is judged to be a generally acceptable level – see Chapter 3.) This might represent a very large clientele. From a much more narrow view, the definition of clientele might be restricted to all those who are described as 'in care' and all those subject to continuing 'case work' (the latter is what is usually meant when workers talk about 'case loads'). This would exclude, for example, those merely in receipt of such services

[7] Hall (1971) presents an interesting case-study of the reception of clients in a Children's Department. He speaks of receptionists carrying out an 'initial interview' and emphasizes the significant effect of their own use of discretion in the way they carry out their work – demonstrating how they can 'suppress' certain clients or act as 'advocates' for others. Rees (1972) in a more abstract analysis of access problems in personal health and welfare stresses the importance of what he calls the 'scouting' services of general medical practitioners and health visitors.

as home helps or meals on wheels, or those elderly people, who attend the department's day centres for meals and social recreation. Clearly this would produce a much smaller figure for the real clientele.

However, we suggest that there is a more useful way of defining clientele than either of these, a way which turns on the apparently trivial matter of registration, in whatever manner it may occur.[8] For although a department no doubt carries accountability in some diffuse sense for all those in need in its locality, when details of such cases are officially known and registered the accountability sharpens very considerably. If, unknown and unregarded, an old lady dies of hypothermia it is one thing: a matter of regret and indicative of lack of initiative or responsibility somewhere or other. If, on the other hand, the old lady is already on the books of the department, and supposedly, for example, receiving occasional visits from a social worker, it is quite another thing. Again, the accountability of the department where a child dies of neglect or cruelty is quite different if the department has been advised beforehand, say by the police or by neighbours, that such a risk is suspected, than if no such information has been lodged.

At the other extreme, the fact that the department (or one of its workers) has judged that active 'case work' is no longer justified in a particular case does not necessarily remove accountability. Although in general it can be agreed that decisions of this kind are quite proper, in any particular case a decision to stop active case work may well be an ill-judged one, for which the department will inevitably be held to blame if things turn out badly. In this sense a department can never close its cases unless the client dies or changes status in some marked way as, for example, when a child legally becomes an adult. The most that can happen is that any one particular worker can be relieved of accountability for a particular case by his own superior. Ultimately (in a hierarchical system) the director of the department continues to carry accountability.

We have then:

Case
- an instance of the situation presented by a person or family registered by the department as in need of help or action by the department to relieve or prevent social distress.

[8] In some departments known as 'indexing'.

Exact definition of 'client' seems more difficult. Where one person only is involved it is easy enough, but where, for example, does one draw the line in a family? Does one include the would-be adopters in adoption work, or the foster parents in fostering? There is no doubt that the department is carrying out work of some sort with both these latter kinds of people. Does one include the recalcitrant employer or the insensitive school teacher? Tentatively we have suggested the following:

Client('s)
  – the particular person or people in a case identified as in need of help or action to relieve or prevent social distress.

Again, the definition turns on the idea of social distress. If the person with whom the social worker is in contact himself suffers from social distress or is at risk of doing so, then he is a client. Otherwise, however integral his involvement and influence in the case, he is not.[9]

However, leaving aside uncertainties as to who exactly does or does not qualify as a client, the hard definition of *case* at any rate allows a sharp definition of what is meant by *screening*, and distinguishes it from *short-term case work*. The formal definition of *screening* becomes:

Screening
  – the process of deciding whether applications or new referrals represent proper *cases* for the department.

To complete the scheme illustrated in Figure 8.2 two further definitions may then be added:

Bombardment (Unscreened)
  – the impact of applicants and new referrals on the department, made in person, by telephone or by writing.

Bombardment (Screened)
  – the impact of new cases on the department, i.e. the incoming work load after screening.

[9] One cannot pretend that this exhausts the discussion. Smith and Harris (1972) in their empirical study of the ideologies adopted by social workers distinguish those who tend to identify *individuals* as clients, those who tend to identify *families* as clients, and those who tend to identify *sub-cultures* as clients (for example teen-age gangs).

Definitions of the Respective Roles of Reception, Duty, and Intake Staff

With the establishment of this general descriptive model of the process of receipt and subsequent handling of incoming work with individuals and families, the way lies open to a clearer conception of the work of such people as receptionists, specialist intake workers, and duty workers, and of the differences between them.

Receptionists in this view carry out *screening work* as here defined, with those who apply in person to the department. Following screening their job is either to deflect or redirect the applicant to another more appropriate agency, or to register details of the case and to direct it to the attention of the social worker on duty or intake work.

The work of *duty officers* can be defined as:

(1) carrying out such *short-term case work* on all new cases as can be accommodated within the duty period, and either concluding work on the case or providing written *case assessments*, including suggestions as to further work or services needed; and

(2) dealing with emergencies on existing cases where the field worker normally responsible is not available.

In addition they may be involved in the screening and registration of certain written applications or referrals, and they may also provide a reference point for all those who are seeking more general information on or about the department.

Specialist intake workers are simply those who specialize in *short-term case work* as it has been defined, within some understood time-limit. In this respect, then, intake work and duty work overlap, though in practice the time scale on which any specialist intake workers operate is likely to be very considerably longer than that in which duty officers operate, even where teams are on duty for a week at a time.[10] (Again the relevance of various theories

[10] Very little seems to have been published on the operation of specialist intake teams in British SSDs. One exception is an informative account of the experimental introduction of a specialist intake team in Hammersmith (Duncan, 1973). This argues (with the support of statistics on the treatment of bombardment before and after the experimental scheme) that the specialist intake team does indeed remove pressure from long-term workers, and offers the new client a better service than is possible under a conventional duty system.

about what can be successfully achieved with various cases in various periods of time is apparent.)

Present State of Work on Reception, Duty, and Intake

This in fact represents the present substance of our work in this particular field. Our experience for the moment is almost wholly based on work with one authority – Wandsworth. Out of this experience we have established the general model for work processes at the intake point described above, and we have identified what seem to be some of the most important requirements for the establishment of successful specialist intake teams – the easy availability of information on resources, good access to specialized supervision, etc. The model in its entirety has now been explored and revised in a number of discussions with various groups of staff in Wandsworth. Over and above this it has been expounded and tested many times in conference discussions, as a result of which it has given rise to specific development work in at least one other local authority.

Case Allocation and Supervisory Review

Let us turn now to the second question posed at the start of the chapter, namely how cases get allocated to specific social workers and how their work gets reviewed.

In the study described above of the various intake and duty systems established by the five Area Teams in the newly established SSD in Wandsworth, we also had the opportunity of studying allocation processes, and again found a wide variety of practice. All the Areas had regular meetings at roughly weekly intervals to allocate those incoming cases which had not already been dealt with and closed by the duty team, or taken on voluntarily for further work by one of the duty team, or by a specialist intake worker where such existed.

The various ways in which these allocation meetings were organized were as follows:

Area One
The whole Area Team, comprising four sub-teams met together for allocation. The Area Officer was present but it was up to each senior social worker to arrange allocation to his own sub-team. The

Area Officer and the seniors met on the day before the meeting for a preliminary discussion, and sometimes seniors had already discussed with the individual concerned the possibility of taking a particular case.

Area Two

The Area Officer, having seen all the cases to be allocated, met two of the four sub-teams at a time, presented a résumé of the cases, and asked for suitable volunteers.

Area Three

Duty seniors brought cases to be allocated to the allocation meeting, which was presided over by the Area Officer. Again for the sake of spreading load equitably, the Area Officer met two of the four sub-area teams at a time.

Area Four

Again the staff met for allocation purposes twice, two sub-teams at a time. Each meeting was presided over by one of the two seniors concerned. The senior introduced each case, the duty worker who had dealt with it amplified the details, and the whole group discussed it. The meeting was used quite deliberately to aid the processes of getting workers formerly specialist, to understand and cope with cases of all kinds. Eventually, with some guidance from seniors, the social workers would choose their own cases. The Area Officer dealt with any cases not disposed of at a weekly Area Team meeting.

Area Five

The Area Officer having seen all cases, they were passed directly to the four sub-area teams, who then sorted out their own allocations.

The last situation was of particular interest because at an earlier stage in the life of this new Area Team the Area Officer and his seniors had decided in advance who should get what case. However, following criticism of the system by social workers in the Area, the more participative system described above had been adopted, though the Area Officer still insisted on the right of the team leaders to intervene if they thought that inappropriate self-allocation was taking place.

Discussions with these and other social workers showed how difficult and delicate they all felt this allocation process to be. Area Officers and Team Leaders would often bend over backwards to avoid the impression of insensitive and authoritarian direction.

But how much genuine democracy was really possible in this matter? It is true that many different procedures are possible and indeed that the adoption of different styles of approach may lead to different attitudes to the process – to a different 'climate' of operation. However, one cannot ignore basic realities of organizational life. Given the existence of a managerial hierarchy, by definition those at the top are accountable for all the work of those lower down; and if this is the situation it seems logical and necessary that final authority to prescribe what shall and what shall not be done must also rest with them. In other words it seems that adequate analysis must distinguish the *style* of working from the underlying organizational *structure*.

Similar problems and hesitancies continue beyond allocation, where any question arises of reviewing how the social worker is actually conducting the case. Significantly, the worker now talks of 'his' case. This has an obvious meaning in terms of immediacy of personal contact and of personal identification, but again one can enquire as to what it means in an organizational sense.

Surely in this sense any social worker in an agency which is hierarchically organized can only speak of 'my' cases by virtue of some explicit or implicit process of allocation by more senior officers. Given a hierarchical organization with managerial relationships at all levels, all cases 'belong', in an organizational sense, to the head of the hierarchy – the Director. It is certainly he who will be held to account by his employing authority for serious shortcomings in the handling of any case.[11] In this situation he will want to establish an adequate system for reviewing work.

However, a further clarification is needed before any so-called review process can be completely understood. For as the word 'review' is commonly used in social work, it bears two distinct meanings: review of the progress of cases with particular clients (sometimes statutorily determined), and review of the work of the individual worker concerned in the case.

Because of the way certain reviews are prescribed in legislation, it becomes easy to confuse the two. For example, legislation[12] covering children in the care of a department who are placed in

[11] But see again the very different implications of the possible non-hierarchical organization of social work discussed in Appendix B.

[12] The Boarding-Out of Children Regulations 1955 (Statutory Instrument No. 1377).

foster homes says not only that there shall be regular reviews of the well-being and progress of the children, but that such reviews shall be carried out as far as possible by a person other than one directly concerned. Usually it is the supervisor of the worker who is visiting. In fact two things are going on here. One is a *case assessment* as we have defined it, which is directed to the needs of the child and possibilities for further action or change in plans, and the second is an authoritative review by a more senior officer of the quality of work carried out by a mere junior – a *supervisory review*. A supervisory review always implies some element of case assessment, but (as has been noted earlier) case assessment does not necessarily imply supervisory review.

Nor (obviously) need a supervisory review await some statutory case assessment. Any discussion of a case, however brief, which takes place between a junior officer and a more senior who carries authority in the matter concerned affords opportunity for – indeed inevitably forces – some review of the quality of the junior officer's judgement and capability. Discussions of apparently limited matters such as the authorization of particular expenditures provide a good example.

However a distinction must be made between such a review and other forms of consultation between two working colleagues. In a supervisory review there is a person present who carries authority to affect in some way subsequent action in the case and maybe even to affect the future career and development of the worker in charge of the case. Inevitably in such situations the senior person concerned has shouldered some responsibility for subsequent events, even if his or her response has amounted to no more than tacit approval of what is heard or discovered. It need not be assumed, however, that in all situations where one worker approaches another to share difficulties and anxieties, or to get advice from one more experienced than himself in a particular field of activity, there is a supervisory element. Obviously many such approaches are quite informal and imply neither authority on the part of the person approached nor any accountability for what subsequently happens. (The third case, where specialist consultant roles are formally established, has already been discussed in Chapter 5. As there argued, in this situation also there would be no supervisory element.)

In the climate of some departments it may sometimes seem that little or no review of the work of the individual social worker is carried out. It was obvious, for example, in the Mental Health Department project in Wandsworth[13] that the prevailing social climate was very non-directive. Workers participated fully in all decisions as to how cases and special duties were allocated, and had apparently unlimited discretion on choice of treatment and allocation of time to particular clients. However, careful analysis revealed all the following potential means of review, either direct or indirect:

(a) immediate, but retrospective, review of all work handled on duty rotas;
(b) review of work at closure points;
(c) review when services or resources were needed beyond the use of the social worker's own time and skill;
(d) review of specific work on receipt of complaints or on request for information from certain other agencies and individuals;
(e) review when workers raised cases for discussion with a senior officer;
(f) review on occassion where other colleagues had to pick up work with clients during duty sessions, during periods of crisis or emergency (this created a pressure to keep work and recording etc., up to date).

So whilst there was no regular systematic review of all ongoing work, it was only where no outside resources or information were needed, no emergency arose, and the worker never identified the need to discuss the work she was doing, that the way in which workers were handling cases would fail to be reviewed at some time or other. Even then, review at acceptance gave room for prescription of work to be done and the closure review ensured a check on use of discretion by the worker in the interim. However, this is not to suggest that all existing review processes were already adequate, or indeed that they were already located in such a way as to harmonize with the fundamental managerial structure. This may well apply more generally.

In the project in the Essex Children's Department, for example,[14] when Child Care Officers wanted authority to spend cash or initiate prosecutions they might bypass the Area Children's Officer and go

[13, 14] See details on page 96.

straight to the Assistant Children's Officer, the Deputy Children's Officer, or even the Children's Officer. A four-monthly review system existed for all children in care, which was operated by the Deputy Children's Officer directly with the residential staff and Child Care Officer involved, though the relevant Area Officer might occasionally attend. In addition, a six-monthly review system operated for all other cases, which might be presided over by any of a number of senior officers according to a rota system – the Area Officer, one of two Principal Child Care Officers, the Assistant Children's Officer, the Deputy Children's Officer, or the Children's Officer. In this situation, in the words of the final report:

> The combined effect of extensive referral to senior officers for *ad hoc* consultation or specific decision ... and the departmental review system could lead to a situation in which a case might be scrutinized by any or all six senior officers in a year, as well as by a supervisor. Given that the advice of these senior officers is viewed as prescriptive and that none has a totality of accountability, there is created in the minds of CCOs an impression of interchangeability between these people. The exact nature of the relationship of senior officers remains unclear though some elements of a *supervisory* relationship are apparent ...

It is perhaps the fact that had the main lines of *managerial* authority been clearly established, the system of formal case reviews might have been acceptable without organizational confusion, given also a special conception of the role of 'case conference chairman' as discussed below.

As a result of these (and other) various pieces of project work, we gradually evolved more precise definitions of *case allocation* and *supervisory review*, and in particular distinguished the latter more clearly from *case assessment*. We also developed in project work in Wandsworth a possible statement of the proper role of Team Leaders and Area Officers in various processes of allocation and supervision.[15] The statement and its accompanying definitions were discussed in a number of meetings and provisionally agreed as follows:

[15] Initial discussions were with the Director and his three Assistant Directors. Subsequent discussions took place in two two-day seminars for senior social work and administrative staff – about seventy in all.

Case Allocation
– is the process by which specific workers become accountable for
action on specific cases. It proceeds either:
(a) by the assignment of a case to a worker by another officer; or
(b) by automatic allocation according to some predetermined principle, e.g. a 'patch' system or a duty system.[16]

A Supervisory Review
– occurs whenever an assessment of a case is discussed by the worker
or workers accountable for the case with another member of the
department who has authority to modify the assessment if needs
be.

*The Roles of Area Officers and Team Leaders in Respect of Allo-
cation and Supervisory Review*
In *duty work* it is part of the function of the Duty Team Leader
('Duty Senior') to see that all new cases or emergency referrals on
existing cases are dealt with, and the Duty Team Leader has
authority to allocate cases to duty workers.
It is also the function of the Duty Team Leader to satisfy himself
or herself that appropriate *short-term case work* is being carried out
during the duty period and if necessary to *review* the work carried
out by duty workers.
Where cases have been transferred from duty teams or specialist
intake workers to other teams for long-term case work, a number of
different means exist for dealing with the process of *case allocation*.
Case allocation can take place, for example, through interaction
between:
– the Area Officer, the Team Leader, and the individual social
worker
– the Team Leader and the individual social worker
– the Team Leader and his or her full team of social workers, etc.
In terms of personal motivation, or good social work procedure,
each of these means of allocation have their pros and cons. However,
it should be recognized that none of these alternatives can ignore
what *managerial* relationships already exist. If the Team Leader has

[16] A further elaboration of *case allocation* formulated in project work
in one Area in Wandsworth suggested that it is properly concerned over
and above assigning accountability with four things;
(1) the clarification and formulation of the social work tasks;
(2) the determination of priorities;
(3) the allocation of resources (mostly social worker time/choice of
worker); and
(4) the development of staff consistent with client needs.

a *managerial* role, then he or she is accountable for ensuring that cases get allocated as efficiently as possible, bearing in mind the needs of clients on one hand and the capabilities and needs for growth of the worker on the other. The Team Leader has authority to assign a particular case either for *short-term case work* or for *long-term case work* to a particular worker without further ado, if needs be. The same would apply to the Area Officer, where he or she is directly concerned in the allocation process.

Where the Area Officer or the Team Leader are concerned in case allocation either have authority in addition to allocating the case:
– to propose specific *tasks* to be adopted in case work;
– to veto *tasks* proposed by the social worker which they do not consider appropriate, or in the ultimate;
– to withdraw the case for reallocation.

(Question: is it only authority to *propose* specific tasks, or is it authority to prescribe them?)

It is the duty of the Area Officer, or where the duty is delegated, of the Team Leader, to carry out:
– all statutory supervisory reviews (e.g. in children's work)
– any regular supervisory reviews laid down by Departmental prescription
– such other supervisory reviews as he or she judges necessary in view of the capability of the social worker concerned, and in the light of the accountability of the Area Officer for the work carried out by the social worker.

In a supervisory review situation, the person carrying out the review again has authority:
– to propose specific new tasks, or reformulation of tasks
– to veto tasks proposed or being undertaken by the social worker which they do not consider appropriate, or in the ultimate
– to withdraw the case for reallocation.

(Again the question of right to *prescribe* specific tasks, rather than merely to *propose* specific tasks, arises.)

It will be seen that at this point in project work, the right of the supervisor not only to *veto* what was to be done, but also (more positively) to *prescribe* tasks to be carried out, was left in doubt. Elsewhere (see the discussion in Chapter 5) we have assumed that the supervisory role *does* carry this positive authority.

At the time of writing, project work continues in Area Teams in Wandsworth, so that this material is likely to receive further test and refinement as work proceeds.

Existing Procedures for Placement in Residential Care

The third question raised at the start of the chapter was how places in residential care are arranged for clients who need them.

For a start it can be taken as given that there is not likely to be, now or in any foreseeable state, an abundance of possible places in departmental establishments from which the most suitable one may be carefully selected for the client in question. Places are hard to come by, and often rough and ready compromises will have to be made. In other words, the placement process is always likely to be experienced as something in the nature of a difficult and anxious search by the field worker who initiates it, more or less urgent according to the nature of the case concerned.

Second, the question of the establishment in which he is placed is likely to be a matter of immense significance for the client himself. As the head of one old person's home put it to us, 'for many old people coming into care is the second most important step in their lives, the first being marriage and the purchase of a house'. Most elderly people in care are likely to be in the home concerned for the rest of their lives. So are many of those who are mentally subnormal. Even for children, there will be some who stay in residential care for many years, perhaps until they are fully adult.

Third, the financial importance of placement decisions warrants stress. Typically, well over half of departmental budgets is spent on residential provision.

Clearly the procedures by which this step is decided demand very careful consideration. We have had the opportunity to study them in two departments – in some depth in Brent and to a lesser degree in East Sussex. As a result of this experience, we have been able to construct again, if only tentatively, a general analytical model of the situation.

The opportunity to study this subject in East Sussex arose as part of our initial project there, which was concerned with the general relationships of the field work and residential divisions.[17] Although the question of placement procedures was not one specifically pursued in subsequent project work, initial discussions with a number of senior staff from both divisions threw up incidental material of some interest on this subject.

It appeared that a number of different systems were in operation

[17] For the specific terms of reference and other details see page 65.

for different kinds of clients. An Executive Assistant on the staff of the Assistant Director (Social Work Services)[18] allocated all places for the elderly and homeless throughout the County. Area Directors or their senior social workers allocated places for all child care establishments in their particular Areas. Places for the majority of mental health establishments were allocated by a senior social worker in one particular Area, who was experienced in the work.

One of the Area Directors commented on the difficulty that the Executive Assistant faced in gauging the real needs and priorities of requests for places for the elderly presented to them by a large number of social workers when they could not possibly know or contact individually. He saw it as necessary for social workers in each Area to sort out the relative priority of their applications before making applications for places, and noticed the developing tendency where resources were particularly sparse (for example, in places for the homeless) for the Executive Assistant to leave the Areas themselves to negotiate respective priorities in their own applications. But in the words of another Area Director, 'the system depends mainly on how eloquent any social worker is in presenting a case to the Executive Assistant, and how hard they continue to push thereafter'.

At the time of discussion, there was a waiting list of about four hundred for places in old people's homes, including about fifty classified as urgent. The views of the Executive Assistant reflected back to him in a report included the following:

> In your view it is the Area's job to assess need, and, given that there are more applications than vacancies, it is your job to try to ensure that the scarce resources are used in the best possible way. Thus you *may* have to decide between competing needs.
>
> You feel that it is not your place to arbitrate in such situations and you refer back to the Area with the information on the vacancy and ask them to select the most appropriate client. Similarly, when clients proposed by different areas seem to have equal weight you refer to the Area Directors to negotiate collaterally and decide which client is the most suitable for admission.
>
> It seems as though some improvement could be achieved by Areas sorting out their own priorities before application is made to H.Q.

[18] The main outlines of the organization of East Sussex SSD at the time of its establishment are shown in Figure 4.2, page 61.

With the more difficult clients, it feels to you as though you have to 'sell' them to the Matrons. It is at this stage that they may well produce some information, e.g. about a staffing crisis, which justifies their reluctance. It is your view that ultimately you have the right to insist on a client being admitted to a Home; however, you would try to avoid this situation as you feel it would not augur well for the welcome and care likely to be offered to the client. You would never insist without checking out the situation with the Residential and Day Care Officer concerned.

The Assistant Director in charge of Residential and Supporting Services strongly emphasized that his complete absence of control over placements was quite at odds with his accountability for the effective functioning of establishments. How could he feel accountable if the overloading of a particular establishment led to a general lowering of standards? The Assistant Director (Social Work Services) completely concurred with this analysis of the situation as it stood, but stated her opinion that in the long run all social work decisions, including those of placement, should properly be made at Area level in any case.

In Brent the initial problem with which the Department was concerned was the establishment of some form of 'central placement bureau' faced with the prospect of Area Teams who were gradually moving from headquarters to various local sites. At the time that our work in Brent commenced in the autumn of 1971, information about vacancies was collated and held in the (central) Administrative Division, whilst decisions on placement were made by a 'Residential Manager' on the staff of the Head of Residential and Day Care Division.[19] Because of the magnitude of the question, it was agreed that in the first instance attention should be concentrated on placement procedures for the elderly. Subsequent discussions revealed many problems similar to those experienced in East Sussex.

For example, the views of the Residential Manager who dealt with placements, as reflected in a report of discussions with her, included the following:

You point out the general difficulty of deciding priorities, particularly since you only have the waiting list card and not the case papers.

[19] See the organization chart for Brent in Figure 4.1, page 60.

You keep a priority waiting list according to Area demand, and in your assessment of priorities are guided by the views of Area Managers. The Area's definition of 'priority' varies widely, and some social workers might almost always put in a case as a 'priority'. Also, applications can come in directly from social workers without the backing of Area Managers or seniors. Overall, you consider that it might unfortunately be the case that 'he who shouts loudest' might be securing preferential treatment for their clients.

One criterion, however, which is used is that any client over ninety is put on the priorty waiting list. (At present there are about 25 clients on the priority list plus 115 on the ordinary list.)

In addition to the waiting list and priority list, there is also a third list comprising residents awaiting transfer to other homes. In practice, therefore, you decide on admissions from amongst the three lists, since to choose from the 'priority' list alone would leave the 'ordinary' and transfer clients with no real prospect of admission.

Clients can move from list to list, that is to say either become priorities, or move from priority to the ordinary waiting list according to circumstance.

Although the client's wishes are taken into account, it is difficult to fit clients to desired homes. Areas are notified of vacancies and the place is held for one week. If the client accepts the place, the Area informs you, and the administration then prepares an admission order to be sent to the matron. In theory the matron should receive the order three days before the client arrives.

The admission order contains the name of the Area Manager and the social worker who dealt with the client. If the matron was unwilling to accept the prospective resident, she would inform the Area Manager. If there was still no agreement, the question would come to you. Theoretically, the issue could eventually reach the heads of the Family Services and Residential and Day Care Divisions.

Discussions with two heads of homes confirmed the thinness of the existing arrangements for introducing the would-be resident to the home. In the words of one:

Some residents may never have seen the Home prior to their admittance. They are not informed of their expected behaviour in the Home, nor are they warned, for example, that they might have to live in a room with four beds and not necessarily in a single-bedded room.

But she added that she did not want to have to choose residents herself, or to assess them before entry to the Home. The other head, however, thought that the Matron or Superintendent should see potential residents not only to introduce them to the home, but also to assess their suitability, for example, their compatability with existing residents.

One of the two Area Managers with whom the subject was discussed described his experience of the existing situation as follows:

> The Area is notified by the Residential Manager when a place is available. There is usually little choice in the matter. The place is kept open for ten days, although a longer period might be requested. The client is visited by the social worker and at maximum would see the home once before entry. There are pressures on the client to accept the place, although he can refuse if he wishes. Likewise, the matron might wish to refuse entry to the suggested resident, but she too would be subject to pressures in favour of acceptance. In the case of a matron refusing to accept a client, even after any other Area Managers, Residential Manager, etc., had been involved, the Area Manager considers that the Assistant Director (Residential and Day Care) would have the final decision. The Area Manager points out that he does not consider himself to have the authority to instruct the matron, and that anyway if the matron refused he does not feel that it would be in the best interests of the client to insist on admission.

At this point a general report was prepared and presented to the various people involved.[20] It summarized some of the existing problems, and presented the following list of prerequisites which participants had emphasized as necessary for any adequate placement procedures:

- the need to obtain maximum knowledge of available vacancies in private and voluntary organizations, with suitable means of communication between Areas
- an adequate system of records
- the need to build in a method of dealing with emergencies
- that placement decisions should be made on the basis of maximum professional (field and residential) assessment
- maintenance of equal assessment standards between Areas
- optimum utilization of resources, avoidance of Area empire building, etc.

[20] The Assistant Directors (Family Services) and (Residential and Day Care), the Residential Care Manager, the Senior Administrative Officer, two heads of homes, and two Area Officers.

- clear-cut and agreed procedures, to avoid costly and frustrating time wasting
- maximum client consultation and agreement, to avoid the difficult process of transfer from Home to Home

The report also offered a general analysis of the placement process. It suggested that in reality placement consisted not of one, but of a whole complex of connected decisions, of which the key ones were those shown in Table 8.1. It also suggested various alternative ways in which this complex of decisions might be handled in Brent.

In fact it was at this point in the Brent project, as described in Chapter 4, that a radical shift occurred in the discussion, from the specific questions of placement procedures for the elderly to the much more fundamental question of how residential care as a whole was organized, and indeed, what exactly it constituted. The next phase of project work was concerned chiefly with these latter questions, and this aspect of the work still continues.

In the meantime, however, Brent have proceeded towards establishing a central placement bureau, taking account of many of the needs revealed by earlier project work, such as for example the desirability of heads of homes being party to placement decisions.[21]

A General Analysis of the Placement Process

As a result of this work in East Sussex and Brent we have been able to evolve a general analysis of the placement process as shown in Table 8.1. There appear to be at least seven distinguishable and critical decisions in the process. The Table suggests how these might most appropriately be placed in the organization, depending, for example, on whether the department concerned was generally organized according to a Model A or a Model B pattern. The proposals are, of course, consistent with two underlying assumptions – first that the work of residential and field work staff brings them essentially in a *collateral* relationship, and second, that each division is essentially organized as a *managerial hierarchy*, so that ultimate rights to review and if necessary to reverse

---

[21] The project work on placement in Brent and the subsequent general analysis based on it is described in more detail by Billis (1974).

DECISION	POSSIBLE LOCATION MODEL A DEPARTMENTS	POSSIBLE LOCATION MODEL B DEPARTMENTS
1. Whether residential care is needed	Fieldworker in Level 2*	Fieldworker in Level 2*
2. Designation as 'urgent' or not	Ditto or Area Officer	Ditto or Area Officer
3. Relative priority in Area	Area Officer	Area Officer
4. Relative priority in Department (or Division – Model B)	Assistant Director (Fieldwork)	Divisional Director, or Divisional Operational Co-ordinator (if such exists); at Departmental Level, Assistant Director (Operations)
5. Suggested matching of clients to vacancies	Staff Assistant to Assistant Director (Residential); or member of his staff	Divisional Operational Co-ordinator (if such exists) or Residential Manager; or members of their staffs
6. Suitability of Home for client	Fieldworker in Level 2	Fieldworker in Level 2
7. Suitability of client for Home	Head of Home, with review by Residential Manager or Assistant Director (Residential) if necessary	Head of Home, with review by Residential Manager or Divisional Director if necessary

* See Chapter 5

Table 8.1   Key Placement Decisions and Their Possible Organizational Locations

the decisions of those at lower levels always rest with those at higher levels (see Chapter 6).

Since its first formulation we have been using conference discussions to test, and where necessary, to modify this general framework.

Case Co-ordination

The general statements made above bring us back, however, to the issues identified at the start of the chapter, and in a sense to the crux of the problem. In the typical situation where several workers are involved in the same case, by what means is successful co-ordination and control to be achieved? Typically it is not by means of straightforward *managerial* relationships at all. The intrusion of, for example, Area Officers (let alone Departmental or Divisional Directors) in case discussions is a rare event in comparison with the many interactions that arise between the workers directly in contact with the clients. Even where the Area Officer is a party to the discussions he is not necessarily in a managerial relationship to all those involved. Gradually, in the course of research we have come to see that control and co-ordination in specific case work is typically achieved through a kind of role that can be described as a *co-ordinating* one.

In general, co-ordinating roles seem to work as follows.[22] Within the framework of some agreed task, the co-ordinator is obliged to monitor general progress, to draw attention to lapses from programme, and to take the initiative in situations of uncertainty. The co-ordinative role does not carry either *supervisory* or *managerial* authority (see Appendix A). It does carry authority, for example, to call meetings, and to require accounts of progress, but not authority to issue overriding instructions in the face of sustained disagreement by any of the parties involved: only managers of the participants concerned have this right.[23] A more specific ver-

[22] The recognition of *co-ordinating roles* as a type of their own first arose in our own work at Brunel in the health field. The precise definition that has been evolved and tested there is shown in Appendix A. We have at this point no reason to suppose that such a conception does not apply as usefully in certain similar situations in social services, or indeed, elsewhere.

[23] It seems from parallel work in the health field that the *co-ordinating role* is the typical means of control too in the multi-disciplinary health team, though managerial relationships may intrude to some degree (See

sion of the definition to fit the particular situation of the co-ordinator in a case work situation might read as follows:

Case Co-ordination
(a) proposing necessary tasks in relation to the total needs, short- and long-term, of the case;
(and then, assuming agreement):
(b) negotiating co-ordinated work programmes and procedures;
(c) arranging the allocation of existing resources to colleagues or arranging the provision of additional resources where necessary;
(d) keeping informed of action and progress in the case;
(e) helping to overcome problems encountered by other colleagues;
(f) providing relevant information to other colleagues, including information on progress;
(g) reporting on progress to superior.

Although (c) above refers to the allocation of such resources as there are, it should be emphasized that few, if any, significant resources may be under the control of the co-ordinator. It is certainly not suggested that case co-ordinators will necessarily have control of the availability of residential places, or be able by some magic to make more money available for material aid, say, or more time available for carrying out case work in depth, however badly such things may be needed.

At the time of writing we are at the point in several projects of trying to identify more clearly with the staff concerned the exact locus of the co-ordinating role in various situations where a number of people are involved in the same case. Almost certainly it rests in the early stages of a case with the field social worker, or the more senior field social worker, involved: there is probably some

---

Rowbottom *et al.*, 1973). The thought that adequate treatment of the client or patient requires the teamwork of a number of different professions or specialisms, often from both health and social services is rapidly acquiring the status of a cliché. Although the Seebohm Report (1968) advocated that the family in need of social care should as far as possible be served by a single social worker (para. 516) it goes on to agree that there would sometimes be reasons for involving other specialist workers as well (para. 519). Where health care staff are heavily involved as in mental health care (see for example the report on the Mental Health Services After Unification (British Medical Association, 1972)) the problems of team organization cannot be ignored. Is the psychiatrist automatically in overall charge? (Seebohm, para. 348) If so, what is his role, *managerial* or *co-ordinating*?

2

08   SOCIAL SERVICES DEPARTMENTS

analogy here with the general medical practitioner in health care. At later stages, or in other cases, it may shift to or rest with heads of residential establishments, or with other senior residential staff.

For example, in East Sussex the possibility of the Residential and Day Care Officer (see Chapter 6) carrying out a co-ordinating role in respect of clients newly-admitted to care, has been under discussion. A possible statement of his duties includes the following:

Convening meetings of interested parties in respect of each client within X weeks of the client's admission to care. The purpose of the meeting will be to agree:
(a) the treatment tasks to be undertaken.
(b) whether the case can be *transferred* to the Head of the Establishment; and if not in the event of collaborative working, who shall co-ordinate in future (it could be the Head of the Establishment, the Field Social Worker, the Residential and Day Care Officer, etc.);
(c) an appropriate date for next review.

The Residential and Day Care Officer will have a duty to convey the decisions or recommendations made to each participant and his manager to ensure ongoing support and supervision.

Chairmanship of Case Conferences

Closely associated with case co-ordination is the question of chairmanship of case conferences and case reviews of various kinds. It appears that it is not unusual for a wide variety of senior departmental staff to chair such events, as evidenced in the system of case reviews in the Essex Children's Department, described above. Often the same case may be chaired by different senior staff at various times. Should one person chair all case conferences, and if so who should it be? What authority should he or she carry?

Some basic analysis may help to clear the ground considerably. Given that directors of departments are not likely to have time to chair all such events (or for that matter directors of divisions in Model B departments either, presumably) then whoever chairs the meeting is not going to be in a *managerial* relationship to all others present. For example, a senior residential officer is not in a managerial relationship to field work staff present, however junior; or vice versa. (As always, one must be on guard against the assumption that difference in *grade* or *status* constitutes in itself difference in organizational *authority*.) Secondly the chairman is not necessarily the natural *case co-ordinator* (as we have just defined it) for all cases under review.

It seems then that the chairman must be seen neither as in a *managerial* role (unless incidentally) to others present, nor necessarily as the specific co-ordinator of action on each case, but as in some sort of more general 'meeting-co-ordinator' role. As for any chairman, it would be his job to steer the discussion, and to 'manage' the agenda. He would have *co-ordinating* authority in respect of these matters, but no authority to make binding decisions in the face of sustained disagreement. It would be seen as his role to help the various parties to reach consensus if possible; but if this were not possible, to take due account of the realities of basic departmental organization, and the existing division of accountability. If the chairman's role is seen in this light, the question of who should take the chair becomes perhaps less critical provided he is senior and experienced enough. In the course of such meetings various decisions, for example about continued collaboration of field workers and residential workers, or deliberate transfer of cases to residential staff, could be made in the way described earlier. The meeting could also consider any question of transfer of the case-co-ordinating role itself, when the moment seemed appropriate to do so, in any given case under review.

Conclusion

In this chapter we have been describing project work which has gone beyond the study of the main shape of departmental structure and the functions of its various parts discussed in previous chapters. Here, the focus has been on the detailed processes by which incoming work is dealt with, assessed, allocated to appropriate workers, and thereafter controlled. We have also examined some of the questions of transfer, collaboration, and co-ordination, which arise where a number of workers are concerned with any one case. We have studied too the processes by which clients get placed in residential care.

Broadly, the result of the first phase of our project work in this area is the provision of analysis which allows some clearer understanding of the *nature* of these processes, and the creation of better-defined language in which to describe them and formulate alternative ways of dealing with them. However, the work has as yet provided little or no experience of deliberate test of some of the possibilities which can now be more clearly seen.

Project work concerned both with specialist intake teams and with duty teams has enabled the creation of a general model of the initial stages of 'case work' (i.e. *basic social work*) with new clients. There appear to be three main elements, for each of which a precise definition has been evolved:

> *screening*
> *short-term case work*
> *long-term case work.*

The model also incorporates definitions of *bombardment, case, client, case assessment, referral,* and *transfer.* In terms of this model it has been possible to offer a detailed analysis of the typical work of such staff as receptionists, specialist intake workers, and duty workers.

Research on the way that allocation and supervisory processes are carried out in practice has led to formulation of the important distinction between *case assessment* and *supervisory review.* A wide variety of different occasions on which supervisory reviews inevitably arise has been identified in current departmental practice. A detailed formulation has been evolved of the proper role of the Team Leader (or Area Officer) in both allocation and subsequent review processes.

Project work on procedures for placing clients in residential care in two authorities has demonstrated some common problems. It is suggested that in 'placement', not just one but a complex of perhaps seven major decisions or processes is involved. The likely locus of these various decisions in Model A and Model B departments has been explored.

Work with particular clients proceeds typically through the combined efforts of a multi-disciplinary team including on occasion people from other agencies or departments. The co-ordination of the work of any particular team through simple *managerial* mechanisms is usually inappropriate if not impossible. Typically (in contrast), it is possible to identify a defined *co-ordinative* role which may rest initially with field work staff and may be transferred later by deliberate decision to residential staff for certain types of client in care. Project work suggests, moreover, that the role of chairman of case conference is not properly conceived either as a straightforward *managerial* one or necessarily as that of a *case co-ordinator*.

9 Further Areas of Expanding Project Work

Harking back to the broad view of the SSD and its social environment which was presented in Chapter 2, it will be evident that projects described in the previous chapters have been concerned largely with the central executive system – its functions, its role structure, and its co-ordinative procedures. Given the nature of this particular research which deals with those problems and only those problems which it is invited to consider by client departments, such a bias or preoccupation is perhaps only to be expected in the first years of a newly reorganized service. We have not yet been presented with opportunities to explore, for example, local authority structure itself, or the roles of local authority members *vis-à-vis* officers of the department. We have not yet had opportunities to work jointly with social services and other agencies and departments. Nor have we undertaken direct work with clients or would-be clients of SSDs.[1]

However, as the new service gradually achieves order in its own house its attention naturally begins to turn outwards, and signs of the reorientation start to be reflected in our own project work. In this chapter we shall describe some emerging areas of work on this broader front. In some of these areas we have started actual

[1] Indeed whether such latter work is possible within the limits of the social-analytic approach as we presently conceive it, is a question which has to be considered in its own right. If it is not possible, one returns to more conventional methods of exploration, such as surveys or detailed case-studies, for this particular area of investigation.

project work in specific departments. In others we rely for the moment mainly on observation and speculation.

Generally speaking, then, these emerging areas of interest are concerned with the relationship of the central departmental structure to other social groups and social systems which lie outside it. We shall describe, for example, some ideas which are developing on the links between social services and health authorities. We shall register some first thoughts on corporate organization within local authorities, and on community participation. We shall offer some suggestions on the likely future development of professional and occupational groups within social work. We shall describe in some detail a project concerned with a staff representative system in one of our client departments. This lies beyond the central executive structure, in the sense that the staff as a group may be thought of as having a distinct existence and social force of their own, regardless of the fact that also, as employees, they man this central structure.

The Present Social Climate of SSDs

By way of introduction to these broader issues it is helpful to take note of certain general trends in thinking and practice which fundamentally condition the present social climate in which SSDs operate. At least six such important trends can readily be identified.

First, there is the increasing acceptance of *the links between the social breakdown of particular individuals and families and the general social environment in which they occur.* No longer is the social breakdown of individuals or families seen in isolation, but increasingly in relation to, and indeed as a result of, matters such as inadequate housing, poor education, uncertain and unsatisfactory employment, and the general poverty of social and cultural environment.[2] We have already noted in Chapter 3 that one effect of this tendency is the more explicit recognition of the need for departments to carry out work at the community level in

[2] It is unnecessary for our purposes here to produce evidence to support the assertion. The main point is that it is widely believed to be true, and that such a belief, more or less consciously held, forms the basis of much planning and action, as will be evident from sampling any leading periodicals in the field.

addition to carrying out 'case work', i.e. work with individual clients and families.

Second, and this is somewhat related, is *the trend to community care* in both social services and in health. Increasingly it becomes accepted opinion that the treatment of many conditions of social, mental, and even physical, distress or damage is most effectively carried out 'in the community' rather than in large and self-contained institutions ('homes', 'hospitals') geographically and socially remote from the places where people pursue their normal lives.[3] One effect of this view is a tendency to opt for organizational arrangements which are decentralized both physically and in terms of organizational control. As SSDs grow in size, Model B structures, where establishments are linked to, and run by, divisional teams, become more attractive than Model A structures, with their emphasis on specialism and central control. In health services, the 'health centre' and the 'community hospital' attract fashionable attention at the expense of the 'district general hospital', or the large remote mental health institutions built in response to earlier ideologies.

Third, there is an increasing emphasis on *corporate* and *joint planning* which also relates to some degree to the two trends identified above. Local authorities are adjured not to plan social services, education, housing, land-use, and so on, in isolation; but to conceive each as part of one grand plan concerned with the general quality of local life, a total 'community plan'. In consequence there is increasing talk of 'corporate management' in local authorities involving all the chief officers. There are proposals for the establishment of general 'policy and resources' committees of local authorities, and of the establishment of general 'research and intelligence' units to feed the planning processes.[4] Recognition that plans for health and social services are inevitably

---

[3] Again this statement is presented uncritically as representing the received opinion of the moment. However, the pressure of a counter-movement is also evident which reasserts the view that better treatment is provided in relatively large, relatively specialized, institutions in certain conditions and cases.

[4] See the Bains Report (1972) on the management and structure of local authorities. See also the work of the Institute of Local Government Studies on corporate planning and management as presented, for example, by Stewart (1971), and Greenwood and Stewart (1972).

intimately linked brings its own specific proposals for joint consultation and joint planning.[5]

Clearly associated with this last trend towards more comprehensive planning at local level is the trend for *greater central government intervention in planning*, as evidenced in the recent (1972) request[6] to all local authorities to produce and submit ten-year plans for the development of their social services. Inevitably, moves to more coherent local planning become linked with moves to more coherent national planning. And thus, as we have discussed at various points, 'strategic planning' becomes a subject of increasing importance in SSDs themselves.

A fifth trend of increasing importance might be described as the *move to greater public participation* in the processes of local government (and in those of other statutory agencies too). If more coherent and comprehensive plans are to be made, then the public want to be in on the act before they become too established and hardened – and not only through the mechanism of their elected councillors. Proposed land-use developments are put to public scrutiny at an early point. Community Health Councils are to be established in each Health District. Within some local authorities special committees of councillors and members of local societies and welfare organizations have been established on a geographical basis to act as local reference points for SSDs. Organized pressure groups grow apace, each with its own particular concern and each intent on influencing the development of policy and allocation of resources that already takes place within the duly constituted processes of democratic government.

The interest of social services departments themselves is a double one here. Not only will they have to learn how to live with various more or less formalized pressures from the 'public', other than these transmitted through elected local authority members, but to some extent (as discussed in Chapter 3) they themselves are in the business of helping to foster the capacity to create such pressures on local authorities and other agencies.

[5] The White Paper on *National Health Service Reorganization* (Department of Health and Social Security, 1972) describes Joint Consultative Committees of local authority and health authority members. The report on *Management Arrangements for the Reorganised Health Services* (DHSS, 1972) describes various 'health care planning teams' which would include local authority social services staff as members.

[6] Department of Health and Social Security, Circular 35/72.

Finally, there is the *trend of growing professionalism in social work* itself, as a force to be reckoned with. With the formation of one main association for social workers,[7] the accelerating increase in professional training, and the improved career prospects which the new larger departments offer, the social work profession increasingly becomes a political force in its own right.

With this broad picture in mind some preliminary thoughts on organizational and procedural issues at various specific points within it will now be offered in turn.

Links Between Health and Social Services

At the level of the health and social services authorities themselves, it is now known that the formal link will be through a Joint Consultative Committee.[8] This will consist of members of the Area Health Authority itself meeting, in effect in a negotiating situation, with members of the corresponding local authority itself – non-metropolitan county or metropolitan district as the case may be. What are the necessary and appropriate links at departmental level?

We have surmised that they might be of three kinds:

(1) those concerned with *strategic planning*, e.g. planning long-term comprehensive provision for the elderly, in hospital, in residential care, and in the community;
(2) those concerned with *operational co-ordination*, e.g. the establishment of detailed systems for the transfer of clients from hospital to the care of the social services and vice versa; or the detailed deployment of social work staff in health care institutions of various kinds;
(3) those concerned with *individual cases*.

Although there has been much talk of the prime need to associate Health Care Districts with Social Services Areas, this is probably somewhat unrealistic in terms of their very different scale and range of functions. Health Care District organizations (led by

[7] The British Association of Social Workers, formed in 1970 by the amalgamation of a large number of more specialized professional associations.

[8] See White Paper on NHS Reorganisation, Department of Health and Social Security (1972).

'District Management Teams') are essentially comprehensive units of health care planning and delivery. In consideration of the economics of modern health care technology, such comprehensive operational units are only· viable for populations of the order of 200–250,000. Area Social Service Teams on the other hand do not in either Model A or Model B departments provide a complete and comprehensive range of social services (see Chapter 4), nor are they the main locus of comprehensive planning in SSDs. Typically they correspond to populations of 30–70,000 – a whole order smaller than the Health District. Even self-contained geographical Divisions in Model B departments are likely to be somewhat smaller than Health Districts – perhaps of the order of 70,000–150,000 populations. Given the arrangements for Health Service organization[9] one may suggest tentatively that the following prime organizational linkages might apply:

Health Authority	Social Services	Joint Activity
1. Area Team of Officers (the Area Medical Officer, Area Nursing Officer, etc.) and their immediate assistants	– Director of Social Services and his immediate assistants	– Strategic Planning and Operational Co-ordination
2. District Management Teams (the District Community Physician, District Nursing Officer, etc.)	– As above. Also the Divisional Directors in geographically-organized departments	– Strategic Planning and Operational Co-ordination
3. Health Care Planning Teams (Geriatrics, Mental Illness, Sub-normality, etc.)	– Senior specialists in the fields concerned – Research and Planning Officers – A Principal Health Care Co-ordinator?	– Strategic Planning and Operational Co-ordination

[9] See *Management Arrangements for the Reorganised Health Services* (Department of Health and Social Security, 1972).

Health Authority	Social Services	Joint Activity
4. Individual Units (Hospitals, Health Centres, Clinics, Group Practices)	– Staff outposted to the Unit concerned *or* designated Liaison Officers – Area and Divisional Officers on occasion	– Operational Co-ordination and individual Case Co-ordination
5. Individual doctors and nurses	– Individual social workers, field or residential workers – Area and Divisional Officers on occasion	– Individual Case Co-ordination

Corporate Management in Local Authorities

In the discussion of corporate management within local authorities one of the prime organizational questions is the intended nature of the much-discussed management teams of chief officers 'led' by a chief executive officer.[10] We assume two possible answers. First, the 'chief executive' might indeed be the head of a unified *managerial hierarchy* (Figure 9.1). In this case each chief officer would be genuinely accountable to the Chief Executive Officer, and to him only. Any direct contact which any had with a particular committee of the local authority must then be seen in the light of each being essentially an assistant to the Chief Executive Officer; and, of course, any policies which were prescribed by particular committees would have to be the subject of discussion with the Chief Executive Officer as well.

Alternatively the Chief Executive Officer might be the general *co-ordinator* of the chief officers group, and chairman of any joint meetings (Figure 9.2). In this case each chief officer would be accountable only to the local authority itself, and subject only to policies set or approved by the authority. Such discussions as we

[10] As described for example in the Bains Report (p. 40 et. seq.). The Report leaves it unclear whether a *managerial* or *co-ordinative* role as discussed below is being prescribed for the Chief Executive Officer.

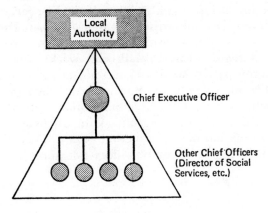

Figure 9.1

have had with Directors of Social Services and other senior staff have indicated that the second picture is considered more realistic and acceptable. Again the chief point is to distinguish a particular (and in this case no doubt very appropriate) *process* or *style* – corporate management – from the underlying *structure* of organizational relationships.

In passing it is worthy of note that similar management groups are becoming increasingly popular at departmental level. The same contrasts of structure and process arise. At the time of our project work in Brent, a management group consisting of the Director, the three Assistant Directors, the Chief Administrative Officer, the six Area Managers, and the Residential and Day Care Manager,

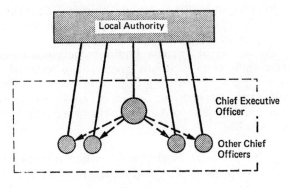

Figure 9.2

were meeting at four-weekly intervals. In East Sussex the Director and his immediate subordinates – four Assistant Directors and six Area Directors – also formed a management group which met together at regular intervals. Project work with the group concerned in this particular situation confirmed that managerial status of the Director did not disappear during such meetings. Rather such meetings were used as a particular method of promoting communication within the group, joint discussion, and the collaborative formation of departmental policy. There is no reason to suppose that the same analysis does not apply elsewhere within SSDs.

Consumer Participation

The subject of consumer participation cannot of course be adequately considered without due account of the prior existence of the democratic control of departments through elected representatives who form the local authority. Nevertheless the question may be posed: what more *direct* links, if any, might be built between clients, consumers, the public, on the one hand, and the department on the other? One thinks here, for example, of such things in neighbouring fields as Community Health Councils in relation to health matters, parent-teacher associations in education, and proposed neighbourhood councils in relation to local authority services generally. The problems are classic.

(1) Who exactly *are* the consumers who are to be represented?
(2) How are they to achieve genuine representation through their own elected representatives as opposed to the mock-representation of appointed (or self-appointed) spokesmen?
(3) How are such representative bodies to be given enough power to make their mark, without giving them so much that they begin to confuse the existing lines of democratic control?
(4) How do such formalized bodies of consumer representation stand in relation to spontaneously-emerging pressure groups of various kinds?

A passing thought – it is obviously easier to conceive institutionalized client-representative systems for those clients who themselves live within an 'institution', for example an old person's home, than for those, to take an extreme case, who arrive individually and in an unrelated fashion at the reception desk of the Area Office.

Professional and Occupational Development in Social Services Departments

In the light of developing professionalism in social work we have constantly been testing the question whether full managerial roles are considered possible in relation to those who might reasonably be classified as fully competent 'professional' workers. So far (as indicated in Chapter 5) the evidence is that not only are they possible, but already more or less fully realized, whether explicitly or not, in most departments. However, a further issue which still remains to be explored is at what point the development of social work as a profession in its own right, with its own particular skills and mysteries, might preclude managerial structure; and what organizational structure might then replace it. Our tentative analysis of this question is developed in some length in Appendix B.

Over and above this, we suggest that an important realignment is likely to take place within the broad occupational category of social work in the coming years. At present there are (roughly speaking) two main sub-occupational groups within social work – field workers and residential workers. (This leaves aside a third ill-defined and heterogeneous collection of workers mainly employed in domiciliary and day care work, including home helps, mobility and communication specialists, and unqualified staff, some of whom might also be reckoned to be social workers.) At present, generalizing somewhat again, the main career paths are constrained within these two sub-categories (see Figure 9.3).

If the analysis and findings accumulated in our own project work are correct, however, there are strong similarities between field and residential social work as it needs to be practised. As was discussed in Chapters 3, 5, and 6, something describable as *basic social work* is possible in both kinds of work and the provision of a number of *basic services* of virtually identical kinds is called for in both. What is chiefly different is the setting in which these activities are undertaken. To a large degree, this applies also to the field of domiciliary and day care.

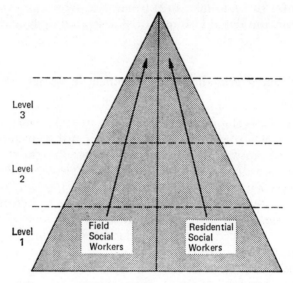

Figure 9.3   Existing Broad Career Paths in Social Work

Increasingly as this situation becomes recognized, it is predictable that common training patterns, and more closely integrated
career structure will follow.[11] (This leaves aside certain occupational groups such as occupational therapists and specialist teachers
who, it can be predicted, will be likely to become even more
clearly distinct from social workers. These are the people who
carry out what we have called *supplementary services*.) However,
this does not preclude the development from a common generic
training of certain specialisms *within* a more closely integrated
social work profession – and indeed such subjects as residential
care, or perhaps community work, form an obvious basis for
specialization.

What is also likely, however, is that as social work grows in
professionalism, auxiliary sub-groups will develop in support of
the main professional group, with their own separate (and necessarily more modest) career progressions. The pattern of occupational groups might therefore become somewhat similar in time

[11] The strong similarities between the arguments developed in this section
and those developed by the National Working Party on Training for
Residential Work (Central Council for Education and Training and Social
Work, 1973) will be evident.

to that found in the health field, where basic generic training for doctors gives rise, at later stages, to choice of a number of special-isms, and where a whole host of ancillary and supporting pro-fessions exist which have developed over the years.

In social work the ancillary group would include many of the people currently employed under titles such as welfare assistants, social work assistants, family aides, care attendants, and residential child care officers. The qualification and training required by this group would not be so stringent as for professional social workers. However, there would presumably be chances to move from the ancillary group to the main social work group by the acquisition of appropriate further qualifications.

The career paths for these two main groups of workers might then be as shown in Figure 9.4. The 'levels' described are as those

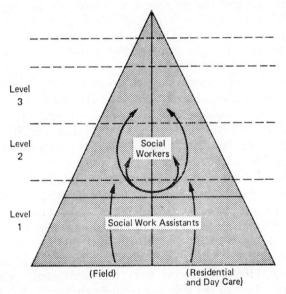

Figure 9.4   Possible Future Career Paths in Social Work

used in previous chapters (see Chapters 4, 5, and 6). Whatever the setting, certain distinct qualities of work could be identified at these three levels. The work and the kind of workers involved might be as follows:

Level 1

The work would be concerned with providing specific *basic services* and carrying out specific parts of *basic social work* under the supervision of Level 2 workers. (The kinds of staff involved would be assistants, trainees, aides, students, and inexperienced social workers.)

Level 2

Workers here would be in charge of cases and fully capable of carrying out *basic social work,* including planning and implementing treatment programmes of various kinds. They would also be capable, as necessity arose, of helping in the provision of *basic services.* (The kinds of staff involved would be capable field social workers, team leaders and specialist practitioners, heads of most residential establishments, and heads of certain day centres.)

Level 3

The work here would be managing groups of Level 2 (and Level 1) workers; establishing policies and development programmes, and ensuring the maintenance of general standards; or carrying out high level specialist activities, or staff work. (The kind of staff involved would be Area Officers, residential group managers and heads of certain more complex residential establishments, specialist co-ordinators, training managers, etc.)

Social-workers-to-be would start in lower grades in Level 1 work as trainees or students, and subsequently, as newly qualified workers, move to a higher grade in Level 1. Thereafter, they could be expected to graduate to Level 2 work within a relatively short period of time as a matter of course. Further promotion would be to Level 3 and beyond.

Social work assistants of various kinds would start in the lower ranges of Level 1 and advance through various grades within Level 1 as they acquired more skill and experience, and perhaps also appropriate formal qualifications. It should be stressed that each organizational level would contain several distinct *grades* – see Appendix A. Thus advancement within a *level* would have very real meaning. However, social work assistants could not be expected to move into Level 2 posts without gaining the sort of qualification necessary to undertake the control and direction of *basic social work* activities.[12]

[12] Unless, conceivably, separate complete sections start to become established to provide *basic services* under separate management, i.e., under Level 2 workers who are not necessarily trained to carry out or direct *basic social work.* This might conceivably arise, for example, out of the extension of home-help activities.

Representative Systems for Departmental Staff – Experience in Wandsworth

In relation to many of the broader issues described above our work for the present is preliminary and speculative. In one particular area however – that of representative systems of staff within departments – we have in fact had some direct project experience.

In April 1971 we were approached by a newly-formed group of field work staff representatives in Wandsworth to see if we might help them collectively to clarify their roles and methods of working. In initial discussions it transpired that each of the five recently-established Area Teams had elected three representatives, and that the total group of fifteen representatives had already started to impress on the Director and other senior staff the strength of concern about certain subjects that existed amongst field work staff. Whilst the inevitable problems of bringing into being a completely new department were recognized, there was nevertheless much concern, for example, about what was considered to be inadequate reception and interviewing facilities for clients and inadequate clerical support for social workers; about the difficulties of communication between top and bottom of the new department; about uncertainty over the roles of various senior administrative staff; and so on. It was interesting to note that almost all the issues, at this point at any rate, were about how the department worked and the quality of service which it gave to clients: they were not about more obviously personal things like conditions of employment for field work staff, payment, and promotion opportunities.

During the next few months, we attended three meetings of the Representative Group, mainly observing, but as time went on making occasional comments as well. We then produced and fed to the Group an analysis directed not towards the specific issues on which they were themselves attempting to communicate and negotiate, but to evident problems about their own roles and procedures. Questions had emerged, for example, of how representatives were to find out just what was of genuine concern to their constituents, and how they were to communicate progress on subsequent action to them. Could existing Area Team Meetings be used? If special Area meetings were called by representatives, attendance tended to be poor. There were also problems of the internal organization of the Group – constant difficulties of finding somebody to take minutes, and of agreeing who was to negotiate particular issues with particular senior officers. Last but not least, we ourselves noted many occasions when representatives seemed to be pressing issues on the grounds that they *personally* happened to believe them important, without any apparent evidence that they were of *general* concern. Our first report to them read as follows:

Notes on Wandsworth Field Workers' Representative Group
This note on the constitution and functions of the Wandsworth Field Workers' Representative Group is produced at their request as a basis for a discussion of these subjects at a forthcoming meeting. It follows the attendance of Brunel researchers as observers at three earlier meetings.

There can be little doubt that the subjects discussed at these and other meetings have real meat in them – intake and allocation procedures, role of sector clerks, establishment and appointments, reception facilities, etc. – but this still leaves the first and fundamental question: *is a representative system necessary, to discuss these or any other questions?* What distinguishes these particular discussions from those that might be entered into for instance by complete Area Teams, or even by spontaneous groups of social workers within areas?

Analysis of the Role of the Representative Group
In principle, representative groups in general may discuss:
  (a) issues which happen to concern them as individuals, or
  (b) issues which they believe to be of concern to the group they represent, either:
    – issues common to all basic grade social workers
    – issues common to all the social workers in a particular Area.

Discussions of a kind (a) are not in accord with the idea of a representative system. Individuals do not need to be elected as representatives to take up such issues in any place that may be appropriate, e.g. in Area Team meetings, or in working parties, or just in individual discussions with senior or Area officers.

Representatives should surely restrict themselves to issues of kind (b). But how do they know which issues are of concern to their constituents?

  – It is suggested that, in principle, representatives need not, and cannot always work on a precise mandate from their constituents – that they have to use judgement about what issues are, or will be of concern to their constituents.

- Nevertheless, at the same time there must be some regular means of communication between represenatives and constituents so that the former can generally keep their finger on the pulse, or so that they can, on occasion, raise specific issues for discussion, or pass on specific information.

Meetings with Constituents

Such a means is obviously a meeting of representatives and their constituents within each Area.

- Can such a meeting adequately be combined with a meeting called and run by the Area Officer? Who decides the frequency of meetings, the agenda, the urgency of particular items? Can members really ignore the presence of the Area Officer in speaking their mind?
- If separate meetings are held can these be justified as 'official business' within work-time? Or should they be considered as 'out-of-hours'?

The attendance of constituents at meetings will surely give a measure of the general strength of feelings about issues needing to be raised. When 'hot' issues arise there will presumably be no difficulty in getting good attendance.

Issues Particular to One Area

Issues particular to one Area should be dealt with at Area level in the first instance – if necessary through discussions between representatives and the Area Officer concerned – only with the failure there of adequate resolution should they become meat for discussion by the full Representative Group.

Administration of Representative Meetings

The present Group has no definite Chairman and rotates the duty of Secretary. One obvious advantage of the latter is a spreading of workload. The obvious disadvantages are:

- that no one 'guides' meetings through discussion or attempts to ensure that a particular agenda is adequately covered
- that there is lack of continuity in the taking of minutes, and a variety of styles employed
- that neither constituents nor senior officers of the department have any definite or obvious point of contact should they wish to communicate with the Representative Group as a body
- that nobody can legitimately speak for, or act for the Group between its meetings.

Representative Role and Executive Role

On one occasion the Director apparently suggested in discussion that a particular social worker might personally pursue, explore and report on an idea which she happened to be advocating (in connection with the Hopton holiday scheme). Again, there is probably an inconsistency here between the everyday (executive) role of the social worker, and the special nature of the representative role. In a representative role, the social worker responds only to the needs, expressed or unexpressed, of his constituents, and cannot be assigned work by any senior officer of the department.

Circulation of Minutes

Minutes are presently circulated to constituents *and* to senior field workers and Area Officers. It is noted that one consequence of this is that if anything were said which was unduly critical of individual senior officers, or groups of senior officers, the criticism would have to be toned-down or modified in minutes. If it were important to communicate the full strength of the particular criticism to constituents this would have to be done separately.

The Representative Group started to discuss the report. About the same time, and in response to pressures from various field work staff, the Group decided that the problem of communication between representatives and the body of field workers might best be met or circumvented if all field workers met regularly in one general meeting to discuss their common problems. A series of such meetings was duly launched (outside normal working hours) which we started to attend in addition to our continuing attendance at the meetings of representatives which usually immediately preceded them.

Many of the issues of internal structure and procedure already noted in meetings of the Representative Group raised their head again in the general meetings, and others too became apparent. The issue arose in discussion, for example, of how far 'management' would be likely to take notice of what representatives said unless they were aware of the possibility that field workers might apply sanctions at some stage – though what sanctions would be appropriate would be another matter. And the issue arose again of how the field worker group as a whole could best organize itself in order to act effectively, and with whom it should primarily deal in its negotiations. We produced a second analysis of the various issues that now seemed to arise and fed it back, this time not only to the representatives but to the full field work group.[13] It read as follows:

The Representation of Field Workers' Views – An Analysis
The purpose of this note is to provide an analysis of the discussion at the general meeting of field workers on 27th October.

It supplements an earlier analysis by the Brunel Team of the workings of the existing Representative System, which has already been circulated to all representatives.

The starting question raised at the general meeting was: 'how can an effective field workers' voice be created?'

Some of the main issues noted from the subsequent discussion are listed below, and a brief analysis of each is suggested.

If these comments are helpful, perhaps they can be pursued at the next general meeting.

Issue	*Possibilities*	*Comments*
1) How wide a range of topics should the 'field workers' voice speak on?	– own interests – clients' interests – interests of department as a whole, etc.	– why not all or any of these issues if considered important by field workers?
2) Who are the 'field workers' involved?	– might include senior social workers – might include Area Officers, etc.	– strength of common interest is probably the key criterion. Noted that at present the group *excludes* senior social workers and Area Officers.
3) What is relationship to NALGO?	– there might be an agreed strict division of function	

[13] The full field work group would number some hundred or so, had all attended. In fact in the three general meetings at which we were present, the attendance ranged between thirty and fifty.

Issue	*Possibilities*	*Comments*
	– or general under-standing of divi-sion, but some overlap of func-tion tolerated – or complete over-lap tolerated.	
4) Should activities be carried out by the total field worker group, or by a smaller group of elected rep-resentatives/ delegates on their behalf?	– Area meetings might mandate a a delegate to report views – or Departmental meetings might mandate a dele-gate to report views – or representatives might interpret views as best they could and act at their own initiative, etc.	– None of these are mutually exclusive. A delegate who can only work on a specific mandate is working in very constrained situa-tion. A repre-sentative who never has a chance to communicate with his constitu-ents as a group is often faced with great uncer-tainty. A system of elected repre-sentatives who can meet together, meet Area field workers, or meet with the field worker group as a whole perhaps gives maximum flexibility.
5) Frequency of meetings (Area meetings, De-partmental meetings, meet-ings of repre-sentatives, meetings with senior officers).	– might be according to a regular pro-gramme – might be *ad hoc* as required.	

Issue	*Possibilities*	*Comments*
6) Application of sanctions	– there might be invariable threat of application of sanctions with each communicated unease. – no sanction or threat of sanction on any occasion other than verbal pressure – sanctions or threats of sanctions according to the degree of unease and the course and circumstances of discussions.	– flexible tactics (the third possibility) may have much to be said for them. An effective system of credible representation which can accurately and rapidly communicate the degree of unease on any issue to senior officers, will hopefully tend to reduce to a minimum the likelihood of the need to consider further sanctions.
7) Which senior officers to communicate with?	– with the Director – with the Assistant Director – with Area Officers – with others	– perhaps with all or any, according to the issue? But any Area Officer would be communicated with only on issues related to his Area, by representatives from that Area (if not by the field work staff of that Area as whole).
8) To what extent are regular chairmen, secretaries, conveners, etc. needed?	field workers associations and their representatives might have no regular officers; work would be done	– elected chairmen and secretaries facilitate the conduct of meetings and the systematic handling of communications.

Issue	*Possibilities*	*Comments*
	and roles played *ad hoc*	
	– certain posts might be filled by election for prescribed and limited periods of time	
9) Should senior officers of the Department attend meetings? Should they see minutes of meetings?	– they might never be invited to meetings or shown minutes	– if officers always attend meetings, and see all minutes certain types of discussion or statements are *bound* to be inhibited thereby
	– they might be present at all meetings and see all minutes	– if on the other hand senior officers never met with groups of field workers, at the initiative of the latter or with their representatives; nor ever received written communications from the field worker group or their representatives, then field workers would not be voicing their views to anyone but themselves.
	– they might sometimes attend meetings and sometimes have the results of meetings relayed to them.	– If these two points are right, it follows that meetings of field workers (or their representatives) by themselves should

Comments

simply be dis-
tinguished from
those with officers,
both being
needed; and
that communica-
tions between
field workers should
be distinguished
from communica-
tions with senior
officers, both
being needed.

The next general meeting tried hard to find time to consider procedural problems, but found itself forced to concentrate on substantive issues which were already under negotiation with the Director and other senior staff. In the meantime, at the invitation of the Representative Group, we helped them draft a possible constitution of a 'field workers association' identifying such things as who exactly were the members, and how various representatives and officers might be appointed.

The third general meeting again was heavily and necessarily involved in substantive issues, but did in fact eventually force itself to debate procedural matters. The proposed constitution was put forward by the representatives, but ran into considerable criticism. Why was a *constitution* needed? Why was the legalistic word *association* being employed? A small but vociferous group expressed what one sensed as a strong emotional antipathy to the very ideas of 'rules' and formalization.

Clearly something was wrong. Perhaps the larger group needed amongst other things to define its own attitude to ourselves, the researchers. We decided not to attend the next general meeting in order to allow them more freedom to discuss the issue.[14] The

---

[14] It is worthy of note in passing that researchers involved found difficulty in establishing an adequate social-analytic relationship in so large and unstructured a group. (This was not so with the smaller Representative

invitation to join their discussions was not in fact renewed, and at this point this particular project lapsed.

Representative Systems for Departmental Staff – General

Before the arrival of this particular project, our previous exposure to Glacier Project material had already alerted us to the conception of representative systems as social systems in their own right, clearly distinct or distinguishable from the main structure of executive roles within organizations.[15] Discussions in our conferences which have drawn people from a wide range of departments have revealed two interesting facts about current representative activity in SSDs. First, it would appear that the phenomenon of social workers (usually field workers) expressing their views through the mechanism of elected 'spokesman' or representatives at various times of stress is by no means uncommon. Second, however, it appears that such activity tends to be sporadic and that very few departments have anything which might be described as an established and continuing representative system.

In general, as departments increase in size one would predict that those at the lower levels might have more incentive to find direct ways of impressing their views and needs on those at the top other than by indirect communication through an increasing number of managerial levels. Where, for example, the hierarchy consists of only three or four tiers in all (that is *organizational levels* as opposed to *grades* – see Appendix A) as was the case no doubt in most former children's, welfare, and mental health departments, it is not difficult for those at the bottom to maintain some direct personal contact, individually or as a group, with the head of the department. Whether this is possible, however, with the typical five-tiered social service department described in previous chapters is another matter.

The possible benefits of representative systems have been presented elsewhere.[16] It certainly goes beyond our particular role to

Group – usually about ten in number.) Our doubts about the technical feasibility of social-analytic work in such a setting contributed also to the decision to withdraw from the general meeting.

[15] See for example the fully formalized and explicit distinction between the Executive System and the Representative System at the Glacier Metal Company described by Brown (1960).

[16] Brown, op. cit.

advocate them universally, or, indeed, in any particular circumstance. And in any case, by the nature of the thing, they can only come into being where some considerable need for them is already felt to exist amongst the staff from whom they might spring.

All that needs to be done here by way of general comment is to draw attention to the existence of this particular kind of social phenomenon, and to draw attention to the need to distinguish it from the phenomenon of normal executive machinery. The representative system where it exists is a social system in its own right with its own internal requirements and logic. Its characteristic role – the elected *representative* – has its own distinct properties (see Appendix A); and though, for example, *managers* and *representatives* are both in a sense 'leaders', the distinction in the role and respective authority of each is crucial.

Conclusion

This chapter has dealt with a number of subjects which are for the moment still at the edge of advancing project work. All are concerned in some way with the relation of the central executive structure of the SSD to its social environment, and hence all in this way reflect the stage to which project work is now evolving.

A broader appreciation of the present nature of this social environment is helped by taking account of certain prevailing trends in social thought and practice. Six trends of particular importance can be identified: increasing recognition of the effect of general social environment on the social breakdown of particular individuals or families; emphasis on the benefits of care 'in the community' in social services (and in health) rather than on care within closed institutions; a marked trend to corporate and joint planning, and an accompanying trend to greater intervention by central government in planning processes; a general move towards greater public participation in the running of public services; and finally a growing professionalism within social work itself.

The development of project thinking with regard to those various aspects of the broader social environment is far from even, but several areas of developing thought or experience have been described, as they happen to exist.

In regard to links between social services and health services, it is hypothesized that several distinct kinds will be necessary at departmental level – those concerned with strategic or long-term planning; those concerned with operational co-ordination, e.g. the development of matching systems and procedures; and those concerned with co-ordinating work in relation to individual clients or patients.

In regard to corporate planning, a preliminary question has been raised on the role of the local authority 'chief executive officer' in the chief officers team – is it *managerial* or *co-ordinative?* Parallels are noted with 'management groups' within SSDs themselves. Some preliminary thoughts have been expressed on the broad subject of public participation.

In regard to professional and occupational development in social work, two ideas have been noted. First, taking into account demonstrable similarities in the nature of the work which they might be expected to be doing, it is likely that a closer professional integration of social workers in field work, residential, and day care, settings can be expected. On the other hand, an increasing differentiation can be expected to be recognized between relatively highly-qualified social workers in any setting, and the less well-qualified social workers who help them in that setting. Separate career patterns can be identified for two broad groups of staff, and related to three distinct levels of work.

Finally, project work on a staff representative system in one particular department has identified a number of critical issues for effective functioning, and the possible ways of dealing with them. It is suggested that as SSDs get bigger, there will be an increasing likelihood that a need for explicit and established staff representative systems will be felt.

10 Conclusion

What the Project has Achieved So Far

As was indicated at the start of this book, it is our fundamental assumption that project work of the kind we are undertaking must grow out of organizational problems as they are directly experienced and must be orientated to change. We see our role as helping the departments with which we work to understand and analyse their organizational problems more clearly, and to implement and evaluate remedial action. Thus two results might be expected – an output of better knowledge of the nature of organizational problems in SSDs and of solutions to them; and an output of actual change. The two are different but not, of course, independent. It is only by experiment and change that one tests the validity of knowledge.

Dealing with the second output first, so far it is very difficult to assess how much change has taken place as a direct result of project work.

In fact, in designing the project, change was sought at two distinct levels – change in individual departments as a result of intensive project work within them over extended periods of time, and change nationally through the dissemination of ideas in written form and through the national conference programme, the latter being referred to loosely as 'training'.[1] Now the difficulties

---

[1] As commented in Chapter 1, we now see in fact the possibilities of a three-level change process:

    (1) *intensive social-analytic project work* within a limited number of individual departments, aimed at working sooner or later at all levels and in all parts;

    (2) *intermittent consultancy activities* with a further number of depart-

of assessing the lasting effects of training are notorious. Moreover, the shortness of these particular conference programmes does not increase confidence about their possible impact. Nevertheless we have over the past three to four years run a succession of apparently successful conferences,[2] and we do assume that they themselves have created some modest measure of change.

Again, the assessment of change in individual departments is difficult. At a very basic level we are assured by many concerned that our continuous intervention over a period of years in some of these departments has had the effect of raising generally the sophistication of thinking about, and dealing with, organizational problems. This is a vague statement (though important if true) and impossible to substantiate with hard evidence. However, over and above this, we are just now reaching the point in relationships with several authorities where action which is a direct result of project work or which takes explicit account of project work is either being planned or actually being taken. Hence opportunities now arise for deliberate test of explicit organizational formulations, with the possibility of systematic evaluation or review by the client department concerned.[3]

Given that the introduction and subsequent test of explicit organizational change was always seen as one of the principal goals of the collaborative process, it is perhaps appropriate to consider why it has taken so long to reach this point. Partly, no doubt, shortcomings in our own method of work, which in any case we have had to revise and develop considerably during the course of the project, provide some explanation. Without any doubt, too,

---

ments probably restricted to senior levels, but still oriented to the particular problems of the department concerned;

(3) *general dissemination* of ideas through conferences, lectures, and publications, aimed at national coverage.

[2] Mostly two weeks in length, sometimes one week, involving altogether (as reported in Chapter 1) nearly five hundred senior staff from SSDs throughout England and Wales, and from the Social Work Service Group of the Department of Health and Social Security.

[3] Note again that it is the *client department* which must evaluate, not ourselves; although we will naturally participate in their evaluation processes as we do in all other processes concerned with the project. If the systematic collection of factual data is needed to aid evaluation it will be the responsibility of that client department to decide what they want and how to get it; though again we will help them to analyse what they need.

the coming to an end of the children's, welfare, and mental health departments, and the formation of the new integrated social services departments has had its effect. The period of changeover was one of such intense activity and stress for those in the service that it virtually precluded the start or continuance of systematic project work until late in 1971. Above all this, our experience leaves us to believe that organizational change based on systematic analysis of the fundamental needs and realities of work (as opposed to change in response to specific administrative or political pressures) is a process whose time scale must probably be measured in years rather than in months.

As far as demonstrable results from project work are concerned, then, they lie for the moment mainly within the first area mentioned above – that of increased knowledge of the nature of organizational problems in SSDs and increase in awareness of the various possibilities of tackling them. Given that the method of work does not attempt to provide a systematic survey of the incidence of particular problems throughout a wide range of SSDs, what has been achieved might be described more precisely as the creation of an analytical framework for the study and practical solution of certain sorts of problems. To continue the analogy, the analytical framework has two main tiers or levels.

The bottom or basic tier consists of a whole system of *defined terms and concepts* to enable the more accurate recognition and description of organizational and procedural problems in SSDs. For convenience of reference, all the separate definitions have been brought together in Appendix A. Some refer to organizational relationships – *managerial, co-ordinative, representative,* etc. Some refer to procedures – *transfer, case assessment, supervisory review,* etc. Some refer to more basic concepts – *task, policy, authority, power,* etc.

The second tier consists of a number of possible *models and formulations,* drawing support as it were from the tier below. These have been outlined at various points within the previous text, following descriptions of the particular projects which have given rise to them. Each can be expected to be modified or supplemented in the light of further detailed research work and increasingly (we hope) in the light of actual trial and test. In the meantime, these general formulations as they stand at present may be summarized as follows.

Summary of Main Formulations

The Social and Organizational Setting (Chapter 2)

(1) This project has found inapplicable any simple two-part model of social work organizations in terms of a professional element on the one hand and an agency or bureaucratic element on the other. Instead, a model has been developed involving the interaction of a number of separate social systems – the executive role structure, governing institutions, staff representative systems, professional associations, pressure groups, and other agencies – which it is suggested is closer to the complexities of reality. This is a pluralistic picture. Moreover the social systems involved are of many forms – *hierarchies, committees, coalitions, co-ordinated groups,* and so on.

(2) As far as the central executive role structure is concerned, there is a strong finding to report that it is almost universally acknowledged as hierarchical at the moment, and considered likely to remain so for good reasons. Here 'hierarchy' is used in the precise sense of successive *managerial* relationships, and does not necessarily carry connotations of a high degree of formality, centralization, depersonalization, or rigidity. These latter elements are considered to be independent variables. (An alternative to hierarchical structure along the lines described in Appendix B, based on medical organization, has been tested in many discussions but for the reasons given has found little support.) Moreover, the basic hierarchical structure is not the only one of account in SSDs. Increasingly, co-ordinated groups cut across the main hierarchical lines, giving rise to multi-dimensional patterns – what is becoming known as 'matrix' organization.

The Work of the Department (Chapter 3)

(3) It is strongly suggested that no adequate and comprehensive definition of the work of social services departments can be made in terms of the various conventional categories usually employed – case work, group work, community work, etc., or field work, residential work, day care, and domiciliary services, etc. Considering first work with individual clients and families, we suggest that this can best be described as aiming to provide more or less comprehensive combinations of *basic social work, basic services,* and *supplementary services* (as these terms are themselves detailed in Table 3.1) for those living in various

settings: their own homes, foster homes, residential establishments, hospitals, and so on. But this is not the only operational
work or 'output' of departments. Departments are also expected
to provide demonstrable results, i.e. 'output', at community
level, in such things as carrying out mass screening for social
distress, creating public knowledge of services and rights, assisting voluntary welfare activity, and stimulating self-help groups.

(4) A comprehensive statement of the work of the department must
add to these two main categories of operational work a number
of others which do not themselves directly result in 'output':
  – *research and evaluation*
  – *strategic planning*
  – *public relations*
  – *staffing and training*
  – *managerial and co-ordinative work*
  – *logistics*
  – *finance*
  – *secretarial work.*

Alternative Departmental Structures (Chapter 4)
(5) Theoretically, departments might choose to organize their
operational work according to any of a number of different
bases: *function or kind of work, place, kind of client, kind
of worker, method of work.* In practice the choice of prime
division is likely to be either by *function,* that is for example,
field work, residential care, etc. (Model A departments) or *place,*
that is geographical division (Model B departments).

(6) In either model, decisions must be made about how to organize
the other, non-operational work. Model A departments will
perhaps need a senior officer in charge of *research and planning*
and one in charge of *administration* – defined here more precisely as a combination of *financial work, secretarial work,* and
some share of *logistics* and *staffing work.* Model B departments
will need both these plus a further *operational co-ordinator* in
a *staff officer* capacity to deal with much detailed planning and
control across the various geographical divisions. (In Model A
departments such work depends largely on mutual interaction
between the heads of the various operational divisions.)

(7) Both specialists in various aspects of operational work (e.g.
in group work, or social work procedures, or work with the
mentally ill) and training staff are likely to be best placed on

the staff of this operational co-ordinator in Model B departments. In Model A departments, the most appropriate place for such specialists and trainers is less clear. Conventionally (but for no good logical reasons), they are often attached to field work divisions.

(8) Although the prime division of the department is likely to be either in terms of *function* or in terms of *place*, none of the other possible bases can be ignored. Various organizational mechanisms for co-ordinating, for example work with particular kinds of clients, will have to be devised. The result is a multi-dimensional or matrix organizational pattern only one of whose dimensions is hierarchical.

(9) Given nevertheless the existence of this main hierarchical structure, the question arises of the optimum number of levels within it for effective and responsive operation. Tentatively it seems that the answer may be five levels (including the lowest, non-managerial, level) for departments in the normal range of size, perhaps four in some smaller departments, and conceivably six in the largest. (The distinction here between *managerial levels* and *grade* is crucial – see Appendix A.)

Organization of Field Work (Chapter 5)

(10) Our research shows evidence of much confusion about the appropriate manner, and even the basic propriety, of the supervision of field workers. One of the things often quoted is the need to respect 'due professional independence'. But does due professional independence equate to genuine *professional autonomy* or to what might be called *delegated discretion?* The overwhelming evidence from our work is that social workers do, when the point is put to them in this way, believe that they are working in SSDs within a managerial hierarchy, and therefore working essentially within the limits of delegated discretion rather than with genuine professional autonomy – as available, for example, to medical consultants. The question is confused by another important one, namely the necessary difference in professional and executive capability for a satisfactory and accepted managerial relationship to exist between supervisor and supervisee.

(11) A definition of supervisory work is offered which pays due regard to the need of professional social workers to exercise considerable degrees of delegated freedom, according to their

various capabilities. At the same time the need of the supervisor to review and to prescribe authoritatively what is to be done in the interests both of the client and of the development of the social worker concerned, is emphasized. More specifically, a possible way of doing this is through definition and delegation of particular tasks.

(12) Actual examples of specific definitions of *task* (defined pieces of work with specific planned end points in time) are offered from project work. Examples are described both in the relatively abstract field of helping the individual to achieve better capacity for adequate social functioning, and in more concrete fields like arranging or providing specific services.

(13) Several models of Area Team organizations are offered based on analysis of specific field situations. The essential idea is put forward of two levels of work (and worker) within the Area Team. It may be that whilst Team Leaders *manage* a variety of workers at the lowest level (Level 1) their relationship is only *co-ordinative* to certain other 'career grade' social workers who are working essentially at the same level as themselves (Level 2).

(14) Evidence now appears that clerical and administrative staff working alongside Area Teams cannot be assigned either wholly to the control of the latter, or wholly to the control of the central administrative division. They are probably best recognized as being in an *attachment* situation (see Appendix A).

(15) However, social workers who are so-called 'attached' to hospitals, clinics, etc., are more likely in the terms developed in this project to be *outposted* or *seconded* (see Appendix A).

Organization of Residential Care (Chapter 6)
(16) Our research reveals much evidence of the organizational isolation of heads of residential establishments from the rest of the department. Intermittent links exist with staff from many divisions, but which staff carry authority, and more particularly, which carry accountability for the full support and management of establishments is often quite unclear.

(17) Analysis of the actual work and tasks of residential staff suggests that no satisfactory division can be made between 'care'

matters and 'case work' matters. However, research has revealed frequent attempts to allocate responsibilities for these two subjects to residential and field work divisions respectively. In some ways, this mirrors the equally unreal division between 'professional' and 'administrative' matters. Our work leads us strongly to the conclusion that effective residential management must be concerned with both these aspects. Put in another way, any effective residential division must be concerned both with *basic services* and with *basic social work*.

(18) Drawing on evidence of work with 'homes advisers' and suchlike staff, the proposition is advanced that there is typically a *missing managerial level* in residential management – the one immediately above heads of establishments – although the warning is also made that all heads may not themselves be working at the same managerial level.

(19) Research work on the relationship between field and residential workers points strongly to the appropriateness of a *collateral* relationship. Each, if doing their job fully could be carrying out exactly the same kinds of work, though in different settings. They form (level for level) natural colleagues, and by implication they require parallel if not similar training.

(20) However, in dealing with particular cases, it is likely that one or other may need to play a defined *co-ordinating* role at a particular period of time. More generally there may be a need for defined *liaison* roles for particular field workers in relation to particular establishments.

Organization of Day Care and Domiciliary Services (Chapter 7)

(21) We have little direct project experience in the day care and domiciliary field, but an analysis of what the work involves is nevertheless offered, and the problem of the professional identity of some of the staff concerned noted. Some of the work in this field which can be expected to be carried out by clerical and administrative staff is identified. The inevitable 'dual influence' situations (see Appendix A) of certain staff such as Area Home Help Organizers and occupational therapists working in Areas is also noted.

Co-ordination and Control of Work with Individuals and Families (Chapter 8)

(22) Project work concerned both with specialist intake teams and with duty teams has enabled the creation of a general model

of the initial stages of 'case work' (i.e. *basic social work*) with new clients. There appear to be three main elements, for each of which a precise definition has been evolved:

- *screening* .
- *short-term case work*
- *long-term case work*

The model also incorporates definitions of *bombardment, case, client, case assessment, referral,* and *transfer.* In terms of this model it has been possible to offer a detailed analysis of the typical work of such staff as receptionists, specialist intake workers, and duty workers.

(23) Research on the way that allocation and supervisory processes are carried out in practice has led to formulation of the important distinction between *case assessment* and *supervisory review.* A wide variety of different occasions on which supervisory reviews inevitably arise has been identified in current departmental practice. A detailed formulation has been evolved of the proper role of the Team Leader (or of the Area Officer) in both case allocation and subsequent processes of review.

(24) Project work on procedures for placing clients in residential care in two authorities has demonstrated some common problems. It is suggested that in 'placement' not just one decision, but a complex of perhaps seven major decisions or processes is involved. The likely locus of these various decisions in Model A and Model B departments has been explored.

(25) Work with particular clients proceeds often through the combined efforts of a multi-disciplinary team, including on occasion people from other agencies or departments. The coordination of the work of any particular team through simple *managerial* mechanisms is usually inappropriate if not impossible. Typically (in contrast) there may be identified a defined *co-ordinative* role which may rest initially with field work staff and may be transferred later by deliberate decision to residential staff for certain types of client in care. Project work suggests, moreover, that the role of the chairman of a case conference is not properly conceived either as a straightforward *managerial* one or necessarily as that of a *case co-ordinator.*

Further Areas of Expanding Project Work (Chapter 9)
(26) A tentative picture has been drawn of the way in which links might develop between social services and health authorities.

At departmental level links of three kinds might be required, each with its own separate organizational machinery:
- (a) those concerned with *strategic planning,*
- (b) those concerned with *operational co-ordination* (the establishment of matching systems and procedures),
- (c) those concerned with *individual cases.*

(27) A speculative look at corporate management teams at local authority level, consisting of Chief Executive Officers and other chief officers, raises a major issue of organizational relationship. Is the Chief Executive Officer in a *managerial* or a *co-ordinative* role to the others? At departmental level, work with one management group, consisting of the Director of Social Services and his senior staff, has confirmed that the *managerial* role of the former is necessarily sustained in such events, though this does not detract from the importance of the process being undertaken or prescribe the most appropriate *style* of interaction.

(28) Consideration of the way in which professional and occupational groups in social services are likely to develop, suggests that two things may happen. First, a closer professional integration of social workers in field, residential, and day care settings can be expected, and welcomed as being appropriate to the work to be done. Second, increasing differentiation can be expected to arise between relatively highly-qualified social workers in various settings and less highly-qualified social work assistants who help them in those settings. The possible career patterns of resulting broad groups of staff can be traced in relation to three distinct levels of work below higher management.

(29) Project work with members of a *staff representative system* in one department has identified a number of critical issues for effective functioning, and some possible ways of dealing with them. It is suggested that as SSDs get bigger, the likelihood of a need being felt for explicit and established staff representative systems will also increase.

Postscript

As was indicated in the introduction, what is presented here is in a very real sense a progress report on a continuing project.[4] Further

[4] At the time of writing the project is financed (by the DHSS) on a four-year rolling programme, re-negotiable annually.

series of national conferences are planned. Further specific projects are reaching completion, in hand, or just about to be launched in our several client departments. We are experimenting with new less-intensive methods of intervention in other departments. We are beginning to establish working links with various central agencies and organizations.

Although our method of work changes and evolves, its principle object is still the institutional machinery through which social services are transmitted. By this we do not just mean the 'management structure' of departments, but the whole complex of established social relationships within the department, between the department and other agencies, and between the department and the various bodies which provide more or less authoritative public participation and control. We mean also the whole network of procedures and systems by which the department decides what needs it has to meet, decides (or recommends) how they are to be met, and reviews after the event how well they have been met, both in individual cases and in its total operation.

That such institutional machinery is not the be all and end all of social service provision is obvious enough; but that well-conceived developments in it may lead to better service to the community and better careers for the staff concerned, can hardly be doubted.

Appendix A. A Basic Vocabulary for the Analysis of the Work and Organization of Social Services Departments
(*In Alphabetical Order*)

The object of this appendix is to bring together in a succinct form all the basic conceptions which have evolved so far from this and associated research as prime tools of analysis for the problems of organization and management of SSDs. In most cases a formal definition is offered accompanied by a short commentary – not so long as to duplicate seriously any more extended discussion which has already taken place in the previous text.

The point is worth making again, that without a rigorous definition of basic organizational and procedural concepts there can be no useful statement of existing situations, no unambiguous statement of possible improvements, and no chance of providing formal training in management with the certainty that what is taught is an accurate reflection of the situation in which the trainee is to work. In a word there can be no science.[1] However, it must be understood that these definitions, like all other scientific endeavours, may be subject to review and development as research proceeds.

[1] See Wilfred Brown's essay 'Organization and Science' on this theme – Brown and Jaques (1965).

ACCOUNTABILITY

Accountability is an attribute of a role which indicates the likelihood of the occupant of the role to be subject to positive or negative
sanctions according to assessments of his performance in the role.

The accountability inherent in a given executive role, and the
range of functions to which it relates can usefully be distinguished
from the *sense of responsibility* which any particular occupant
may feel, and which may spread well beyond the bounds of his
particular executive role. People frequently feel some responsibility for all that goes on in their social environment. Again,
social workers, for example, often talk of 'responsibility to their
clients'. This may be valid, but is different from their accountability, which is clearly to their employers.

ATTACHMENT (see also *Dual Influence Situations*)

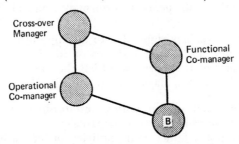

Attachment arises where it is desired to *manage* the work of B in
technical, occupational, or professional respects, in conjunction with
that of other practitioners in the same function or field, whilst
leaving intact a clear line of operational accountability. This is
achieved by B's functional manager *attaching* him to the staff of
some operational manager. Since both then carry elements of managerial authority in respect of B, they become in effect 'co-managers'.

The arrangement relies on the existence of a 'cross-over' manager
who can set or approve policies which are binding on both co-
managers, and who can adjudicate on any unresolved issue which
divides them.

Specifically, the functional co-manager is accountable in respect
of B:

– for helping to select him according to professional criteria,
  and for inducting him in matters relating to the field concerned;

- for helping him to deal with technical problems in the field concerned;
- for co-ordinating his work with that of other similar participants in the field;
- for keeping himself informed about B's work;
- for discussing possible improvements in standards with him and for reporting to the operational co-manager any sustained or significant deficiencies or lapses from established policy in B's work;
- for appraising his technical competence;
- for providing for his technical training.

The operational co-manager is accountable in respect of B:

- for helping to select him and for inducting him in operational matters;
- for assigning work to him and for allocating resources;
- for appraising his general performance and ability.

Each co-manager has right of veto on appointment, right to provide official appraisals, and right to decide if B is unsuitable for performing any of the work for which they are accountable.

The functional co-manager can give instructions provided that:

- they are given within policies established by the 'cross-over' manager, binding on both co-managers;
- they do not conflict with policies or operating instructions issued by the operational co-manager.

Since the functional co-manager is accountable for B's functional competence, he must have the authority to monitor the operational co-manager with respect to policy in the functional area, to ensure that B's competence is being utilized in a professionally appropriate way.

In SSDs it seems likely that area administrative staff are often in *attachment* situations. So too may occupational therapists who work in specific geographical areas.

AUTHORITY

Authority is an attribute of a role which indicates the right of the occupant to act at his own discretion.

The authority in a role may be to expend cash or material resources at discretion, for example to spend money on clients, or to receive them into care. Alternatively it may be to act in some way in relation to other members of the organization – to give them instructions at will, to censure or reward them. Just as accountability may be distinguished from sense of responsibility, so may authority be distinguished from *power* (q.v.). The exercise of power – the ability to act or cause action at discretion – may or may not be legitimate or irregular. Acting with authority implies acting in a legitimated way.

BASIC SERVICES
Basic services is a general term for certain kinds of provision to individuals and families in need, such as the provision of food, clothing and accommodation. No precise definition is offered, but its content is indicated in Table 3.1, where it is contrasted with two other broad areas of work with individuals and families – *basic social work* and the provision of *supplementary services*.

BASIC SOCIAL WORK
Basic social work is a general term for the basic or central core of social work with individuals and families, singly or in groups. No precise definition is offered, but its content is indicated in Table 3.1, where it is contrasted with two other broad areas of work with individuals and families – the provision of *basic services* and the provision of *supplementary services*.

BOMBARDMENT
Unscreened bombardment is the impact of applicants and new referrals on the department, made in person, by telephone, or in writing.
Screened bombardment is the impact of new *cases* on the department, i.e. the incoming work after *screening*.
(See *screening*.)

CASE
A *case* is an instance of the situation presented by any person or family registered by the department as in need of help or action by the department.

Here *cases* are contrasted with individuals or families who are referred to the department or apply themselves, who may or may not turn out to be suitable cases for the department to 'take on' – see *bombardment*.

CASE ALLOCATION

Case allocation is the process by which specific workers become accountable for action on specific cases. It proceeds either:
  (a) by the assignment of a case to a worker by another officer; or
  (b) by automatic allocation according to some predetermined principle, e.g. a 'patch' system or a duty system.

CASE ASSESSMENT

Case assessment is the process, at any stage of a case of:
  (a) considering the needs of the case;
  (b) considering the resources available in the department, and the priority of the case;
  (c) deciding or recommending whether to continue with the case, and if so what action to take.

Case assessment may take place at any stage of a case and at least implies some recording of the results of the process. It may or may not be accompanied by *supervisory review* (q.v.).

CASE COLLABORATION

Case collaboration is the agreement to divide accountability for future work on a case from a given moment of time amongst two or more parties (individuals, sections, agencies). It may also be agreed in this situation that one of the parties acts as *case co-ordinator*.
(See also *Case Referral, Case Transfer*.)

CASE CO-ORDINATION

Case co-ordination involves:
  (a) proposing necessary tasks in relation to the total needs, short- and long-term, of the case;
(and then, assuming agreement):
  (b) negotiating co-ordinated work programmes and procedures;
  (c) arranging the allocation of existing resources to colleagues or arranging the provision of additional resources where necessary;
  (d) keeping informed of action and progress in the case;
  (e) helping to overcome problems encountered by other colleagues;
  (f) providing relevant information to other colleagues, including information on progress;
  (g) reporting on progress to superior.

A *case co-ordinating* role is a particular example of the more general *co-ordinating role* (q.v.). In the first stages of work it will presumably be held by a field worker. Later, for clients in residential care, it could by specific agreement be transferred to an appropriate member of the residential division.

CASE REFERRAL
Case referral is the process of passing details of cases to the department or from one person or section of the department to another, or to another agency, for:
  (a) proposed transfer,
  (b) proposed collaboration, or
  (c) prescribed treatment or services.
(Referral requires an answer.)
(See also *Case Transfer, Case Collaboration*.)

CASE TRANSFER
Case transfer is the agreed transfer of accountability for a case at a given moment of time, from one person or section of the department to another person, section, or agency (i.e. from the head of the section concerned to the head of another section or agency).
(See also *Case Referral, Case Collaboration*.)

CASE WORK, SHORT-TERM AND LONG-TERM
(Case work in this particular context may be taken as synonymous with *basic social work*.)
Short-term case work is the process of *basic social work* in new cases up to the point where *case assessment* produces either,
  (a) the need for *long-term case work*, or
  (b) a decision to close the case, or
  (c) a decision to proceed only by future provision of certain *basic or supplementary services*.

This process is usually expected to be completed in a short term, a matter of a few weeks, or even (in certain duty systems) in one day. The time limit – X days or weeks – will be an administrative decision.

Long-term case work is further *basic social work* in a case which is expected to be needed for some period much longer than that allowed for *short-term case work*.

The question of defining long-term case work only arises where special intake sections are established to carry out *short-term case work*. The criterion for transfer has to be that further work is seen to be needed as far as can be judged for some period much longer than the X days or weeks allowed at maximum for *short-term case work*. Otherwise the case will stay with the intake section for completion.

CLIENT
Client or *clients* are the particular person or people in a case identified as in need of help.

(This definition is relatively untested. The point is to distinguish clients from others, for example, foster parents or teachers who may be deeply involved in a case.)

COLLABORATION – See *Case Collaboration*

COLLATERAL RELATIONSHIP

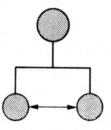

A *collateral relationship* arises where the work of two people ultimately subject to the authority of a common manager interacts in such a way that mutual accommodation is needed in certain matters, and where neither has authority over the other. (Their tasks may be complementary, or they may be supplementary, or they may be unrelated apart from use of common resources.)

Each person in the collateral relationship is separately accountable:
– for accommodating to the other's needs, as far as is reasonable;
– for referring to his own manager any significant problem of mutual work which he has been unable to resolve.

Where collateral colleagues fail to reach agreement, ultimate resolution can only be found at the cross-over point represented by the common manager.

Common examples of collateral relationships in SSDs are where

two field workers, or a field worker and a residential worker, collaborate in the same case.

COMMITTEE

A (true) *committee* is the meeting in some explicit undertaking of
a group of people who bear or represent a common interest, and
who then carry identical roles under the co-ordination of an agreed
chairman. By implication decisions are authorized by majority
acceptance.

True committees cannot exist within *managerial hierarchies*,
but examples in social services can be found at local authority level
itself.

CO-ORDINATING ROLE

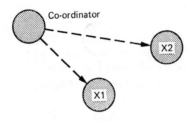

A *co-ordinating role* arises where it is felt necessary to establish
one person with the function of co-ordinating the work of a number
of others *in some particular field* and where a managerial, supervisory, or staff relationship is inappropriate. The activity to be
co-ordinated might for example be:
  – the production of a report, estimate, plan or proposal;
  – the implementation of an approved scheme or project;
  – the overcoming of some unforeseen problem affecting normal
    work.
The co-ordinator can only carry out his role to the full within
the framework of some generally agreed task, although he amongst
others may propose such tasks for the group where a need is discerned.
  The co-ordinator is accountable:
  – for proposing appropriate tasks where a need is discerned;
and following general acceptance of this or any task-proposal:

- for negotiating the general form and content of co-ordinated work programmes;
- for arranging the allocation of existing resources or seeking additional resources where necessary;
- for keeping himself informed of actual progress;
- for helping to overcome problems encountered by X_1, X_2, etc.;
- for providing relevant information to X_1, X_2, etc., including information of progress;
- for reporting on progress to his superior (if such exists) or to those who established the co-ordinating role.

In carrying out these activities the co-ordinator has authority to make firm proposals for action, to arrange meetings, to obtain first-hand knowledge of progress, etc., and to decide what shall be done in situations of uncertainty, but he has no authority in case of sustained disagreements to issue overriding instructions. X_1, X_2, etc., have always the right of direct access to the higher authorities who are setting or sanctioning the tasks to be co-ordinated.

Examples in social services are provided by *case co-ordinating roles*, specialist co-ordinators working in particular fields, and more generally leaders of working parties. It is possible that so-called chief executives of local authorities play a *co-ordinating* rather than a *managerial* role in respect of other chief officers.

DEPUTIZING AND ACTING MANAGEMENT

In the absence of any *manager* from his normal place of work, certain decisions may need to be made by one of his subordinates. Which decisions must be made, and which may be left for referral to the manager on his return will be determined to a great extent by the expected duration of his absence.

One of the subordinates will need to be assigned this *deputizing* function whether or not the word 'deputy' figures in his title.

Where the deputy in the absence of his superior takes on so much of his superior's role in relation to the other subordinates, as to be perceived as carrying accountability for their work, and as carrying authority to assess them and if necessary, to apply sanctions to them, *deputizing* changes to *acting management*. (The implication is that the deputy has the personal capacity to carry the full weight of his superior's role, with the further implication that he is unlikely to be satisfied with a more diminished role on the return of his superior.)

It has not proved possible to assign any significance to the word 'deputy' other than that described above; that is, it has not proved possible to identify any function for a deputy as such which survives the return of his superior. However it is possible that there often is an implicit expectation that deputies play a continuing role as 'operational co-ordinators' – see Chapter 4.

DUAL INFLUENCE SITUATIONS

Dual influence situations arise where a person is subject to organizational influence or control which may potentially at least be *managerial*, from two sources:
  (a) a more senior person in the operational field in which he works;
  (b) a more senior person from the same function or specialism at some higher or more remote echelon of the organization.

Such situations arise in social services, for example for administrative staff, occupational therapists, and for home help organizers working in Areas; or for social workers 'attached' to clinics, hospitals, schools, etc.; although the precise organizational position (see below) is usually far from clear in any of these cases. Discussion suggests that not one but a number of organizational formulations may be appropriate in such situations, according to various circumstances and needs. It is probable that at least four choices of organizational formulation arise: *outposting, attachment, functional monitoring and co-ordinating,* and *secondment* (q.v.).

DUTIES

Duties are the functions prescribed for a particular position within an organization, or for a particular organization, or any part of it.

Duties are ongoing and open-ended, in contrast to *tasks* which imply some specific objective and time limit.

FUNCTIONAL MONITORING AND CO-ORDINATING

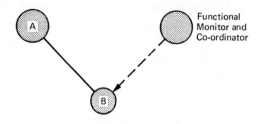

Functional monitoring and co-ordinating arises where it is desired to *monitor* the work of B in technical, occupational, or professional respects and to *co-ordinate* it with the work of other practitioners in the same function or field, whilst leaving intact in all its essential elements the managerial or directive relationship between A and B.

Specifically the functional monitor and co-ordinator is accountable in relation to B:

– for helping to select him (either in an advisory role or with right of veto);
– for providing advice to him in the specialist field concerned, where such is needed;
– for co-ordinating his work with that of other similar participants in the field;
– for *monitoring* the adherence of B to any established policies or practices in the specialist field concerned;
– for providing for B's technical training.

The functional monitor and co-ordinator does not have authority to provide official appraisals of B's work, or to initiate his transfer or dismissal. Such authority rests with A.

A may be an individual manager of B, or a composite body to whom B is directly accountable.

We do not as yet have any clear examples of functional monitoring and co-ordinating within social services. Occupational therapists or home helps within Areas may be in such a situation. So may, for example, the Chief Administrative Officer of the SSD in relation to the Clerk to the Local Authority, or the Treasurer.

GRADE – see *Managerial Levels and Grades*

HIERARCHY – see *Managerial Hierarchy*

LEVEL – see *Managerial Level*

LOGISTICS
Logistics is an activity which encompasses the provision of all material and other real resources (other than the provision of personnel) in support of operational or other more primary work.

MANAGERIAL HIERARCHY
A *managerial hierarchy* is a system of roles built upon successive layers of *managerial relationships.*

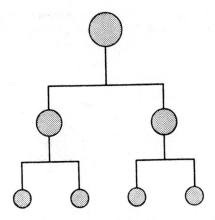

Managerial hierarchies can be contrasted with other institutionalized role systems, for example *committees* (q.v.), coalitions of different interest groups (e.g. 'joint committees' of different authorities) or simply co-operatives or partnerships (e.g. general medical practices).

In general, the word 'hierarchy' can of course be applied to any set of characteristics which can be ordered. In organizations it can be applied to status or *grade*, or even to discernable increments in authority whether managerial or supervisory. A hierarchy of full managerial roles has the characteristic that the person at the top carries as clear and unlimited accountability as is possible for the work of all those beneath. For this reason it is a form which is frequently chosen or accepted by governing bodies for their subordinate executive systems where other circumstances allow it.

MANAGERIAL LEVELS AND GRADES

Grade is an attribute of an organizational role or position which indicates a particular level or range of pay and particular condition of employment.

Managerial Level (or *Rank*) is the level of any organizational role which is part of a *managerial hierarchy*.

It would seem that these concepts are easily separable, but they are regularly confused in practice. It is so often assumed in an unthinking way that differences in *grade* imply some particular relationship of organizational authority – that senior social workers automatically carry authority in respect of basic grade social workers, for example, or Assistant Directors in respect of (more lowly graded) Area Officers. This may or may not be so. Since there is usually a need to employ more steps in a total grading structure than there is possibly room for in terms of managerial levels, it is quite conceivable for managers to have subordinates at several different levels of grade, thus:

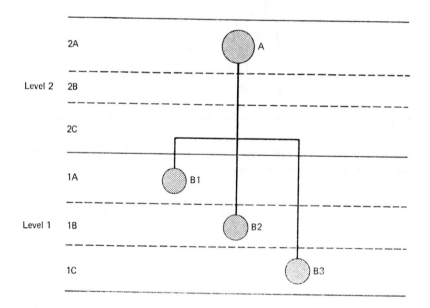

Here, two successive levels in a *managerial hierarchy* have been broken for convenience into three successive *grades* each.

MANAGERIAL ROLE

A *managerial role* arises where A is accountable for certain work and is assigned a subordinate B to assist him in this work. A is accountable for the work which B does for him.

A is accountable:
- for helping to select B;
- for inducting him into his role;
- for assigning work to him and allocating resources;
- for keeping himself informed about B's work, and helping him to deal with work problems;
- for appraising B's general performance and ability and in consequence keeping B informed of his assessments, arranging or providing training, or modifying role.

A has authority:
- to veto the selection of B for the role;
- to make an official appraisal of B's performance and ability;
- to decide if B is unsuitable for performing any of the work for which A is accountable.

Clear examples of managerial roles in SSDs are provided by Directors themselves in relation to their immediate Assistants, or by Area Officers in relation to their own immediate staff.

MONITORING ROLE

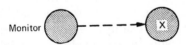

A *monitoring role* arises where it is felt necessary to ensure that the activities of X conform to satisfactory standards *in some particular field,* and where a managerial, supervisory, or staff, relationship is impossible or needs supplementing. The aspect of performance being monitored might, for example, be:
- adherence to contract of employment (attendance, hours of work for example);
- safety;
- financial propriety and security;
- level of expenditure;
- progress on specific project;
- personnel and organizational matters.

Specifically, the monitor is accountable:
- for ensuring that he is adequately informed of the effects of X's activities in the field concerned;

– for discussing possible improvements with X or with X's superiors;
– for reporting to the higher authorities to whom he is accountable sustained or significant deficiencies in the field concerned;
– for recommending new policies or standards where required.

The monitor has authority:

– to obtain first-hand knowledge of X's activities and problems;
– to persuade X to modify his performance, but not to instruct him.

He does not have authority to make or recommend official appraisals of X's work. He does not have authority himself to set new policies or new standards.

Note:

It is possible that certain *scanning* roles exist with accountability for reporting serious deficiencies to higher authorities, but with no accountability for discussing them or negotiating changes.

Although they are no longer called inspectors there is little doubt that Regional Staff of the professional Social Work Service of the DHSS still carry a monitoring function amongst others, in relation to the staff of SSDs. Within the SSD itself there seems less obvious scope for such roles, since monitoring is in any case an integral element of such roles as managerial, supervisory, and staff. However, one clear example of a monitoring role arises in administrative staff, who invariably have the job of monitoring expenditure incurred by all departmental staff against various budget limits.

OPERATIONAL WORK

Operational work is that which arises directly out of the given objects or aims of the organization – the work of providing the services that the organization is in existence to provide.

In SSDs all activities which prevent distress or give direct relief to distress are operational. Operational activities can be contrasted with other necessary organizational activities such as research and evaluation, strategic planning, public relations, staffing and training, managerial and co-ordinative work, logistics, financial, and secretarial work (see Table 3.1).

ORGANIZATION

An *organization* is a system of people who play complementary roles and observe common procedures and policies in pursuit of some common and specific aims.

According to most sociological commentators, an organization is distinguished from other forms of human groups – crowds, cliques, families, communities – by two features. The first is the formal and often explicit nature of the internal role structure. The second is the existence of specific or specifiable aims – though there may well be vigorous discussion as to what exactly these are at any moment of time. Other features of organization are the possibilities of establishing both common procedures and common *policies* (q.v.) to guide action.

SSDs are themselves organizations by this definition. They are part of the larger organization of local government, which exists within the context of a further organization – central government.

OUTPOSTING (see also *Dual Influence Situations*)

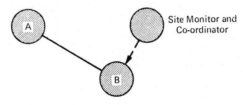

Outposting arises where A is required to make the work of his assistant B available on some physically remote site, whilst retaining the main elements of managerial control of that work.

A is accountable for carrying out the full range of managerial functions in respect of B.

The site monitor and co-ordinator is accountable:

– for inducting B into the local situation;
– for *monitoring* the adherence of B to local regulation and practice;
– for *co-ordinating* the work of B so far as local problems or developments are concerned.

In social services it is likely that field workers are *outposted* to various clinics, hospitals, schools etc. Alternatively, some may be *seconded* (q.v.) to work under given local heads.

POLICIES

Policies are enduring prescriptions which limit or guide work across a number of organizational roles.

Policies are not only set by governing bodies, but in fact by any manager in respect of his own subordinates. (Though any manager must obviously himself work within policies established at higher levels.) Some policies limit authority without directly implying the creation of separate duties (example: 'employ only qualified staff for this post'). Others create new duties for a range of people, or for the whole organization (example: 'better provision should be made for the elderly'). As seen in these examples, policies can range from the very specific to the very general: it is not their generality which defines their character, it is their enduring nature, and applicability to numbers of roles.

POWER

Power is an attribute of an individual or group and indicates the *ability* to act or cause action at discretion.

In contrast, authority expresses the sanctioned *right* to act at discretion (see *authority*). Power rests both on personal qualities – personality, knowledge, expertise, and so on, and on the extent of control of other human and other material resources.

PRESCRIBING RELATIONSHIP

A *prescribing relationship*[2] is similar to a service-seeking relationship (see *service-giving*) but it has this difference.

Provided the prescription is within established policy the person who is to meet the prescription cannot in the face of difficulties refer the problem back to the prescriber, but must somehow contrive or seek resources so as to carry out the prescription at the time required.

[2] Formerly referred to in research at Brunel as a *treatment-prescribing* relationship (Rowbottom et. al. 1973). The modification was introduced in recognition of the fact that more than 'treatments' are usually prescribed in such relationships.

The prescription thus has the force of an *instruction*, rather than a *request* as is the case in service-seeking. The prescribing relationship arises where the action required is seen as meeting an absolute need in its own right, as is the case, for example, in the medical treatment of individual patients

The prime example of a prescribing relationship is that between a doctor and a nurse. It seems to embody the organizational recognition of higher technical or professional skill where a managerial relationship (for example) is not for various reasons appropriate. No instances of prescribing relationships have been discovered at this point within social services, nor, for example, between doctors and social workers. This negative finding is of considerable significance.

REFERRAL – see *Case Referral*

REPRESENTATIVE ROLE

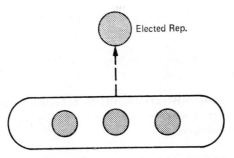

Where any group wish to express the consensus of their views and feelings, or to negotiate with another body, they may choose to do so through the medium of an elected representative.

The elected representative will carry some degree of discretion in presenting views or negotiating, unless he is specifically mandated. (A *delegate* is a representative who works only to a specific mandate.) He is accountable to the group for what he says and does, and if he is judged inadequate by them they will be able to replace him.

Representatives of various groups of staff in SSDs are by no means unknown. However, elected representatives must be distinguished from individuals appointed, for example, to sit on working parties or advisory committees because they are judged typical of the group from which they come.

RESPONSIBILITY

Responsibility may be thought of as a personal attribute – having a sense of responsibility – in contrast to *accountability* (q.v.) which is an attribute of a particular role.

Just as effective organization requires people with personal capacity (power) to use the authority in their roles, so it requires people with an adequate sense of responsibility to accord with their accountability in a role.

ROLE

Role may be briefly described as a set of expectations of behaviour in a given social situation.

Organizational roles can be explored and defined in terms of
  (a) the *duties* or *functions* which fall to the occupant,
  (b) the *authority* available in carrying these out, and the limits to it which exist,
  (c) (sometimes) the particular *tasks* which structure activity in the role,
  (d) the *accountability* of the occupant for his performance.

SCREENING

Screening is the process of deciding whether applications or new referrals represent proper cases for the department to consider.

Screening is commonly carried out by receptionists though sometimes, especially in the case of written applications or referrals, by trained field workers.

SECONDMENT (see also *Dual Influence Situations*)

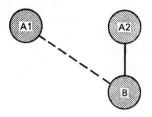

Secondment arises where it is required to transfer B from his original manager A1 to some other manager A2 for some limited period, such as the time for B to gain some desired training or experience.
  In this situation the new manager A2 will:
  – be accountable for inducting B into his new position and assigning work and allocating resources to him;

- be accountable for reviewing B's work and for providing A1 with appraisals of his performance;
- be accountable for helping B's personal development in his work during the time of his secondment;
- have authority to initiate his return, should his performance prove unsatisfactory.

The original manager A1 will:
- be accountable for providing a continuing official appraisal of B's work;
- be accountable for providing for B's formal training, and for making appropriate plans for his career development.

In certain situations it appears that field workers may be seconded to work part-time under medical consultants. In future junior field workers may perhaps be seconded for finite periods to work under team leaders at particular hospital sites.

SERVICE-GIVING RELATIONSHIP

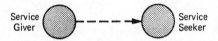

Service Giver — — — → Service Seeker

A *service-giving* relationship arises where it is required to provide access at discretion to certain services without accompanying accountability for managing the work of the person or people who provide the services.

The services offered may include the provision of physical resources, information, or advice, or the carrying out of certain specific tasks.

The service-giver is accountable:
- for providing any service specified by the service-seeker so long as it is within the limits of established policy on kinds of service available;
- for notifying the service-seeker if at any time it is seen to be impossible to provide the service he requires, and discussing possible alternatives;
- (within the limits of delegated authority) for negotiating with the service-seeker any changes or reductions in the kinds of service to be made available.

The service-seeker is accountable:
- for keeping informed of the quality of service actually provided;
- for discussing shortcomings with the service-giver and negotiating changes or improvements;

– for reporting sustained or significant deficiencies in service to the service-giver's superior or to his own superior, as appropriate.

Examples of service-giving in social services arise where clerical and administrative sections at various levels provide on demand such things as typing services, staff recruitment, provision of food or transport.

STAFF OFFICER ROLE

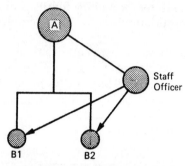

A *staff officer role* arises where a manager A needs assistance in managing the activities of his subordinates (B1, B2) in some particular dimension of work such as personnel and organizational matters or the detailed programming of activities and services.

The staff officer is accountable to A:

– for helping him to formulate policy in the field concerned, taking into account the experience and views of A's other subordinates;

– for seeing that agreed policies in the field concerned are implemented by A's other subordinates, interpreting agreed policy, issuing detailed procedures and programmes, and ensuring adherence to these programmes.

In carrying out these latter activities the staff officer is able to issue instructions. If B1 does not agree with the staff officer's instructions he cannot disregard them, but must take the matter up with A. The staff officer has no authority to make official appraisals of the performance and ability of B1, nor to recommend what the appraisal should be.

In social services, training officers probably play appropriately a staff officer role. The proposed 'operational co-ordinator' roles in Model B departments at departmental level (and divisional level too, if they occur there) are essentially staff officer roles.

SUPERVISORY REVIEW

A *supervisory review* occurs whenever an assessment of a case is discussed by the worker or workers accountable for the case with another member of the department who has authority to modify the assessment if needs be.

Note the distinction from *case assessment* (q.v.) which does not necessarily imply the intervention of a second person.

SUPERVISORY ROLE

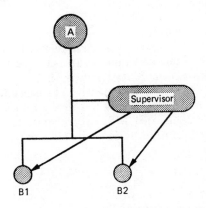

A *supervisory role* arises where a manager A needs help in managing the work of his subordinates B1, B2, etc., in all its aspects.
  The supervisor is accountable to A:
  – for helping to induct B1, B2, into their roles;
  – for helping to assign specific work to B1, B2, and helping to allocate resources;
  – for helping to keep A informed of the work of B1, B2, in all aspects;
  – for helping B1, B2, to deal with work problems that arise;
  – for helping A both to appraise the performance and ability of B1, B2, and to decide appropriate response.
  The supervisor has authority to give instructions to B1. If B1 does not agree with the supervisor's instructions he cannot disregard them, but must take the matter up with A, his manager. He has the authority to recommend to A what the appraisal of the performance and ability of B1, B2, should be and to recommend the exercise of sanctions where necessary.

At earlier stages in the research we assumed that team leaders (senior social workers) frequently carried *supervisory* as opposed to *managerial* roles in respect of certain if not all members of their teams. Deeper consideration of the nature of the supervisory process as the phrase is conventionally used in social work suggests, however, that this inevitably implies managerial capacity and a full managerial relationship.

However, distinct *supervisory* roles as here defined probably do occur at Level 1 – 'shopfloor' level – in roles such as senior clerks, or assistant and deputy heads of establishments, or assistant home help organizers.

SUPPLEMENTARY SERVICES

Supplementary services is a general term for certain kinds of provision to individuals and families in need, such as the provision of communication and mobility training, sheltered employment, formal education etc. Typically it is purveyed by specialists of various kinds. No precise definition is offered but its content is indicated in Table 3.1 where it is contrasted with two other broad areas of work with individuals and families – *basic social work* and the provision of *basic services*.

TASK

A *task* is a piece of work with a specific objective which is to be met within some definite time scale.

Within an organization tasks may arise
   (a) at the discretion of the performer in response to some (continuing) duty;
   (b) sometimes by direct assignment.

The distinction between *tasks* and *duties* has been noted and is crucial. (Examples of basic social work tasks of field workers and residential workers are given in Chapters 5 and 6 respectively.)

TRANSFER – see *Case Transfer*

Appendix B. Possible Alternatives to Hierarchical Organization in Social Services

As was described in Chapter 2, one firm finding from project work is that of the widespread acceptance by staff in the service of the appropriateness of the hierarchical texture of SSDs. Here 'hierarchical' is used in the particular sense of a structure of successive *managerial* relationships. The basic hierarchical texture is widely accepted, but the need is also seen for additional patterns of *co-ordinated groups* to meet various purposes, and sometimes, for accompanying staff representative systems as well.

However, throughout our three years of work we have been constantly at pains to test and retest the validity of this acceptance. Throughout discussions we ourselves have thought that the best test was not simply to enquire whether hierarchical organization (in the sense defined) was acceptable or adequate, and to leave it at that; but to press as far as possible in exploring the viability of any possible alternatives.

This in turn depends on the ability to conceive genuine alternatives – in contrast to what might turn out on examination to be nothing more than redefined versions of hierarchical organization with emphasis, say, on diminished bureaucratic characteristics, or on enhanced participative styles.

At least one basic structural alternative was known to us from several years of research in the field of hospital organization which has been undertaken at Brunel.[1] In this Appendix, drawing from

[1] See Rowbottom *et al.* (1973).

the health care field we shall speculate on what a pattern of non-hierarchical organization along the lines of the medical model might look like in SSDs, and under what conditions it could be expected to develop. Finally we shall touch on the possibility or otherwise of even more radical alternatives.

Professional Autonomy in Hospital Organization

Typical organization of a Hospital Group in the 1948 Health Service is shown in Figure B.1. To avoid the additional complications that the dual system of Hospital Management Committees and Regional Hospital Boards introduce, a Teaching Group has been illustrated, operating under the direction of an appointed Board of Governors, though most of what follows applies equally to HMC Groups.

At first sight, hierarchy still predominates: large parts of the Group are hierarchically organized, as here defined. The chief administrator (or 'House Governor') is head of a hierarchy of administrative, clerical, and hotel services staff; the chief nurse, by whatever name, is head of a large hierarchy of nurses; the treasurer is head of more administrative and clerical staff, and so on for the other chief officers.

On the medical side too, many grades of staff – registrars, house officers, medical and clinical assistants, and a variety of technicians – find themselves in effect in an (organizationally) straightforward subordinate relationship to a surgeon, a pathologist, a radiologist, or some other medical consultant.

But the consultants themselves are different. They are not hierarchically organized. Although the usual variety of experience, seniority, and professional and executive capability, can be supposed to obtain amongst their ranks *none is in a managerial relationship to the other*. Moreover, no other officer is in a managerial relationship to any of them (with the disappearance, or one should say, transformation, of the medical superintendent where he previously existed). Nor is the governing body itself. In fact, provided the individual consultant stays within certain well-understood bounds of professional codes and ethics, and adheres to the limits implicit in his contract, and to the law, he is not answerable to anyone. No-one has the right to prescribe with authority what work he should or should not do. The governing body, the officers,

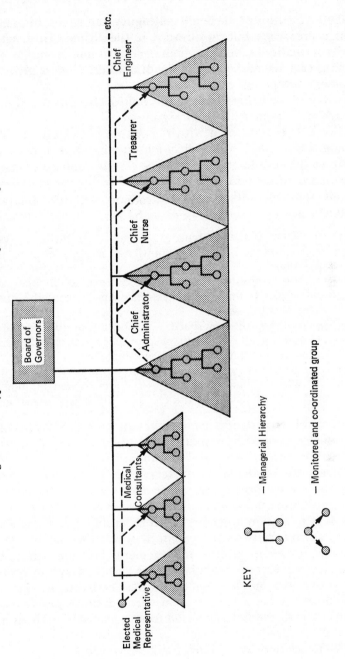

Figure B.1 Typical Structure of a Hospital Group

Board of Governors

Elected Medical Representative

Medical Consultants

Chief Administrator

Chief Nurse

Treasurer

Chief Engineer

etc.

KEY

— Managerial Hierarchy

— Monitored and co-ordinated group

and above all his professional colleagues, can advise him, persuade him, coerce him: but they cannot, in the ultimate, instruct him or apply formalized sanctions – not, again, so long as he stays within certain established bounds of conduct. Here then is genuine professional autonomy.

Why should medical consultants hold such a privileged position? There are two main lines of argument.

The first is concerned with the nature of profession.[2] Without attempting to reach a final decision on what does or does not constitute a 'profession', there would be certain consensus amongst the theorists that the more fully-professionalized an occupational group becomes, the more likely it is to exhibit some or all of the following characteristics:

(1) that there is the existence of a body of scientific or systematic knowledge, and that the knowledge is applicable to practical problems;

(2) that the profession has exclusive competence in understanding and applying this knowledge – to the 'layman' the knowledge is mysterious, esoteric;

(3) hence the profession itself must be responsible for the transmission and development of knowledge, and for the control of entry to and exit from the profession;

(4) that members subscribe to a prime ethic of service rather than self interest, but at the same time aim to remain independent of the value-systems of the clientele (detached–involvement).

Of these characteristics, it might be argued that the idea of a core of knowledge which is beyond 'lay' apprehension, and thus to some degree mysterious, is central and definitive.

Given this particular characteristic, it will at once be obvious that the more advanced the profession – and it is rarely doubted that medicine qualifies as an advanced profession – the more difficult it is to sustain a managerial relationship across a professional boundary, i.e. between a layman, however capable, and a professional, however in need of management. For how can a manager adequately prescribe his subordinate's work, how can he possibly make any full, rounded, and authoritative assessment of that work, and how can he 'zoom-in' to his subordinate's problem-areas to deliver the sort of help expected from a manager, without any real

[2] See Goode (1969) and Jackson (1970).

appreciation of the central elements of knowledge and technique concerned?

These arguments, then, suggest the difficulty of establishing for a highly-developed profession a full managerial relationship outside the profession. They do not however imply that there can be *no* effective lay control of such professionals either through officers or governing bodies: merely that such control cannot properly encompass the full range of what we have defined above as managerial authority. Nor again do they explain in the case just considered why consultants should not be subordinate to some 'super-consultant' within the profession itself.

Here a second consideration emerges. Present hospital consultants do not just supply a professional service. They, like general medical practitioners, provide a *personal* service. It is a service in which the patient has the right to choose which doctor he attends, even if on occasion he does not, or indeed cannot, use this right. It is a service in which he is essentially in the care of one personally identified doctor and in which he is free to change this doctor should he wish. It is unlike the *agency* service provided by doctors in the public health field. The patient is receiving care from Doctor X and his assistants, not from the medical department of the hospital authority concerned.

As we have said, hierarchical organization is not totally absent from this situation – the doctor in charge, as has been noted, has his assistants, many of the status of apprentices. But hierarchical organization above the level of the doctor in charge of the case is indeed incompatible with a 'personal' service.

To return to the typical hospital organization pictured in Figure B.1, there is no one person directly accountable to the Board of Governors for the totality of work carried out under its auspices. Instead there are a large number of people directly accountable to it, in two main groups:

(1) chief officers, each the head of a certain occupational or professional group, with varying degrees of professional independence, but all subject ultimately to the policy-making authority of the governing body;
(2) professional clinicians or therapists employed to act as independent practitioners, with full autonomy to select and act in referred cases as they think best provided they stay within well-established limits: not subject to the policy-making authority

of the governing body as far as their own individual work is
concerned.

Of course, the work of all these people must be brought together,
co-ordinated, and controlled, in some degree and by some means.

The research quoted has definitely confirmed the absence of
full managerial roles at this level, but it has shown in their stead
a number of *co-ordinative* and *monitoring* roles instead. Detailed
definitions of these terms are shown in Appendix A, but certain
essential features may be stressed again at this point.

> *Co-ordinating roles* involve, within the framework of some agreed
> task to be carried out by a group of people, for example
> – calling co-ordinating meetings
> – drawing up programmes of work
> – monitoring and reporting progress
> – resolving obvious uncertainties and indecision.
> The co-ordinator has no authority to issue overriding instructions
> in case of sustained disagreements, and no authority to apply
> managerial sanctions.
> *Monitoring roles* involve in relation to certain defined aspects of
> the work of a number of people
> – ensuring that the monitor is adequately informed of the actual
>   performance in the field concerned;
> – negotiating improvements with the person or persons concerned
>   where there are shortcomings;
> – reporting significant or sustained shortcomings to a higher
>   authority.
> Again the monitor has no authority to prescribe work, and none
> to apply managerial sanctions.

In the hospital situation the chief administrator typically plays
a monitoring and co-ordinating role in relation to his fellow chief-
officers, and in some respects in relation to consultants. However,
the substantial co-ordination of the work of consultants is typically
provided by 'heads of departments' or 'chairmen of committees'
chosen by consultants themselves from amongst their own number.

A Possible Alternative Structure for Social Services – A Personal Service with Professional Autonomy

Here, then, are examples of something truly different from the
managerial hierarchy. The basic organizational element in each

case is the monitored and co-ordinated group, which may be shown
thus:

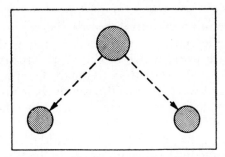

in contrast to the hierarchy, which may be shown thus:

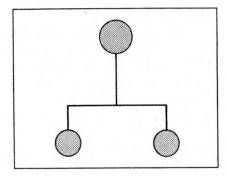

Using the hospital situation as a model, it is possible to see
what an analogous social services organization would look like provided certain conditions prevailed.[3] Let us boldly sketch a picture
of such a fully-fledged professional social service organization as
follows.

The key workers of the agency are now the 'consultant' social
workers, who offer a personal service to clients on demand, and
enjoy complete professional autonomy in the way in which they
handle cases. Not every qualified social worker by any means is in
this category. On the contrary, an extended period of practical
experience under the managerial control of such a 'consultant',
plus a further qualification, is needed before junior social workers

[3] The result provides at least one possible concrete interpretation of
Etzioni's 'fully fledged professional organization' (1964).

reach professional independence.[4] That is, the majority are still subject to hierarchical organization.

Certain agency activities – provision of meals, domestic help, keeping of accounts and central records, staffing, and training work, etc. – are still hierarchically organized. So too, perhaps, is residential and day-care work, which at this stage has differentiated into the relatively highly skilled individual therapy and case work handled by social workers, and the relatively lowly skilled general caring work (analogous to nursing) handled by other workers hierarchically organized.

In this picture, the post of Director would dwindle or disappear, as has that of medical superintendent in hospitals. In his place we should expect an agency 'chief administrator', in a central co-ordinating role, though with managerial control of some or all of the residual agency functions.

Does this appear realistic, now or at any date in the future? It is as well to remember that independent personal practice is not unknown in social work. (It is commonplace for instance in the U.S.A.) However, for social services provided by statutory agencies two serious objections to this model arise.

First, it is doubtful to say the least, whether social work is regarded by the public in general, or members of statutory authorities in particular, as being possessed of an exclusive, science-based, or esoteric, body of knowledge. Without this premise, it is unlikely that the precondition for independent professional practice exists for social workers who are publicly employed and financed.[5]

[4] According to the Report on the Responsibilities of the Consultant Grade (Department of Health and Social Security, 1969) the average age of achievement of medical consultant status in England and Wales is 38-39. Interestingly the National Association of Social Workers in the U.S.A. recommend at least five years experience under supervision as a necessary qualification for independent practice in their guide on 'Requirements for Private Practice' (N.A.S.W., 1967). Toren (1969) is on the same track when she talks (p. 181) of the 'assumption of autonomy' by the social work practitioner after a stipulated number of years of supervised work.

[5] Perhaps in this context Etzioni's (1969) designation of social work along with teaching and nursing, as a 'semi-profession' is after all the most accurate. See Toren's detailed analysis within this context of the uneasy professional status of social work (pp. 141-150). Wilensky and Lebeaux (p. 287) point out that social workers' move towards professionalism 'will not be fully successful without the delimitation of a clear area in which

Second, social workers in statutory agencies have a strong and well-defined monitoring function. For example, they must investigate, and if necessary intervene, in cases of suspected cruelty to children, or in cases of those who must be compulsorily taken into care by reason of failing powers or mental disorder. They now commonly undertake systematic screening of all the chronically sick and disabled in the locality. Such functions are most readily undertaken within the framework of a hierarchically organized agency service: they fit uneasily in the voluntary relationship between the independent therapist and his self-appointed client.

In effect, the argument so far has run thus. At least one genuine structural alternative to the hierarchy exists – the co-ordinated group. Significantly, in one real-life setting in which it can be seen as the major form, it is associated with advanced professional development. Since social work has claims to professional status it is interesting to sketch a picture of what local authority social services might look like organized through co-ordinated groups of professionally autonomous workers, but the resulting picture raises many doubts.[6] Perhaps, however, even more radical alternatives should be considered.

The Radical Critique

What has been considered so far amounts to what might be called a professional critique of hierarchical organization. But we are all now well aware of social forces that strive far beyond this. The new radical critique of existing social structures and institutions has as little time for the traditional tweed-coated professional as it has for the legendary grey-suited bureaucrat.

Now it is difficult to trace in the present day radical writings

---

social work, and no other occupation, has technical competence' (p. 287), but warn that 'social work' must not necessarily be treated as one homogenous occupational group (p. 291). Both Toren (p. 164) and Wilensky and Lebeaux (p. 326) point out that professionalism in social work tends to be associated with, and depend on, the therapeutic content of the 'social reforming' type work.

[6] As has been noted earlier, a Working Party on Professional Integrity in the Children's Service (Association of Child Care Officers, 1969) reached a similar conclusion in rejecting as unreal the notion of a social worker with individual responsibility, and accepting a continuous line of accountability, through the chief officer to representatives of the public.

any very specific analyses and criticisms of hierarchical machinery. It is also difficult to discover any detailed specification of the alternatives to be preferred. Attacks tend to be at a general, far-ranging level, and this is significant. Essentially perhaps, the aim is not for new redesigned machinery: it is simply for a new spirit.[7]

If, however, in keeping with the main preoccupation of this book the discussion is deliberately forced back to the consideration of structure, the question is one of trying to discern what basic possibilities really do, or could, exist other than the two which we have already identified, the managed group (or managerial hierarchy), and the co-ordinated group.

In fact there is apparently one further radical possibility: the genuine co-operative. It may be designated thus:

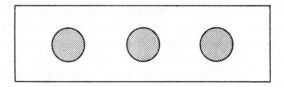

This is an organizational form in which no difference in role is identified for any one of those involved, nor is any special authority or accountability specified. All have an equal voice in affairs, and each plays his part purely according to willingness and capability. Under the name 'partnership' it finds clear existence in law, for example. The trouble as far as organizational theory is concerned is that it is a non-form. Without some institutionalized division of functions, duties, or rights, there is literally no organization. In practice, of course, groups of people working together in such a supposedly unorganized way informally assume complementary functions – that is what 'working together' means. Moreover, where there are many of them, and they work long together, it is impossible to believe that the informal separation of roles will not become *institutionalized* over the course of time. In this situation any continued insistence on the absence of organizational structure will therefore assume the proportion of myth, propaganda, or self-

[7] As Reich (1972) says, the crucial thing in the radical movement is the adoption of a new life-style. 'Structure is not irrelevant ... but it is useless to seek changes in society without changes in consciousness. Consciousness is *prior* to structure.'

deception. Can one for example imagine a typical local authority social services agency employing many hundreds of staff in providing care, meals, aids, transport, advice, supervision, and a multitude of other specific services, managing over the years without some differentiation and formalization of structure? There seems no alternative but to renew the search for structures more complex than the simple co-operative for enterprises other than the very smallest.

One further point must be added, however. Even noting the expressed desire of the radical for a change of *spirit* or *life-style* in organizations, it would be interesting to say the least, to test out how far one particular *structural* development would remove some of the causes of his discontent. The structural change in question is that of the general development of adequate employee representative systems (as discussed in Chapter 9). Such developments might aid acceptance of the inevitability of strong executive role structure, whether managerial or co-ordinative in nature, in order to achieve the aims of the enterprise. In essence, this executive structure could be thought of as the means of effective expression of the power of those who establish the organization. At the same time, through the development of representative systems, a systematic means could be established of expressing the countervailing power of the employees.

In 'social engineering' approaches such as described in this book, attention is shifted from broad, and ultimately meaningless questions such as whether people actually concerned in social services should be left to work out for themselves, in co-operation with their clients, what sort of activities to pursue. Instead attention can be focused more practically on issues like the optimum size and structure of such social agencies in order to allow the governing authority, the employees and, indeed, the immediate clientele, to exert their own due influence on the course of events.

Appendix C. Sample Project Reports

It may be clear from what has been said in the previous text, as well as elsewhere,[1] that the social-analytic method of work does not include at any point the systematic collection and recording of data as the process is normally conceived in social research. Progress ensues by the gradual accumulation and testing of insights into organizational problems, and is registered by the production and agreement of what are in effect joint reports. As each report is produced it often makes obsolete to some degree the previous reports from the sequence of discussions involved. (Over and above this researchers keep their own personal notes of discussions and observations – but these are not available as publishable 'data' until cleared with the clientele concerned.)

Typically, each discussion or sequence of discussions with each individual concerned in any given project gives rise to a report. At the appropriate point various individual reports are summarized and distributed with the summary to the whole group. Discussion then commences with the group as a whole, as a result of which one or a sequence of group reports is produced.

Two samples are shown below, an individual report and a group report. Other samples are available in Chapter 6, where a large part of a report of group discussions on the subject of residential organization in East Sussex is reproduced; in Chapter 8, where a

---

[1] For more detailed discussion of the social-analytic method see Jaques 'Social-Analysis and the Glacier Project' Brown and Jaques (1965), and Appendix B 'Social Analysis in Large-Scale Organizational Change' in *Hospital Organization* (Rowbottom *et. al.* 1973).

large part of a group report on the subject of intake work in Wandsworth Children's Department is reproduced; in Chapter 9 where two complete reports on the subject of staff representation in Wandsworth are reproduced; and at many other points through the text where shorter excerpts from individual and group reports are reproduced.

The first sample is the report of a single three-hour discussion with the Superintendent of an Adult Training Centre in East Sussex. Notice how, although precise terms of reference already exist for the project (paragraph 1), the researcher has felt free to explore various branches from the main track during the course of the discussion.

The second sample is a report of discussions with a group of senior field and residential staff from Brent on the subject of placement procedures for the elderly.

Generally, our reports have tended to become more informal in style as research work has proceeded. We do not eschew the use of precise technical language – that is what the work is about in a sense – but only introduce it as and when it is needed, and then with a strong sense of wishing to test and retest its adequacy on each occasion. It has become increasingly clear that what is involved is at the opposite pole from the systematic collection of data according to a standardized form. Thus increasing responsibility is thrust on each researcher to judge as best he may how frequently to produce reports and what material to include in them. (By and large the frequency of feedback to clientele has greatly increased over the first few years.) As a consequence, reports increasingly reflect the researcher's own particular style and method of work. The ultimate goal may be objective, general and scientific, knowledge, but the path to it demands subjective judgement and scrupulous attention to the concrete and to the particular.

(SAMPLE 1)

RESIDENTIAL & DAY CARE PROJECT – EAST SUSSEX NOTES ON DISCUSSION WITH MR. X, SUPERINTENDENT, ADULT TRAINING CENTRE (AUGUST 1972)

Introduction
1. We met in conjunction with the research project designed:

a) to develop a detailed role specification for Residential and Day Care Officers;

b) to obtain specification of major decisions to be taken by staff in respect of clients, and to establish the respective discretion of County Hall, Establishments or Area Staff to make such decisions.

2. Such formulations must be seen in relation to the particular establishment. You described the Centre to me as existing to provide training for employment (open or sheltered), and related social training for 60 (presently 78) mentally and/or physically handicapped persons and a few formerly mentally ill. Trainees, male and female, range in age from 16 – 60 plus. Twenty-six are resident in the local authority Hostels.

3. In theory trainees should flow through the Centre and the 'permanent' trainee would be an exception. At one time 25% – 30% of trainees per annum were placed in open employment. However the current high national unemployment rate mitigates against the trainees. The work centres are not developed to take the remainder.

4. You are assisted by a deputy and six or seven instructors. You have considerable discretion to organize your own work and social programmes and are accountable for costing and contracts for work undertaken. You usually arrange employment for local trainees and provide support in the first few weeks. For trainees from further afield you have to rely on the social workers to do this.

5. There is a Committee for the Centre including local trade union and business interests. This provides a useful network for establishing work contracts, obtaining gifts of machinery, and finding work for individual trainees.

6. Organizationally speaking:
   6.1 you believe that you are primarily accountable to the Training Officer who is a specialist in your kind of work and with whom you relate on a professional level;
   6.2 you believe that the local Residential and Day Care Officer is concerned with the bricks and mortar and domestic aspects;
   6.3 you note that both the Training Officer and the R & DCO are the subordinates of the Assistant Director (Residential and Supporting Services, and from time to time this Assis-

tant Director visits the Centre personally and you have the
opportunity to discuss things with him;

6.4 you believe that you are in a collateral relationship (neither
side having authority to override the other) with Area Social
work staff and with residential staff at the hostels.

Problems

7. By and large you feel your organizational situation has been
little affected by the integration,[2] though there has been some
dilution of your contact with the social workers. You still relate
primarily with those who were formerly mental welfare officers.
We shall return to this later – suffice it to say that you believe
there are ways in which work could be better co-ordinated.

8. Note has already been made of the way in which shortage of
resources in terms of both open and sheltered employment
opportunities defeats the training objective of the Centre in
the sense that many trainees are permanent attenders.

9. You are concerned about the transition from the Junior Schools
to the Adult Training Centre and believe that there are ways
in which this could be better achieved – we shall return to this
later.

The Role of the Residential and Day Care Officer.

10. We discussed the policy to decentralize accountability for the
management of establishments to Area Directors at some time in
the not too distant future. We noted that provided resources
increased at a reasonable rate this decentralization would provide
opportunities for closer working together between all staff
delivering direct services to clients.

11. It was recognized however that just as the Assistant Director
who is presently accountable needs assistance in managing establishments, so will the Area Director. We discussed whether the
role of the Residential and Day Care Officer could be broadened
in scope to be concerned with all activities in your centre.

12. In particular you felt that the R & DCO could act as a co-
ordinator of Centre, social worker, and Hostel activity with

[2] The integration referred to is that of the Mental Health, Welfare, and
Children's, Departments in 1971.

trainees by convening case conferences designed to obtain agreement about the training plans for the individual and the kind
of work which needs to be done with his family, or using community resources; by seeing that reports necessary for such
meetings are prepared and circulated; by seeing that decisions
of the collaborating workers are recorded; and by reconvening
the group at an agreed suitable point for further review. The
first case conference would be held soon after the trainee's
admission and thereafter according to the needs of any trainee.

13. Within the agreement reached about the trainees' programme,
the R & DCO would be a continuing point of referral for any
member of staff concerned if the programme was getting out of
gear.

14. In your case the role of the Training Officer is going to be of
continuing importance. Presently for example, he is involved
in the selection of trainees and as far as you are concerned he is
the specialist in the Department. We discussed how this specialism could continue to be available to you in the form of a
staff officer role – establishing criteria governing your work,
providing procedural instruction and high level advice – instead
of as now in a quasi-managerial relationship.

15. You feel that there is so much work to be done with trainees
and their placement in the community that you think that as
an alternative to, or as well as, the R & DCO occupying a co-
ordinating role between field and residential workers, there
may be a case for having a social worker fully (or more or less
fully) attached to the Centre. Such a person could set up relationships with industry etc.; and could help to initiate, with the
local education authority, a scheme to integrate the junior
school transfers by having them in their last year at school
attending the Centre a couple of days a week, learning to use
public transport etc.

Decision Making
16. You believe in an establishment like yours, with an active
treatment programme and an objective of a flow-through of
trainees, that you will always be in a collaborative working
situation with field and residential social workers. All decisions
whether to admit, what treatment to engage in, when to transfer
etc., must be made in agreement with the other workers concerned. In the post-decentralization era, the Area Director will

constitute a closer 'cross-over point' to resolve occasional sustained disagreements that exist within the present structure.

(SAMPLE 2)

PROJECT: RESIDENTIAL ACCOMMODATION FOR THE ELDERLY, BRENT
REPORT OF SECOND GROUP DISCUSSION (JULY 1972)

Introduction
1. This short report attempts to summarize the two Project Group meetings which took place on the 15th June and 7th July, 1972. Many of the points incorporated were presented in the first Group Report but this paper can be taken to represent a further step in the ongoing clarification, especially in view of the fact that for the first time the entire Project Group was present.

2. Concerning some issues a fair degree of consensus was obtained. In other cases it was made clear that opinions were made with considerable reservations, usually caused by the sheer complexity of the potential ramifications of the issues.

3. The approach of this report will be first to reiterate those areas of reasonably solid consensus and then to consider subjects which seem to be more open to disagreement or alternative interpretation.

Areas of Consensus
4. The attitude, expressed in the First Group Meeting, that the *role of the Residential and Day Care Division must be clarified* before effective placement procedures can be introduced, was reiterated at the Second Project Group meeting. Despite its avowed intention to devote time to the 'nuts and bolts' of placements, the Group found itself returning to a more detailed examination of the points raised in the first Group Report.

5. There was no disagreement that the present policy, whereby Areas have 'liaison responsibilities' for specified Homes, has failed.

6. The point made in the first meeting, that some Heads of establishments are confused about accountability for their work, was

reinforced by comments made by the two Heads who were present in this second meeting.

7. There is 'a general desire to move away from the 'last refuge' approach – towards a more treatment-orientated approach.

8. The role of the R & DC Advisers requires detailed clarification.

The Management of Residential Care
9. In the previous document a number of alternative choices were suggested to the Department on the assumption that the present structures are inadequate. Some movement must be made towards a more requisite pattern. The alternatives that were suggested were:

9.1 total management of establishments at Area level;
9.2 total management of establishments in R & DC Division;
9.3 establishments subject to a 'dual influence' situation;
9.4 some establishments managed at Area, some at Headquarters level.

The second Group Meeting concentrated its discussion around alternatives 9.1 and 9.2. There appeared to be an implicit agreement that 9.3 and 9.4 were not suitable alternatives.

10. At the beginning of the discussion there appeared to be a wide gap between those participants who felt that with appropriate support from Residential Advisers, Area management (in the fullest sense) of residential establishments was possible. Further, bringing residential establishments into the Area framework would increase promotion prospects for residential staff. On the other hand the reservations of some establishment Heads and others concerning the ability of the Area Managers, and indeed some of the present Advisers, to manage Homes, was strongly voiced.

'My Adviser doesn't know problems of Old People's Welfare.'

'Area Managers have no expertise to manage Homes.'

'Our work is different from that of field workers – We have to live and deal with problems 24 hours a day.'

'We should be managed by the R & DC Division.'

11. By the end of the discussion many of these objections to Area management *seemed* to have lessened and the Group was entering a practical discussion of how a decentralized system might work. For example:

     11.1 what would be the function of the new R & DC Division – the problem of supply and maintenance;

     11.2 whether Heads would go through Area Managers for supplies;

     11.3 whether Seniors could manager Day Centres;

     11.4 the changing role definition of R & DC staff.

12. However, on balance it is probably inaccurate to claim that a 'solid consensus' was reached in favour of either of the two alternatives (9.1 or 9.2). What did seem to emerge, was the feeling that whilst a decentralized system might work, many questions would require a much more detailed and finer clarification than is possible within the framework of this particular Project Group, whose initial terms of reference were much narrower.

Future Project Work and the Achievements of the Present Group

13. At the onset of the researcher's commitment to Brent it was made quite clear that action can only be taken by the relevant executive mechanism of the Department. Project Group perceptions and reports represent analysis of problems and possible alternative approaches for Departmental decision-making. There can be little doubt that much of the earlier Project work will provide the Department with the material to begin the change process to a more requisite system of placements for the Elderly.

14. It is also no secret that the departure of the present Assistant Director (Residential and Day Care) has inevitably lead to a a change in the programming of future project work. It had, for example, been intended to proceed immediately to a similar and more complex project with regard to placements of children into care. This has temporarily been postponed.

15. One of the major achievements of the present Project Group is the way in which the analysis has contributed to executive discussion of divisional structures. The ambition of the researcher is that the method of work will whilst avoiding personal anxieties assist Departmental organization to optimize service to clients.

Bibliography

ALBROW, M. (1970), *Bureaucracy*, London: Macmillan.

ALGIE, J. (1970), 'Management and Organization in the Social Services', *British Hospital Journal*, Vol. LXXX, pp. 1245-1248.

ARGYRIS, C. (1964), *Integrating the Individual and the Organization*, London: Wiley.

ASSOCIATION OF CHILD CARE OFFICERS (1969), *Report of the Working Party on Professional Integrity in the Child Care Service.*

BAINS, M. A. (Chairman) (1972), *The New Local Authorities – Management and Structure*, Report of Study Group appointed jointly by the Secretary of State for the Environment and local authority associations, London: H.M.S.O.

BECKHARD, R. (1969), *Organization Development – Strategies and Models*, Reading, Massachusetts: Addison Wesley.

BENNIS, W. G. (1969), *Organization Development; Its Nature, Origin and Prospects*, Reading, Massachusetts: Addison Wesley.

BENNIS, W. G., BENNE, K. D., and CHIN, R. (1969), *The Planning of Change*, 2nd edn., London: Holt, Rinehart & Winston.

BILLIS, D. (1974), 'Entry into Residential Care', *Brit. J. Social Work*, 3, 4.

BLAU, P. M., and SCOTT, W. R. (1963), *Formal Organizations*, London: Routledge & Kegan Paul.

BRITISH ASSOCIATION OF SOCIAL WORKERS (1971), 'Social Action', Working Party's Discussion Paper, *Social Work Today*, 2 (13), pp. 13-16.

BRITISH MEDICAL ASSOCIATION (1972), *The Mental Health Service After Unification*, Report of a Tripartite Committee with the Authorization of the Royal College of Psychiatrists, the Society of Medical Officers of Health, and the British Medical Association, London.

BROWN, W. (1960), *Exploration in Management*, London: Heinemann.

BROWN, W., and JAQUES, E. (1965), *Glacier Project Papers*, London: Heinemann.

CAPLAN, G. (1970), *Theory and Practice of Mental Health Consultation*, London: Tavistock Publications.

CALOUSTE GULBENKIAN FOUNDATION (1968), *Community Work and Social Change*, The Report of a Study Group on Training (Chairman: Eileen Younghusband), London: Longmans Green.

CAPLAN, G. (1970), *Theory and Practice of Mental Health Consultation*, London: Tavistock Publications.

CENTRAL COUNCIL FOR EDUCATION AND TRAINING IN SOCIAL WORK (1973), *Training for Residential Work* (Discussion Document).

COHEN, P. S. (1968). *Modern Social Theory*, London: Heinemann Educational Books.

DEPARTMENT OF EMPLOYMENT (1972), *Report of the Buttersworth Inquiry into the Work and Pay of Probation Officers and Social Workers* (Buttersworth), London: H.M.S.O.

DEPARTMENT OF HEALTH AND SOCIAL SECURITY (1969), *The Responsibilities of the Consultant Grade* (Godber), London: H.M.S.O.

DEPARTMENT OF HEALTH AND SOCIAL SECURITY (1972), *Management Arrangements for the Reorganised National Health Service*, London: H.M.S.O.

DEPARTMENT OF HEALTH AND SOCIAL SECURITY (1972), *National Health Service Reorganisation: England* (White Paper), Cmnd. 5055, London: H.M.S.O.

DEPARTMENT OF HEALTH AND SOCIAL SECURITY (1972), *Intermediate Treatment* – A Guide for the Regional Planning of new forms of treatment for children in trouble. London: H.M.S.O.

DONNISON, D. V., CHAPMAN, V. *et al.* (1965). *Social Policy and Administration*, London: Allen & Unwin.

DUNCAN, T. M. (1973), 'Intake in an Integrated Team', *Health and Social Services Journal*, 10 February, pp. 318-319.

ETZIONI, A. (1964), *Modern Organizations*, Englewood Cliffs, N. J.: Prentice-Hall.

ETZIONI, A. (ed.) (1969), *The Semi-Professions and Their Organization*, New York: The Free Press.

EVAN, W. M. (1966), 'The Organization-Set: Toward a Theory of Interorganizational Relations', in THOMPSON, J. D., *Approaches to Organizational Design*, Pittsburgh: University of Pittsburgh Press.

FOREN, R., and BROWN, M. J. (1971), *Planning for Service, An Examination of the Organisation and Administration of Local Authority Social Service Departments*, London: Charles Knight.

GOLDBERG, E. M. (1970), *Helping the Aged: A Field Experiment in Social Work*. London: Allen & Unwin.

GOODE, W. J. (1969), 'The Theoretical Limits of Professionalisation', in ETZIONI (ed.) (1969), op. cit.

GRAICUNAS, V. A. (1937), 'Relationships in Organization', in GULICK, L., and URWICK, L. (1937), op. cit.

GREENWOOD, R., and STEWART, J. D. (1972), 'Corporate Planning and Management Organization', *Local Government Studies*, 3, pp. 25-40.

GULBENKIAN REPORT, see CALOUSTE GULBENKIAN FOUNDATION.

GULICK, L., and URWICK, L. (1937), *Papers on the Science of Administration*, New York: Columbia University.

HAGE, J., and AIKEN, M. (1970), *Social Change in Complex Organizations*, New York: Random House.

HALL, A. S. (1971), 'Client Reception in a Social Service Agency', *Public Administration*, 49, pp. 25-44.

HARTMAN, A. (1971), 'But What is Social Casework?', *Social Casework*, July, pp. 411-419.

HERAUD, B. J. (1970), *Sociology and Social Work, Perspectives and Problems*, London: Pergamon.

HODDER, J. (1968), 'Management of Children's Department Residential Services', in *Residential Staff in Child Care*, Residential Child Care Association.

HOME OFFICE (1968), *Children in Trouble* (White Paper), London: H.M.S.O.

HOME OFFICE *et al.* (1968), *Report of the Committee on Local Authority and Allied Personal Social Services* (Seebohm), Cmnd. 3703, London: H.M.S.O.

HORNSTEIN, H. A. *et al.* (1971), *Social Intervention – A Behavioural Science Approach*, New York: The Free Press.

HUMBLE, J. W. (1970), *Management by Objectives in Action*, London: McGraw-Hill.

HUNTER, T. D. (1967), Hierarchy or Arena? The Administrative Implications of a Sociotherapeutic Régime, in FREEMAN. H., and FARNDALE, J. (eds.) (1967), *New Aspects of the Mental Health Services*, Oxford: Pergamon.

JACKSON, J. A. (ed.) (1970), *Professions and Professionalisation*, London: Cambridge University Press.

JAQUES, E. (1967), *Equitable Payment*, 2nd edn., Harmondsworth: Penguin.

JAQUES, E. (1965), 'Social Analysis and the Glacier Project', in BROWN, W., and JAQUES, E. (1965), *Glacier Project Papers*, London: Heinemann.

KATZ, D., and KAHN, R. L. (1966), *The Social Psychology of Organizations*, New York: Wiley.

KING, R. D., RAYNES, N. V., and TIZARD, J. (1971), *Patterns of Residential Care*, London: Routledge & Kegan Paul.

KINGDON, D. R. (1973), *Matrix Organization, Managing Information Technologies*, London: Tavistock.

KOGAN, M. (1969), *The Government of the Social Services*, The Sixteenth Charles Russell Memorial Lecture, London: The Charles Russell Memorial Trust.

KOGAN, M., and TERRY, J. (1971), *The Organisation of a Social Services Department: A Blueprint*, London: Bookstall Publications.

LAWRENCE, P. R., and LORSCH, J. W. (1967), *Organization and Environment: Managing Differentiation and Integration*, Boston: Harvard University Press.

LEISSNER, A., HELDMAN, K. A., and DAVES, E. V. (1971), *Advice, Guidance and Assistance: A Study of Seven Family Advice Centres*, London: Longmans Green.

LEONARD, P. (1966), *Sociology in Social Work*, London: Routledge & Kegan Paul.

LIKERT, R. (1961), *New Patterns of Management*, New York: McGraw-Hill.

LIPPITT, R., WATSON, J., and WESTLEY, B. (1958), *The Dynamics of Planned Change*, New York: Harcourt Brace.

MCGREGOR, D. (1960), *The Human Side of Enterprise*, New York: McGraw-Hill.

MARCUSE, H. (1964), *One Dimensional Man*, London: Routledge & Kegan Paul.

MILLER, E. J., and RICE, A. K. (1967), *Systems of Organisation*, London: Tavistock Publications.

MINISTRY OF HOUSING AND LOCAL GOVERNMENT (1967), *Management of Local Government (Volume 1)* (Maud), London: H.M.S.O.

MOUZELIS, N. P. (1967), *Organisation and Bureaucracy*, London: Routledge & Kegan Paul.

NATIONAL ASSOCIATION OF SOCIAL WORKERS (1967), *Handbook on the Private Practice of Social Work*, New York: N.A.S.W.

NEWMAN, A. D., and ROWBOTTOM, R. W. (1968), *Organization Analysis*, London: Heinemann.

PARSONS, T. (1960), *Structure and Process in Modern Society*, Glencoe: The Free Press.

PERROW, C. (1961), 'The Analysis of Goals in Complex Organizations', *Amer. Social. R.*, 26, 6, p. 855.

PETTES, D. E. (1967), *Supervision in Social Work, A Method of Student Training and Staff Development*, London: Allen & Unwin.

RAPOPORT, L. (1970), 'Crisis Intervention as a Mode of Brief Treatment', in ROBERTS and NEE (eds.) (1970), op. cit.

REES, A. M. (1972), 'Access to Personal Health and Welfare Services', *Social and Economic Administration*, 6 (1), pp. 34-44.

REICH, C. A. (1972), *The Greening of America*, Harmondsworth: Penguin.

REID, W. J., and SHYNE, A. W. (1969), *Brief and Extended Casework*, New York: Columbia University Press.

RESIDENTIAL CHILD CARE ASSOCIATION *et al.* (1966), *The Residential Task in Child Care*, Report of a Study Group at Castle Priory College, Wallingford.

RIGHTON, P. (1971), 'The Objectives and Methods of Residential Social Work', *Child in Care*, December 1971, pp. 11-19 (Residential Child Care Association).

ROBERTS, R. W., and NEE, R. H. (eds.) (1970), *Theories of Social Casework*, Chicago: University Press.

ROWBOTTOM, R. W. *et al.* (1973), *Hospital Organization, A Progress Report on the Brunel Health Services Organization Project*, London: Heinemann.

ROWBOTTOM, R. W., and HEY, A. M. (1973), 'Organizing Social Services – A Second Chance', *Local Government Chronicle*, 5526, pp. 127-131.

ROYAL INSTITUTE OF PUBLIC ADMINISTRATION (1971), *Supportive Staff in Scottish Social Work Departments*, London: R.I.P.A.

SCHON, D. A. (1971), *Beyond the Stable State*, London: Temple Smith.

SEEBOHM REPORT – see HOME OFFICE *et al.* (1968).

SILVERMAN, D. (1970), *The Theory of Organisations*, London: Heinemann Educational Books.

SIMON, H. A. (1964), 'On the Concept of Organizational Goals', *Admin. Sci. Q.*, ix, pp. 1-22.

SMITH, G. (1970), *Social Work and the Sociology of Organizations*, London: Routledge & Kegan Paul.

SMITH, G., and HARRIS, R. (1972), 'Ideologies of Need and the Organization of Social Work Departments', *British Journal of Social Work*, 2 (1), pp. 27-45.

STEWART, J. D. (1971), *Management in Local Government, a Viewpoint*, London: Charles Knight.

TOREN, N. (1969), 'Semi-Professionalism and Social Work: A Theoretical Perspective', in ETZIONI, A. (ed.) (1969), op. cit.

WILENSKY, H. L., and LEBEAUX, C. N. (1965), *Industrial Society and Social Welfare*, New York: The Free Press.

WILLIAMS, G. (Chairman) (1967), *Caring for People – Staffing Residential Homes*, Report of a Committee of Enquiry set up by the National Council of Social Service, London: Allen & Unwin.

WOOTTON, B. *et al.* (1959), *Social Science and Social Pathology*, London: Allen & Unwin.

Index